A Temporary Future

A Temporary Future

The Fiction of David Mitchell

Patrick O'Donnell

Bloomsbury Academic
An imprint of Bloomsbury Publishing Inc

B L O O M S B U R Y
NEW YORK • LONDON • NEW DELHI • SYDNEY

Bloomsbury Academic
An imprint of Bloomsbury Publishing Inc

1385 Broadway	50 Bedford Square
New York	London
NY10018	WC1B 3DP
USA	UK

www.bloomsbury.com

BLOOMSBURY and the Diana logo are trademarks of Bloomsbury Publishing Plc

First published 2015

Patrick O'Donnell, 2015

All rights reserved. No part of this publication may be reproduced or transmitted in any form or by any means, electronic or mechanical, including photocopying, recording, or any information storage or retrieval system, without prior permission in writing from the publishers.

No responsibility for loss caused to any individual or organization acting on or refraining from action as a result of the material in this publication can be accepted by Bloomsbury or the author.

Library of Congress Cataloging-in-Publication Data
O'Donnell, Patrick, 1948-
A temporary future : the fiction of David Mitchell / Patrick O'Donnell.
pages cm
Includes bibliographical references and index.
ISBN 978-1-4411-7122-1 (hardback : alk. paper) –
ISBN 978-1-4411-5728-7 (pbk. : alk. paper)
1. Mitchell, David (David Stephen)–Criticism and interpretation. I. Title.
PR6063.I785Z75 2015
823'.914–dc23
2014029885

ISBN: HB: 978-1-4411-7122-1
PB: 978-1-4411-5728-7
ePub: 978-1-4411-1613-0
ePDF: 978-1-4411-9301-8

Typeset by Integra Software Services Pvt. Ltd.

Contents

Preface and Acknowledgments   vi

Introduction: Many Worlds, Real Time   1

1   A Company of Strangers: *ghostwritten*   23
2   City Life: *Number9Dream*   51
3   Time Travels: *Cloud Atlas*   69
4   Timepiece: *blackswangreen*   103
5   Minor Histories: *The Thousand Autumns of Jacob de Zoet*   123
6   A Secret War: *The Bone Clocks*   155

Epilogue: Toward a Fiction of the Future   181

Notes   186
Works Cited   206
Index   213

Preface and Acknowledgments

The purpose of this book is to serve as a critical introduction to the work of the British contemporary novelist David Mitchell and to engage in a close reading of his six novels to date, from *ghostwritten* (1999) to *The Bone Clocks* (2014). In the fifteen years since his first published novel, Mitchell has risen to be one of the premiere novelists of his generation. His novels are, on the one hand, complex, detailed, and challenging, and call for close scrutiny; on the other hand, they are accessible to a broad audience, in no small part due to Mitchell's power as a storyteller and his belief that the transmission of stories is, and always has been, a key to the survival of the species. I have organized the discussion along straightforward lines: first, an introduction, which provides a summary of Mitchell's career and, then, considers his canon thus far within the contexts of narrative form and genre, the placement of his writing within the frameworks of the postmillennial British novel, his engagement with cosmopolitanism, metamodernism, and the many worlds interpretation, and above all Mitchell's intensive interest in temporality and the construction of the future in its relation to a human past replete with cultural and political violence. Following the introduction are discussions of the six novels in chronological order, each intended to incrementally build linkages and trace throughlines as his writing has developed over these fifteen years, while also paying close attention to the specificities of each novel. I close with a brief conclusion on Mitchell's fiction of/in the future. Throughout, especially as this book is an early entry into what predictably will be a number of substantive discussions of his work to come, I have attempted to proceed in ways that will contribute to an understanding of Mitchell's fiction for the broad audience of his work as well as provide leads or strands of inquiry for those interested in advancing the critical conversation.

In writing this book, I am indebted to my good friend and colleague Justus Nieland, who read the entire manuscript and provided invaluable commentary at each step along the way. Haaris Naqvi has proved to be the most patient and considerate of editors; his support for this book as it has unfolded has been essential to its completion. I am grateful to the College of Arts and Letters at Michigan State University for granting release time from teaching and support for travel to Ireland essential to the completion of this book. My thanks to Angela Denney for her wise counsel and advice during the final stages of the book's completion and to Kate Birdsall for a meticulous job of data-checking the proofs. I am most appreciative of the time David

Mitchell set aside to discuss his work with me on an invigorating September morning and afternoon in Clonakilty, for his generous correspondence with me by e-mail, and for arranging to have his publisher send me the advances of *The Bone Clocks*. I am grateful as ever, and more than ever, to my wife Diane, both for her careful, expert proofreading of the manuscript and for so many other good things in our life together.

East Lansing, Michigan

July, 2014

Introduction: Many Worlds, Real Time

Austerlitz, the titular protagonist of the last of W.G. Sebald's novels to be published during his lifetime, speaks at one point of Parisian streets haunted by the past, and of his belief that "all the moments of our life occupy the same space, as if future events already existed and were only waiting for us to find our way to them at last, just as when we have accepted an invitation we duly arrive in a certain house at a given time" (*Austerlitz*, 257–58). The novels of David Mitchell, from the first, *ghostwritten*, to the most recent, *The Bone Clocks*, might be considered as narrative invitations to explore Austerlitz's sense of the future as anterior to our arrival at the certain time and place of its manifestation in event, its realization in the present. At the age of forty-five as of this writing, Mitchell has rapidly established himself as a major presence in contemporary literature, certainly on a par with writers of the just-previous generation such as Ian McEwan, A.S. Byatt, and Kazuo Ishiguro. From the beginning, Mitchell's novels have demanded an immersion into the countless details of multiple times, spaces, and worlds intersecting and overlapping, culminating in stories written and received, thus "given," but intimating a host of possible stories and worlds in the offing, awaiting habitation. Mitchell's fiction invokes multiplicity. Contingency—that collision of randomness with facticity—is the plotful measure of his novels where characters and their ancestors or descendents transmigrate across stories set in universes that operate according to principles of spatial and temporal compression and dilation. The "certain" house at which one arrives in reading Mitchell—the novel one holds in one's hands—is typically composed of many parts and genres, the architecture being neither carpenter's gothic nor that of the sedimented multinovel, but a capacious assemblage of narratives connected to each other in differential patterns. Those patterns, detected by readers through variable acts of attention, can shift and fluctuate depending on the circumstances of one's reading, the narrative thread that draws one's notice at a given moment, the emergence of a sequence that compels one to recall something in a given novel's "past," or something that seems to be lurking in its "future." Mitchell's novels are fluid, mutable, and granular: they register change over time both thematically and architectonically. They invite readers who want to engage with the novelist in generating navigable realms consequential for an understanding of how we inhabit the world(s) that we have before us.

Born in the seaside town of Southport, Merseyside in 1969 and raised in Malvern, Worcestershire, Mitchell published *ghostwritten* at the age of thirty during an eight-year residency in Hiroshima teaching English to technical students. Just as his upbringing in the West Midlands informs his fourth novel, *blackswangreen* (2006), so his tenure in Japan and his travels in Asia most directly inform his second, *Number9Dream* (2001), and his fifth, *The Thousand Autumns of Jacob de Zoet* (2010). But Mitchell is not so much interested in the conversion of autobiographical experience into fiction as he is in disrupting any notions of singular identities or worlds with the phantasmagoric, manifold nature of human experience dispersed across the time and space of a life or millennia. He has discussed aspects of his own life in the many interviews he has given, including the challenges of growing up with a stammer, his university career at the University of Kent, where he pursued an M.A. degree in "the postmodern novel" ("The Art of Fiction," n.p.), and his decision to move to the West Cork town of Clonakilty, where he and his wife could raise a family in a place removed from the cosmopolitan furor of London and the high cost of living in Japan. The revelation of these details, however, is consistently turned toward the illumination of his writing, and away from the construction of a personality. I follow suit in this introduction to his fiction. Where a life detail is occasionally brought into the discussion, it is for the purpose of better understanding a narrative strategy or a thematic development, not for creating linkages between the "life" and "art" of David Mitchell. Stammering, for example, is of primary concern not as "speech impediment" suffered by the author, but as it contributes to an understanding of Mitchell's career-long engagement with translation and the relation of languages to world-building; uninterested in the cult of self, when he discusses his stammer, Mitchell is characteristically analytic, ironic, and self-deprecatory. Accordingly, the gaze, here, falls on the writing, in all of its richness and complexity.

From the beginning of his writing career, Mitchell has been the recipient of avid attention from reviewers, critics, and award juries. *ghostwritten*, a novel in ten parts that relates the stories of roughly contemporaneous protagonists scattered in locations from Okinawa, to St. Petersburg, to New York, won the John Llewellyn Rhys Prize for the best work of literature in the Commonwealth by a writer under the age of thirty-five.[1] *Number9Dream*, whose single protagonist enters the urban labyrinth of Tokyo in search of his father on a journey that requires the traversal of multiple realities, was short-listed for the 2001 Man Booker Prize, along with such notable works as Ian McEwan's *Atonement*, Ali Smith's *Hotel World*, and Peter Carey's *True History of the Kelly Gang*, which was selected for the prize. *Cloud Atlas* (2004), Mitchell's most widely read and well-known novel, and the first to be adapted for film, is an assemblage of six nested narratives that occur in times ranging from the mid-nineteenth century to a postmillennial future, and in locations from the deck of a British sailing ship in the South Seas to a tribal village in the remote future on the big island of Hawaii. *Cloud Atlas* was also short-listed for the Booker Prize, won in that year by Alan Hollinghurst's *The Line of Beauty*, and was the winner of the British Book Award for 2004. Just two years later, *blackswangreen*, a novel set in Mitchell's native Worcestershire and made up of a series of vignettes depicting the life of its thirteen-year-old protagonist during a critical year of domestic upheaval and national folly, was nominated for numerous prizes, including the Booker (long list), the Costa Book Awards, and the *Los Angeles Times* Book Prize. Mitchell's fifth novel, *The Thousand Autumns of Jacob de Zoet*, set in the Dutch East India Company trading post of Dejima in Nagasaki Bay on the cusp of the nineteenth century, won the Commonwealth Writers Prize, was long-listed for the Booker and short-listed for the recently instituted Walter Scott Prize for historical fiction. *The Bone Clocks* traces the life of Holly Sykes from the age of fifteen in 1984 to the age of seventy-four in 2043. A complex network of stories that circulate around Holly's involvement with larger historical, temporal, and cosmological forces, the novel alternates between fantasy and realism in projecting chronoscapes where the future of the planet is at stake.

In addition to this extraordinary succession of novels, Mitchell has written the libretto to Dutch composer Michael van der Aa's *The Sunken Garden*, which premiered at the English National Opera on April 12, 2013. The opera is described on van der Aa's website (http://www.vanderaa.net/sunkengarden) as "an occult-mystery film-opera" and was positively reviewed in such venues as the *New York Times*, the *Wall Street Journal*, and *The Observer* as a powerful experiment that combines 3-D film with live performance in portraying the plight of art and the artist in the digital age. Mitchell has also collaborated with his wife, KA Yoshida, in the translation of *The Reason I Jump* (2013), the remarkable diary written by a thirteen-year-old autistic boy, Naoki Higashida, arranged as a series of questions and answers. In the Introduction to the book, Mitchell candidly discusses his own experiences as the parent of an autistic son, and the ways in which Higashida's book "allowed me to round a corner in our relationship with [him]. Naoki Higashida's writing administered the kick I needed to stop feeling sorry for myself, and start thinking how much tougher life was for my son, and what I could do to make it less tough" (*Reason*, 10–11). The connections between these projects in other genres and Mitchell's hybridic fiction are many: the mixing of genres is a key element of Mitchell's novels to be examined later, but these recent forays into opera and translation highlight his ongoing interest in the way form enables specific narrative trajectories that can radically shift direction when genre boundaries are crossed.

Mitchell's ventures into multiple genres and his remarkable ability to capture the stylistic signatures of genre are well known. Indeed, they are a hallmark of his novels, each a story-assemblage containing numerous interrelated tales and multiple narrative trajectories. His readers have come to expect to encounter a bevy of voices and stories in successive novels: the flight of a terrorist, a history of modern China related through the eyes of an old woman living on a mountainside, or the transcript of New York talk radio show in *ghostwritten*; an escape from an asylum, political conspiracy at a California nuclear power plant, or the story of an escaped slave in the twenty-second century in *Cloud Atlas*; naval battles, the inner works of late-eighteenth-century Japanese court society, or the tale of a gothic blood-sacrifice cult in *The Thousand Autumns of Jacob de Zoet*. In these novels, the reader may recognize elements of the *noir* thriller, spiritual autobiography, *bildungsroman*, travelogue, science fiction novel, and survival narrative jostling up against each other. Multiple discursive entities occupy the same space in Mitchell's fiction as well: letter, diary, note, story and story-within-a-story, poem, song, dream, joke, sketch—most or all of them can be found in each of his narrative assemblages. Perhaps most visibly in the six recursive narratives of *Cloud Atlas*, one can detect the myriad intertextual "voices" that echo throughout his fiction: Melville and Conrad in the "The Pacific Journal of Adam Ewing"; Nabokovian petulance in "Letters from Zedelghem"; the self-incriminating wit of Anthony Burgess (especially the Burgess of *Earthly Powers* [1980]) in "The Ghastly Ordeal of Timothy Cavendish"; or Russell Hoban's *Ridley Walker* (1980) in "Sloosha's Crossin' An' Ev'rythin' After." Calvino's *rashoman* narrratives, Borges' forking paths and infinite libraries, Murakami's hallucinatory dreamscapes—all can be seen as echoed in Mitchell's fiction writ large.

Yet Mitchell does not view himself as a characteristically "postmodern" writer, engaging in metafictional experiments and mashups or writing under the aegis of magical realism or postmodern pastiche. As he says in a recent discussion with the *Guardian*'s Stuart Jeffries on the film adaptation of *Cloud Atlas*, "I don't want to project myself as this great experimenter—I'm not. In any case, the words 'experimental novelist' must make your heart sink as much as the words 'British magical realism'" (Jeffries, n.p.). In part, Mitchell's desire not to be identified as an experimentalist in the postmodern tradition is related to his investment in "story" as an immersive, polyglot medium for which self-reflexivity is a component among others—as it has been in the novel since *Don Quixote*—but not necessarily the primary ingredient.² True, Mitchell "plays" with genre; his novels characteristically exhibit quantum or calendrical intricacies of plot and form; across separate novels, he populates tiled, contingent fictional worlds with recurring characters, clearly signaling the incorporation of metafictional elements into his writing (self-parodically so in the character of "Goatwriter," a nomadic bard chasing after his lost text in one of the alternative universes of *Number9Dream*). But these moves are primarily indicative of his own immersion into deep storytelling traditions—written and oral—that have always relied upon an awareness of the narrative medium as a form of mediation. In Mitchell's hands, these techniques are put into the larger service of articulating "thick" fictional worlds in which the narrational contexts informing action, character, event, setting, sequence, the navigation of space, and the fluctuation of time are integral to an understanding of "story" as a social and cultural force.³

It is certain that Mitchell has been deeply influenced by "classic" postmodernism, at least in terms of some elements of form and technique; after all, there is the aforementioned M.A. degree in "the postmodern novel" and the homage to Calvino and Murakami discernible in *Cloud Atlas* and *Number9Dream*, respectively. But beyond or beside postmodernism, there are a number of revealing frameworks for a consideration of Mitchell's fiction and its place in contemporary writing. Mitchell has been viewed as a "cosmopolitan" writer by Berthold Schoene, whose excellent *The Cosmopolitan Novel* includes a chapter entitled "The World Begins Its Turn with You, or How David Mitchell's Novels Think," which discusses *ghostwritten* and *Cloud Atlas* as embodying

> Mitchell's ambition...to imagine globality by depicting worldwide human living in multifaceted, delicately entwined, serialised snapshots of the human condition, marked by global connectivity and virtual proximity as much as psycho-geographical detachment and xenophobic segregation....Mitchell's fiction summons humanity's world-creative potential as well as its tragic (self-) destructiveness into a kind of literary communality which his readers are not only invited to relate to, but must partake of as inhabitants of one and the same world. (98)

While I do not agree that it is "one and the same world" resulting from the "world-creative potential" that Mitchell activates in his readers, but multiple worlds traversed by mobile identities, Schoene's formulation eloquently captures the investments of Mitchell's novels in connectivity, occurring across time, space, region, and domain. It is the connection between locations, characters, and spatiotemporal zones, globally scattered, that is at the heart of the cosmopolitanism evidenced throughout Mitchell's writing. The effect of connectivity in Mitchell—quite different from "connection" in writers such as Thomas Pynchon and Don DeLillo—is not conspiratorial, the standing condition of late capitalist postmodernism; but neither is it neoliberal or humanist in any traditional sense, a twenty-first-century version of E.M. Forster's "only connect" as the solution to the dilemma of cultural estrangement. Connectivity in Mitchell can be seen as the semirandom convergence of identities and events in narratable patterns that militate against official histories, territorial agendas, and social hierarchies in proffering the possibility, in Schoene's terms, not of "a particular destiny for the whole of humanity," but (based on Jean-Luc Nancy's philosophy of community) an open, indeterminate, and temporary future, the "spacing of a world, a world that is always 'to come'" (98).

Mitchell's cosmopolitanism can be seen as a matter of both plot and style. His novels contain numerous scenes in which characters on rhizomic journeys stray from the pathways of a nominal world and reality and, in the process, discover alternative communities, worlds, and impermanent, nondestined futures that they can only project in the anterior mode as proceeding from randomness and surprise. Neal Brose, the compromised lawyer of *ghostwritten* working for an international firm engaged in shady financial dealings, simply does not go to work one day; his wandering through the maze-like pathways of a holy mountain leads to a confrontation with the transitory nature of his existence and the recognition of realities close by that he never knew existed. A "fabricant" escaping her enslavers in "The Orison of Sonmi~451" (*Cloud Atlas*) stumbles upon a community of outcasts from the corporate, racist governmental hierarchy of twenty-second century "Nea So Copros" (Seoul, Korea); the members of the community, housed in an abandoned convent, give her temporary refuge and represent a version of human existence based on hospitality to strangers. A similar community is discovered by Jason Taylor, the adolescent protagonist of *blackswangreen*, when he wanders too far into the woods bordering the English middle-class town of the novel's title and discovers an encampment of travelers who eventually welcome him into their midst and protect him from the threats of bullies. On each of these occasions, the new path or community is discovered by accident, as forms of contingency that were always there, but hidden from the heretofore constricted view of the observer. In Mitchell's novels, the discovery of other worlds and realities almost exclusively occurs as the result of wandering or escape, such that his cosmopolitanism, as plotted, envisions circumstantial itineraries and the serendipitous crossing of the multiple paths of those roaming outside the matrices and orders of a normative reality.

The many nomadic sojourners of Mitchell's novels represent an aspect of a modernist cosmopolitanism that Rebecca Walkowitz suggests has its origins in the nineteenth-century tradition of the *flâneur*, he or she who wanders through the city streets noting its oddities, its hidden pockets of humanity, and its underworld, thereby discovering radical alterities of city life. Further, Walkowitz describes in her compelling analysis of modern and contemporary cosmopolitan writers ranging from Joyce and Woolf to Ishiguro and Sebald a "cosmopolitan style" that Mitchell both shares and from which he deviates. According to Walkowitz, modernist cosmopolitan style

> registers the limits of perception and the waning of a confident epistemology, the conflict between the exhaustive and the ineffable, the appeal of the trivial, the political consequences of uniformity and variousness in meaning, the fragmentation of perspectives, and the disruption of social categories. (20)

There are a number of moving parts to this description, and indeed, the "cosmopolitan style" of Mitchell's fiction reflects perceptual limitation and "the waning of a confident epistemology" in its multiperspectivalism and in its insistence on the partiality of knowledge as a condition of time passing. His novels are often engaged in revealing the political consequences and sheer brutality of uniformity and totalization in the regimes of civilization it depicts, from the Enlightenment and age of colonialism to postapocalyptic tribal cultures. The "appeal of the trivial" in his work can be seen in the seemingly endless lists of brand names noted by Jason, immersed in commodity culture, in *blackswangreen*; the "disruption of social categories" is enacted in the hodgepodge assemblage of identities that circumstantially come together throughout Mitchell's novels.

At the same time, his own version of "cosmopolitan style" incorporates significant variations on this theme. Mitchell is not so much interested in a "fragmentation of perspectives" as he is in the way that multiple divergent perspectives can haphazardly overlap or collide, though never adding up in their multiplicity to some singular composite "world" or view. This tendency is consonant with his formalistic decision to bring a number of genres into play in his novels in order to generate a hybridity of tiled worlds marked by connective variations in temporality and localization.[4] Nor is "the ineffable" in conflict with "the exhaustive" in Mitchell's fiction in the ways Walkowitz suggests: an example exists in Joyce's catalogs of signs and objects in *Ulysses*, in contrast to the quasi-profane, quasi-mystical nature of Molly's desire or Stephen Dedalus' metaphysical sensibility. For Mitchell, specifically, the ineffable of "the human," registered in noncorporeal sentient intelligence of *ghostwritten*, the birthmarked protagonists of *Cloud Atlas*, and the "atemporal" sojourners and returnees of *The Bone Clocks*, is embodied materially and corporally in identities scattered across time and space, whose futures, imagined and unimaginable, are precarious in the face of material exhaustibility. Mitchell's cosmopolitan style is thus infused with temporality: knowledge, identity, consciousness, perception, and difference—all become visible only as traces of time's passing and as glimmers of what a temporary precarious future may hold.

Stylistically, Mitchell's cosmopolitanism reveals itself in the centrifugal, extra-referential lines of flight that can often be observed in the mental observations and digressions of his characters. Hugo Lamb, of *The Bone Clocks*, offers a telling example. He is a Cambridge University student who also appears at a younger age as Jason Taylor's cousin in *blackswangreen*. Hugo's mind wanders following sex with Mariângela Pinto-Pereira, a Brazilian nurse who is one of, apparently, several current girlfriends and sex partners:

> Mariângela's dream-catcher swings when I biff it, and I find my lover's crucifix among her boingy curls. I hold the Son of God in my mouth, and imagine him dissolving on my tongue. Sex may be the antidote to death but it offers life everlasting only to the species, not the individual. On the CD player, Ella Fitzgerald forgets the words to "Mac the Knife" one broiling night in Berlin over forty years summers ago. A District Line rumbles down below. Mariângela kisses the fleshy underside of my forearm, then bites, hard. "Ow," I complain, enjoying the pain. "Is that Portuguese for 'The Earth moved for me, my lord and master, how was it for you?'" (126)

The passage is both casual—a tangle of spontaneously associative mental threads—and, yet, circuitously relevant to several of the concerns around which Mitchell's novels orbit. *The Bone Clocks*, in part, is a novel-long reflection on mortality, its title referring to chronometer of the body that measures its demise with each tick of the clock. The scandalous address to Mariângela's crucifix—as the host in a communion rite after hot sex—recalls the blasphemous religiosity of the demonic cult leader in *The Thousand Autumns of Jacob de Zoet*, as well as the corporeal basis of Christianity to which Mitchell draws our attention throughout his novels. Ella Fitzgerald's rendition of "Mac the Knife" from the 1960 live album *Ella in Berlin* plays in the background. Recorded at the height of the Cold War and divided Berlin by the great African American jazz singer, the track is infamous because Fitzgerald forgot the lyrics to the song and made up her own on the fly. This implicitly speaks to notions of story and history as improvisation that one encounters both in the forms and the plots of Mitchell's fiction, as well as to the capacious knowledge of jazz and pop displayed by Mitchell's protagonists: a song list of the titles referenced by Jason Taylor in *blackswangreen*, for example, would include hundreds of titles. Hugo's notation of the decades that have passed between the world's "then" and his "now" touches upon the mutable temporalities and time-jumps of Mitchell's fiction, and the shifting historical contexts to which his characters' mental wanderings always consciously or unconsciously refer. Mariângela's love bite is recognized as body language translatable (or not) into "Portuguese" for an English expression—a subtle reference to Mitchell's interest in both translation and the somatic language of the body. The laid-back affect of passage conceals its thematic and historical reach beyond the singularities of the individual and the moment; such reflections are typical of characters' thought patterns in the novels, and indicative of their worldliness, even in a seemingly offhand instance.

There are other frameworks conjoining and overlapping with the cosmopolitanism of Mitchell's novels that illuminate the specificities of his fiction. Especially relevant to the view of Mitchell as a cosmopolitan novelist is that of Tom LeClair, who, in a review of Hari Kunzru's *Gods Without Men* (2012), identifies Mitchell along with Kunzru, Thomas Pynchon, Don DeLillo, and Tom McCarthy as an "anthropological novelist": "a writer who presents individual psychology and current society through the long and wide lenses of cultural systems—religious, historical, political, technological—as they are affected by a particular physical environment" (LeClair, n.p.).[5] LeClair's insight is crucial to an understanding of how Mitchell's fiction works. Rather than viewing Mitchell and the company he keeps in more familiar terms as an "encyclopedic novelist" in the tradition of Cervantes, Melville, Joyce, and Pynchon, whose novels are noted for their erudition and archival depth, LeClair regards Kunzru, McCarthy, and Mitchell, tangentially and locally, as writers who move across regions and regimes to probe the connections between the disparate elements, cultures, and social orders of the planet they inhabit.[6] To be sure, Mitchell's writing throughout his career is "encyclopedic" in its discursive array. In *ghostwritten*, for example, particle physics, the history of modern China, an impressive playlist of contemporary jazz melodies and pop tunes, descriptions of walking itineraries of Hong Kong, St. Petersburg, and London, Buddhism, and transcripts generated by global telecommunications systems intersect at multiple points in the stories of strangers seemingly connected only by chance. Yet it is the kernel of contingency at the heart of worldly circumstances that comprises Mitchell's "anthropology." His novels convey the sense that everything is laterally connected not because of some monolithic notion of "the human race" inhabiting a singular global environment, but because humans are only one of countless life-forms existing in a shared spatiotemporal realm where technology, among other things, is making increasingly obvious the extent to which micro- and macro-cultures affect, constitute, and are responsible for each other.

The anthropology of Mitchell's fiction, or more precisely, the archaeological anthropology of work equally invested in the material and social dimensions of human cultures, can be further defined in contrast to vertical fictional archaeologies such as that of the popular American novelist James A. Michener, who, in *Hawaii* (1959), *Centennial* (1974), and *Chesapeake* (1978) layers stories in chronological order from historical periods ranging from the prehistoric to the contemporary in an attempt to foreground the progressive evolution of the transcendent "human" amidst mutable cultural circumstances. We shall see how Mitchell lateralizes this synchronic genetic concept of "deep" history and storytelling in *Cloud Atlas* into the networks of contingency evident throughout his fiction. Nor is Mitchell's fiction merely to be considered in the category of neural or network narratives that David Bordwell has defined for a number of contemporary films, including *Babel* (2006), *Crash* (2005), and *Syriana* (2005), which "open up a social structure of acquaintance, kinship and friendship beyond any one character's ken. The narration gradually reveals the array to us, attaching us to one character, then another ... [who] have diverging purposes and projects, and these intersect only occasionally – often accidentally" (Bordwell, 190; cited in Peters, n.p.). The "six degrees of separation" evident in such films can all too easily be read as facile versions of New Age global interconnectivity about which Mitchell is deeply suspicious.

More accurately, while Mitchell's novels, as they unfold, reveal an increasingly complex set of connections that exist between stories, histories, characters, and itineraries, they do so in the service of representing human interaction across what Mary Louise Pratt has termed "contact zones," or "social spaces where cultures meet, clash, and grapple with each other, often in contexts of highly asymmetrical relations of power, or their aftermaths as they are lived out in many parts of the world today" (Pratt, 34). Beginning with his first, Mitchell's novels depict cultural "zones" and the identities who inhabit them in spatiotemporal adjacency. The adjacencies and contingencies of his fiction are as often differential, frictional, and laden with the asymmetries of power as they are indicative of any sense of implicitly harmonious human connectivity. The characters of his novels frequently encounter each other and life-altering circumstances as a matter of sheer (and, sometimes, bad) accident, though the multiple linkages available in and across Mitchell's novels often suggest that the coincidental, viewed after the fact, is at the same time the fated and fatal.

As Pieter Vermeulen has suggested of *ghostwritten*, Mitchell's fiction "rigorously refuses a privileged perspective or a unifying voice"; it represents characters and voices, locales and routes of traversal notable for their differences, even the intransigency of their adjacency, existing "side by side as different parts that do not add up to a coherent whole" (Vermeulen, 382). Vermeulen further notes that Mitchell can also be regarded as the novelist of globalization whose fiction, citing Michael Annesley, touches upon "tourism, climate change, Jihadi terrorism, the power of international brands, mass migrations, the spread of the English language, and the rise of trans-national media conglomerates" (Annesley, 112). In the novels, these topics are treated in contiguous narratives often dispersed across a spatial-temporal horizon indicative of Mitchell's sense that the "global" is an assemblage of contact zones, migratory (and transmigratory) routes, minor histories, and contrasting and overlying cultural systems. To Annesley's list might be added Mitchell's interest not only in "the spread of the English language" but also in translation as a process that reveals the *portmanteaux* as well as the intransigencies of linguistic difference; his depictions of cultural violence as having origins in national or sovereign agendas that militate against human survival in the historical long view; his sense of the "planetary" delineated by Susan Stanford Friedman as "a consciousness of the earth as a planet, not restricted to geopolitical formations and potentially encompassing the non-human as well as the human" (Friedman, 495), and an observance of "an interactional set of relations throughout the globe that may also manifest differently in particular places and times" (Friedman, 478). Mitchell's novels portray "relations" between cultures and identities in precisely this manner, the differential particularities of time and place an essential component of the content of his fiction.

Regarded in this light, Mitchell is part of a larger, diverse company of contemporary writers who reflect "planetarity" in their depictions of hybrid localities and cultures that are relatable via the diverse identities that traverse them, either corporeally or virtually. We might include in a list of such writers Zadie Smith, whose *White Teeth* (2000) portrays cultural and racial conflicts in first- and second-generation immigrant families living in "mixed" neighborhoods in contemporary North-West London; Orhan Pamuk, who, in novels such as *The New Life* (1998) and *Snow* (2004), depicts nomadic figures undertaking geographical and spatiotemporal boundary crossings; Andrés Neuman, whose *Traveler of the Century* (2012) portrays a man who wanders into and out of a city dislocated in space and time, much like that of Kazuo Ishiguro's *The Unconsoled* (1995); China Miéville, whose *Perdido Street Station* (2000) and *The City & the City* (2009) depict the metropolis as a place of identity-assemblages (some of them interspecial) that move through a realm of strict hierarchical systems and zones; Haruki Murakami, whose *The Wind-Up Bird Chronicle* (1997) and *1Q84* (2011) are admixtures of history, fantasy, and dream featuring characters in search of family and identity; or Paolo Bacigalupi, whose similarly named *The Windup Girl* (2009) is a dystopic novel set in future Thailand depicting a genetically enhanced slave who seeks escape from a nightmarish landscape of environmental disaster where bioterrorists, nomads, and corporate militia freely roam the city. The list could be extended indefinitely, but it is worth noting that all of these very different novels, published during the cycle of Mitchell's own writing career, share a common interest with Mitchell in understanding the "global" not as a totality, but as a series of shifting planes and contingent zones crossed by individuals whose itineraries are often a matter of circumstance.

Miéville's fiction, in particular, is suggestive of another framework common among writers of planetarity and useful for considering Mitchell's fiction—that of psychogeography. Historically, psychogeography develops out of the Situationist philosophy of Guy Debord, who defines it as "the study of the precise laws and specific effects of the geographical environment, whether consciously organized or not, on the emotions and behavior of individuals" (Debord, "Introduction," 8). One of the principles of psychogeography, according to Debord, is that of the *dérive*, an activity in which "one or more persons during a certain period drop their relations, their work and leisure activities, and all their other usual motives for movement and action, and let themselves be drawn by the attractions of the terrain and the encounters they find there" (Debord, "Theory," 62). Contingency and chance operate in tandem in the *dérive*, neither having ascendency since the activity involves moving through a composite environment, such as a city, organized into routes and districts, but one that is replete with serendipitous encounters and hidden byways:

> Chance is a less important factor in this activity than one might think: from a dérive point of view cities have psychogeographical contours, with constant currents, fixed points and vortexes that strongly discourage entry into or exit from certain zones.
>
> But the dérive includes both this letting-go and its necessary contradiction: the domination of psychogeographical variations by the knowledge and calculation of their possibilities. (Knabb, 1279–81)

From his first novel onward, as I shall emphasize in the discussion of *ghostwritten*, Mitchell's novels proceed psychogeographically, their protagonists pursuing itineraries through complex landscapes. These, in effect, become available to them because, willingly or not, they have "dropped their relations" with normality. In so doing, they are subjected to the contradiction that exists between the "calculus" of the material realms they inhabit and the chance encounters and events that abound everywhere once they are liberated from the navigation of reality solely through the matrices of Euclidean space and chronological time. For the reader, the exposure to multiple worlds and temporalities inhabiting the same novelistic domain instigates the possibility of varying futures as the novel is being read. As the community of readers that has grown around Mitchell's novels attest in blogs and reader reviews, second- and third-time readings of a novel can inspire identifications and forms of attention to detail-sets and plot threads that culminate in an entirely different itinerary through a given novel than was the case with the first reading. As will be seen in the readings to follow, Mitchell's novels are situational and "psychogeographic" for both protagonists and readers, as each party navigates narrative terrains that continuously shift in terms of affect, relationality, and connectivity.

Even though the term was developed by a twentieth-century Marxist social theorist, the novel, arguably, has always been a psychogeographic genre, and historians of psychogeography have traced its effects back to Defoe's *Robinson Crusoe* (1719) and *Journal of the Plague Year* (1722), and forwards from that point through the writings of Charles Dickens, Edgar Allan Poe, Thomas de Quincey, Robert Louis Stevenson, and Arthur Machen to contemporaries such as Will Self, Peter Ackroyd, Iain Sinclair, J.G. Ballard, and W.G. Sebald.[7] All of these writers approach cities and landscapes as opportunities for understanding the relation between human identity and built and natural environments. For each, the exploration of local conditions in their materiality is a combination of chance and circumstance: an obstruction leads to a new route, and something unseen in previous journeys; a hidden pathway leads to a different sequence of events than one had expected, or that had been prefigured by the narrative trajectory of one's previous orientation; and the connections between past and future—where one has come from, and where one is going—are tentative and frayed.

We can consider Quasar, the protagonist of "Okinawa" in *ghostwritten*, as an example. Having executed a terrorist gas attack in a Tokyo subway, he escapes to a village on the small island of Kumejima in Okinawa, and discovers on his solitary walks and his encounters with inhabitants manifestations of strangeness and eccentricity that trouble his ingrained perceptions of nature, politics, and human behavior; his fate is to be lost and confused in an environment that is both self-contained ("The road looped back to the port, as all the roads on this island eventually do" [31]) and infinitely opaque ("Clouds begin to ink out the stars, one by one" [31]). His story, like the stories of many of Mitchell's protagonists, is an itinerary, the navigation of a landscape that his both familiar and alien. Like Quasar, many of Mitchell's protagonists navigate the islands scattered across Mitchell's global landscape: Adam Ewing, in *Cloud Atlas*, temporarily stranded on the Chatham Islands; Jacob de Zoet, clerking for the East India Company on the artificial island of Dejima in *The Thousand Autumns of Jacob de Zoet*; Eiji Mayake, in *Number9Dream*, leaving and returning to Yakushima, the island domain of his boyhood; Mo Muntervary, in *ghostwritten*, escaping from the C.I.A. to her childhood home of Clear Island off the coast of Southwest Ireland; a group of survivors living on Hawaii in the postapocalyptic future. For Mitchell, islands embody a paradox in that they are circumscribed, contained topographies—their margins or borders a matter of different elements, yet fractal as they are always changing in size and shape, their interiors replete with hidden recesses, and their histories signposted by remnants and ruins. They exist as forms of provisional space.[8]

Mitchell's islands are not just those that are named on a map: seagoing vessels, crowded pubs, bureaucratic offices, homes for the elderly, city zones, museums, restaurants, educational institutions, and amusement parks—all exist as time-bound, islanded spaces with more or less permeable barriers, each containing a singular culture (though often heterogeneous within), yet by virtue of that singularity, indicative of the fact that it is one among many. Hugo Lamb again provides an example while navigating toward the bar of a student pub in 1991 Cambridge. The description of the crowd is characteristic of Mitchell's "centrifugal" style, as well as his extraordinary ability to capture period mise-en-scène:

> The Buried Bishop's a gridlocked scrum, an all-you-can-eat of youth: "Stephen Hawing and the Dalai Lama, right; they posit a unified truth"; short denim skirts, Gap and Next Shirts, Kurt Cobain cardigans, black Levi's; "Did you see that oversexed pig by the loos, undressing me with his eyes?"; that song by the Pogues and Kristy MacColl booms in my diaphragm and knees; "Like, *my* only charitty shop bargains were headlice, scabies, and fleas"; a fug of hairspray, seat and Lynx, Chanel No. 5, and smoke; ... high-volume discourse on who's the best Bond; on Gilmour and Waters and Syd; on hyperreality; dollar-pound parity; Sartre, Bart Simpson, Barthes's myths; "Make mine a double"; George Michael's stubble; "Like, music expired with the Smiths"; urbane and entitled, for the most part, my peers their eyes, hopes and

futures all starry; fetal think-tankers, judges and bankers... they're sprung from the loins of the global elite.... (109–10)

The mob scene at the Buried Bishop, which is recorded Altman-style by the flâneur Hugo as he takes note of the discourse of 1990s "global elite" youth culture, exists on a single and singular plane, one of *The Bone Clocks'* thousand plateaus that intersect in the multiple times and spaces of the novel.[9] Its eccentricity lies in the multiple speech registers of Hugo's overhearing that extend outwards to the economic, historical, aesthetic, and philosophical in the stray references to feminism, global capitalism, poststructuralist philosophy, and grunge fashion that Hugo detects. The potential connectivity of his many islands—both to each other and to the "ev'rythin' after" of their localized styles, discourse, and histories—constitutes Mitchell's fiction as an assemblage, a navigation of variegated plateaus.

In Mitchell's novels, the linkages between characters, topographies, events, itineraries, and histories are always in a process of formation. Although his writing may be different in many ways from that of W.G. Sebald's, Mitchell shares with him the characteristic of asynopticism observed by fellow contemporary British novelist Will Self, whose *Psychogeography: Disentangling the Modern Conundrum of Psyche and Space* (2007) offers one of the most insightful commentaries on the movement. For Sebald, according to Self, "a synoptic view is quite impossible.... at every turn, Sebald confounds his own achievement...: the dead are not dead, time is inconsistent—no river running smoothly from past to future, but eddies and crosscurrents of chronology—while coincidences are none the less hugely significant" (Self, n.p.). While Sebald's narrative confounding often takes place through observation, description, and the digressions of memory stirred by a chance encounter, Mitchell's occurs through the movement of characters amidst shifting temporalities and locations, and the juxtaposition (or collision) of multidirectional narrative trajectories. Mitchell's cosmopolitanism thus conjoins with his psychogeographic tendencies in the articulation of narrative worlds replete with possibilities for proximate connections between nomadic identities over time.

With its mixture of genres, voices, and styles, fluctuating between recognizably traditional narrative modes and those more visibly reflexive and contemporary, Mitchell's fiction resists easy classification, yet it bears some of the traces of the "metamodern." Timotheus Vermeulen and Robin van den Akker have deployed the term to refer to a "structure of feeling" that has come into being in the twenty-first century in the wake of "financial crises, geopolitical instabilities... climatological uncertainties... the disintegration of the political center on both a geopolitical level... and a national level" (4–5).

For Vermeulen and van den Akker, the result in many contemporary cultural forms and expressions is an "abandoning [of] tactics such as pastiche and parataxis for strategies like myth and metaxis, melancholy for hope, and exhibitionism for engagement" (5). They note that "metamodernistic" art forms oscillate "between a modern enthusiasm and a postmodern irony, between hope and melancholy, between naïveté and knowingness, empathy and apathy, unity and plurality, totality and fragmentation, purity and ambiguity" (5–6). Perhaps most pertinent to Mitchell's novels, they write that "the metamodern should be understood as a spacetime that is both/neither ordered and disordered. Metamodernism displaces the parameters of the present with those of a future present that is futureless" (12).[10]

While Mitchell's fiction does not share every feature of metamodernism as defined by Vermeulen and van den Akker, in the conjunction of multiple genres and rhizomic narrative trajectories, it does often affectively "oscillate" between "hope and melancholy," as occurs, for example, in the moment when Jacob de Zoet, returning to Holland after eighteen years of service to the Dutch East India Company on the trading post of Dejima in Nagasaki Bay, projects a future based on memories of the past in his homeland haunted by an alternative future he will never have in leaving Japan behind. The entirety of *Number9Dream* features a protagonist who continuously vacillates between "naïvité and knowingness" as the precondition for survival in the labyrinthine metropolis of Tokyo; and, in all of Mitchell's novels, there is both the structural and thematic alternation between partial, indexical "worlds" that culminate in a fractal assemblage of deeply interconnected stories and events. But most significantly, Mitchell's novels fabricate a "spacetime" in which the fatal and the serendipitous cross paths; where hierarchical, often tyrannical, social orders labor under the illusion of eternal domain in a quantum universe in which, according to *Cloud Atlas*' Timothy Cavendish, "Time's Arrow" has become "Time's Boomerang" (147); and where the primary tense is that of the "future present," implying the coexistence of multiple futures, including the potential "futurelessness" of global apocalypse.

To this last feature of Mitchell's fiction much of my discussion of his novels will be dedicated. Mitchell is interested in time and temporality in multiple domains: scientific, historical, subjectival, calendrical, and epochal. His "interdisciplinary" novels contain portrayals of scientists, doctors, herbalists, astrologers, and navigators, all students of the effects of time passing and time to come upon nature and culture. In *ghostwritten* and *Cloud Atlas* alone, there are, successively, two scientists—Mo Muntervary, an Irish quantum physicist, and Isaac Sachs, an American nuclear engineer—each operating in different worlds, but both working under assumptions about temporality such as that expressed by Sachs:

Symmetry demands an actual + virtual future, too. We imagine how next week, next year, or 2225 will shape up—a virtual future, constructed by wishes, prophecies + daydreams. This virtual future may influence the actual future, as in a self-fulfilling prophecy, but the actual future will eclipse our virtual one surely as tomorrow eclipses today. ... the actual future + the actual past exist only in the hazy distance, where they are no good to anyone. (393)

Sachs' mathematics of temporality is ironically hedged by "actual" circumstances: he is about to be blown up in a plane as part of a conspiracy to silence witnesses to design flaws in an unstable nuclear power plant. His view of temporality as instantiating multiple virtual pasts, presents, and futures that only become "real" in the aftermath, like tracing the path of quarks in a particle accelerator, accords with that of Mo Muntervary, who adds a perspective about the reversibility of time consonant with her research in the field of "quantum chronodynamics" (323) that calculates the slowing down and speeding up of time in relation to mass. Mo posits that theories of relativity and quantum mechanics, applied to the linkage between past, present, and future, result in a "scientific" view of history and temporality that echoes throughout Mitchell's novels: "The double-crossed, might-have-been history of my country is not the study of what actually took place here: it's the study of historians' studies. Historians have their axes to grind, just as physicists do. Memories are their own descendants masquerading as the ancestors of the present" (318). In this relativistic temporality of many worlds, where the future is anterior to the present until realized at the other end of the chronological scale as the "real" past, "each of us," as Mo puts it, is "a loose particle, an infinity of paths through the park, probable ones, improbable ones, none of them real until observed, whatever real means" (329).[11]

The future in Mitchell's novels, as indicated in the title of this book, is a virtual condition, wholly temporary because it is only recognized as *the* future once it has evaporated and been posited as the "what happened," inevitably different from the many things that might have happened, the many identities one might have become, or the many worlds one might have navigated. Mitchell's fiction charts the permutations of this differential equation in its cross-hatched plots, parallel and colliding itineraries, intersections of chance, coincidence, and circumstance, and characters-avatars reborn, marked, transmigrated, and reduplicated across the six novels. Mitchell's characters often speak of time and the movements of bodies through space in relativistic, haphazard terms: for Cavendish, the passage of time (a boomerang) is visible in its reversal; later in his narrative, he revises the metaphor: "Time, no arrow, no boomerang, but a concertina"

(354), temporality having become, for him, a variable set of compressions and dilations. For Goatwriter, the fictional author within a manuscript read by Eiji Mayake, the protagonist of *Number9Dream*, "[t]ime relapsed and collapsed" (227); for Marco, a ghostwriter and musician roaming the streets of London in *ghostwritten*, "[t]ime buckled" as he awaits a fateful spin of the roulette wheel at a casino (304); and for Hugo Lamb of *The Bone Clocks*, gazing at the figure of a retired military officer in a rest home, time is an optical instrument: "I, too, will end up like this vulnerable old man. When I look at Brigadier Reginald Philby, I'm looking down time's telescope at myself" (126). In these figures and dozens of other that recur across Mitchell's novels, a poetics of temporal materiality emerges: time is imagined as a musical instrument, a hunting tool, a sick patient, and a geological plate. Each suggests the mutable relation between past and future founded upon the instability of time itself. If time is a boomerang, then the future will return to the past; if time is a concertina, then past and future overlap in variegated patterns as one moves to and fro between them; in geological time, the buckling of the temporal plate portends a violent set of collisions between shifting pasts and futures. Collectively, Mitchell's temporal figures are indicative of a temporality that encompasses multiple pasts and futures existing in various ratios of relation to each other; how a specific past will be resolved into a specific future depends, in essence, on what "time" it is.

While, on the one hand, the notion of a temporary future is conveyed through the memories, experiences, and imaginative projections of his characters, a countervailing need for temporal determinacy—a *measurable* relation between past, present, and future—is also perceptible in the many clocks, calendars, and chronological devices to be found in his fiction. Throughout, the dating of parts, chapters, letters, and diaries in the novels is a matter of both variation and precision. In *The Thousand Autumns of Jacob de Zoet*, there is a dual chronology that uses both the Japanese calendar ("the ninth night of the fifth month" of "[t]he eleventh year of the Era of Kansei" [2]) and the Western Calendar ("Evening of July 20, 1799" [10]) for the dating of the parts and chapters. In *Cloud Atlas*, we can observe forms of dating that range from the familiar ("Thursday, 7th November" [2]), to the pretentious ("29th-VI-1931" [41]), and the postlapsarian ("Abbess'd teached us Clock Tongue but I'd forgot it, 'cept for *O'Clock* an *Half Past*. I mem'ry Abbess sayin', *Civ'lize needs time, an' if we let this clock die, time'll die to, an' then how can we bring back the Civ'lize Days as it was b'fore the Fall?*" [247]). The manifest time-signature of *The Bone Clocks* is quite visible in its title, its cover showing concentric clock faces, and one of its six parts entitled "An Horologist's Labyrinth."

The relation between the temporal relativism that underlies the "real time" of the quantum universes Mitchell depicts and the human, historicist need for marking and experiencing time diurnally, chronologically, and calendrically is parallel to the relation between contingency and fate in the novels. As Marco puts it when comparing a live football match to one viewed on videotape after the fact of the game, in the latter:

> The past, present, and future exist at the same time: all the tape is there, in your hand. There can be no chance, for every human decision and random fall of the ball is already fated. Therefore, does chance or fate control our lives? Well, the answer is as relative as time. If you're in your life, chance. Viewed from the outside, like a book you're reading, it's fate all the way. (283)

That this reflection exists in a novel *we* are reading might be viewed as one of the many metafictional gestures of Mitchell's writing, which are inevitably directed at the reader's fourth wall engagement with the book she is reading. But Marco's thought experiment also brings together the crucial elements of the temporality of Mitchell's novels: time passing into the future, seen through a rear-view mirror in which objects may be closer than they appear, is both relative and determined, depending on the perspective informing the perception of time as such. Chance can appear to be fatal if one rewinds the tape at a certain speed; what becomes fate in the aftermath might have been, at the time, a matter of sheer circumstance. For Mitchell, the future is always temporary in that it exists as the future only momentarily, and because it is wholly reliant on a measuring of time passing that generates the necessary illusion of anterior determinacy.

The conception of temporality informs a host of key concerns in Mitchell's novels. The rise and fall of empires, for example, whether Roman or American, is often visible in the background of Mitchell's fiction; the utopian aspirations of empires and their dystopic consequences play out in contrast to the future conceived as multiple and temporary. Empires as represented in the novels are inevitably built upon the fantasy of permanence, of a "guaranteed" future of social and cultural stability assured by the universal implementation of a singular, dominant ideology through economic and military conquest. The Thousand Year Reich, the New World Order, and the imperial domains of Rome, Constantinople, Britain, Holland, and a hundred others—all have maintained this fantasy, and all have collapsed into the "alternative" future of its evaporation. Gibbon is thus required reading for Mitchell, and one can spot references to *The History of the Decline and Fall of the Roman Empire* (1776–89) in several of the novels. Written in the age of globalization that, in at least one of its versions, envisions a totalized global order operating under the aegis of universal capitalism, Mitchell's novels are set amidst empires, or societies with pretensions to empire, coming and going, present and past, but all of them subject to the ravages of time and change. *The Thousand Autumns of Jacob de Zoet* takes place primarily at the moment when the reach of the Dutch empire is in steep decline and the British Empire is on the rise—both trajectories signified in trading relationships with a Japanese empire on the verge of modernization. In *Cloud Atlas*, the techno-corporate dystopia of twenty-fourth-century Nea So Copros has been built upon the backs of enslaved clones, whose evolving individual and collective consciousness will inevitably lead to revolt and overthrow (though in the larger historical reach of the novel, global nuclear apocalypse has occurred at some point later in time such that the only remnant of empire of any kind are rival tribal moieties). In *blackswangreen*, Jason Taylor's maturation takes place against the last gasp of the British Empire in the Falklands Conflict. For Mitchell, the condition of the temporary can extend to the instant of the present, the span of a human life, or the age of an empire, but in all cases, the future is a transient state of radical indeterminacy.

For that form of singularity we often term "the individual," temporariness and the indeterminacy of the future offers the occasion for the projection of multiple selves and multiple futures in Mitchell's novels. One way of regarding Mitchell's writing is to see it as the fictionalization of futurity in plot, character, style, and theme. The hallmarks of this writing are many, but the principal signs are the many instances of prophecy, projection, and imagining possible futures that occur in his work. These, combined with the bi-location of characters (e.g. when Holly Sykes of *The Bone Clocks* imagines what would be going on in her house at a given hour; were she there to see it instead of from her observational point on the road as a runaway), the scattering of characters or character-ancestors and descendents among novels, and the multiplication of temporal zones that various characters inhabit, suggest the degree to which identity is plural, not singular in his fiction. This pluralization of identity, enabled, perhaps, above all, by Mitchell's remarkable ability to cast and embody multiple voices in his novels—ranging from that of a fifteen-year-old English girl in *The Bone Clocks* to that of a Dutch physician in the eighteenth century or an American journalist in the twentieth—is inextricably bound to the conception of a temporary future. If "fate," whether that of the individual, nation, or planet, is not determined by chronology, if cause and effect are equal partners with serendipity in the makeup of history, and if identity transpires in overlapping times and spaces, then the future is necessarily always and only a transitory site where alternative narratives are disseminated.

In Mitchell's fiction the uncertainty of the future is both a promise and a danger hedged by mortality, individual and collective. As represented in *Cloud Atlas*, the far future takes place in the aftermath of apocalypse, and as the temporal location for the survival and evolution of a human remnant that survives the brutalities of a continuous past of war, genocide, and racism. The survival of the human—or more precisely, the survival of a record of human life after the human race has nearly annihilated itself—occurs in the sixth, central, narrative of this novel, "Sloosha's Crossin' an' Ev'rythin' After," where the composite of the novel's narrative pasts, including those that take place in the future, are passed into the hands of the reader. Mitchell composes here and throughout his fiction a view of narrative survival and responsibility aligned with orality—the passing on of stories told from generation to generation, taking on alternative forms over time—as well as with the scriptural and the discursive, the writing down of multiple narratives that are entrusted to readers who are engaged in drawing connections between the transmigratory identities and dispersed events of his novels. If "we" survive, Mitchell tells us, it will be because we have a hand in delivering and passing on narratives that offer alternatives to those fatal territorial stories of empire and supremacy, narcissistic agency, and xenophobic fear that tenaciously remain. This is a future he figures for the work of fiction, perched at the limits of what might be and what might have been imagined and seen.

1

A Company of Strangers: *ghostwritten*

> *The world runs on strangers coping.*
> Marco, in *ghostwritten* (293).

When considered from the perspective of an ongoing career or a completed canon, first novels often can be deceptive. Characteristically comprised largely of autobiographical materials, the initial foray of a young novelist is frequently perceived to be imitative and tentative, only opaquely indicative of what will become the mature author's signature, her vision, his repertoire. *ghostwritten*, a novel in ten chapters conveying the stories of nine different protagonists scattered across nine locations ranging from Okinawa to New York, is atypical in this regard. Not only does it evolve many of the patterns and elements that Mitchell will continue to muster in subsequent novels but it also disseminates the autobiographical "I" into the nine first-person narrators—strangers to each other—who inhabit the novel's dispersed and uneven latitudes. In addition to suggesting that it is authored by an immaterial presence, the novel's title foretells its attention to ghosts, the immaterial, aliens, strangers, and estrangement; it suggests the degree to which Mitchell considers the act of storytelling as mediatory, not the imprinting of the author's originary vision but a channeling of voices and identities; it implicates temporality as a mode of conveyance—*ghostwritten*—inscribed in time, in the past.

The nine narrators of *ghostwritten* reflect Mitchell's fascination with a number that occurs throughout his fiction. Examples abound: the title of *Number9Dream* (containing nine chapters, the last one comprised of the single word "nine"); the "Nine Folded Valleys" of "Sloosha's Crossin' An' Ev'rythin' After" in *Cloud Atlas* (where "nine" and "ninety" recur over fifty times, and over half that many again in *blackswangreen*); and the nine "unengifted" sisters praying at the Shiranui Shrine in *The Thousand Autumns of Jacob de Zoet*. Mitchell's use of the number nine is symptomatic of his broader interest in numerology and the fatal or mystical properties of numbers: as some of his readers have discerned, it can be viewed as a structural principle, a means of perspectively organizing the contact zones of a multiverse.[1] The number nine has particularly variant, contradictory meanings across interconnected cultures (in China, it can signify wholeness, completion, good fortune; in Japan, it can be considered as inauspicious as it sounds like the word for "pain"). As such, nine is a particularly apt number for a novel in which nine semi-autonomous, semicollective protagonists, each alienated in some manner from a homeland while both separated from and overlapping each other spatially and temporally, traverse diverse cosmopolitan landscapes.

Several of the narratives of *ghostwritten* are cosmopolitan in Schoene's sense as they portray "serialised snapshots of the human condition, marked by global connectivity and virtual proximity" (98). They are also metropolitan in their depiction of contemporary cities—Tokyo, Hong Kong, St. Petersburg, London, New York—all sprawling assemblages of labyrinthine streets where the itineraries of strangers often intersect. In *The City and the City* (2009), his allegory of divided contemporary metropolises such as Jerusalem, (formerly) Berlin, El Paso/Ciudad Juarez, or Beirut, China, Miélville relates a police procedural that takes place in the politically divided city of Besźel/Ul Quoma, where the inhabitants of one city are trained not to see the inhabitants of the other, even though they live topographically in the same district, often on the same street. There are areas of the city that Miélville's narrator terms "cross-hatched," where divided areas intersect and where citizens of both cities live in intimate proximity but cannot acknowledge the existence of the other—a form of political disavowal that the novel's narrator terms "unseeing." The allegory of the cross-hatched city in *The City and the City* is useful in understanding the narratives and dispersed environments of *ghostwritten* that, collectively, could be considered as charting the streets, paths, and byways of a globalized metropolis in which the proximity of lives is alternatively acknowledged and disavowed, where the "other" is either seen or unseen according to local cultural and political logics. A preliminary accounting of these stories of sameness and difference will begin to reveal how the repetitions and recurrences of Mitchell's first novel—its cross-hatchings of numbers, coincidences, entities, locations, and events ranging from the astronomical to the political—articulates a world in which the narrative weave limns the cultural and political circumstances of the human order on a planet inhabited by many orders of being and nonbeing.

Itineraries

ghostwritten is a novel of particularities and detail. The objects, artifacts, sites, sounds, identities, and cultural manifestations its protagonists encounter on their often, meandering, or circuitous itineraries are both significant and accidental; their stories compel the reader to be both a hermeneutist and bricoleur, at once divining the patterned sense of the text and assembling significance out of myriad details lying about that are stumbled upon through disparate acts of attention. A detailed tour of the novel's nine narratives in ten chapters reveals its through lines as Mitchell navigates the contingent relations between chance and circumstance, the material and the immaterial, cultural location and temporality, and community and estrangement.

1. The first chapter, "Okinawa," plays upon themes of the cultural outsider and the hunted man as it records the flight of a religious cultist and domestic terrorist, Keisuke Tanaka, code-named "Quasar," from the scene of his attack on a Tokyo metro line using nerve gas. The event is clearly based upon the Subway Sarin Incident of 1995, in which members of the Aun Shinrikyo ("Supreme Truth") cult carried out coordinated attacks that killed thirteen people.[2] In its apocalyptism, the Quasar's cult, led by the putatively divine "His Serendipity" (5), which mirrors that of the factual Aun Shinrikyo, initiates the novel's concern throughout with the fragile, treacherous—and indeed, serendipitous—condition of a planet inhabited by peoples seemingly bent on self-extinction.

Quasar escapes to Nawa, the main city in Okinawa, the southern Japanese prefecture consisting of the Ryukyu Islands. When he hears that the cult members are being rounded up by the police, he flees again to Kumejima, a small, remote island that Quasar regards as "a squalid, incestuous prison" (27). There, he failingly attempts to avoid the island's few inhabitants while communicating telepathically via microwaves and animals with "His Serendipity," who has been caught and jailed. Quasar becomes increasingly isolated on the haunted, isolated "lump of rock" seemingly at the end of the world that he reflects was

> once the main trading center of the Ryukyu Empire with China. Boats laden with spices, slaves, coral, ivory, silk. Swords, coconuts, hemp. The shouts of men would have filled the bustling harbor, old women would have knelt in the marketplace, with their scales and piles of fruit and dried fish. Girls with obedient breasts lean out of the dusky windows, over the flower boxes, promising, murmuring.... Now it's all gone. Long gone. Okinawa became a squalid apology for a fiefdom, squabbled over by masters far beyond its curved horizons. (27)

Laden with the fantasy and exoticism of orientalist versions of island history that Mitchell will explore at much greater length in *Cloud Atlas* and *The Thousand Autumns of Jacob de Zoet*, Quasar's image of Kumejima's dynastic past infers the mutable, dialectical relation between center and periphery that plays out across deep time and changing empires, while prefiguring Clear Island, the "island as old as the world" (312) which is the homeland of Mo Muntervary, the protagonist of the novel's eighth chapter. At the end of "Okinawa," a partial story foreshadowing the stories to follow as embodiments of pasts and futures awaiting connection with each other, Quasar appears to be fatalistic about the possibility of ultimate escape while a typhoon approaches and clouds begin "to ink out the stars, one by one" (31).

2. In "Tokyo," a jazz saxophonist named Satoru is serving time as a record store clerk while waiting for his future to unfold. Like Quasar, Satoru is a cultural outsider, abandoned by his father (this will become a thematic recurrence in Mitchell's fiction). His mother is a Filipino club "hostess" working in Tokyo; she has been deported after the birth of her illegitimate child. Alienated in an impossibly crowded "city [that] never stops rewriting itself" and often viewing the world affectively composed as a series of liner notes from an impressive repertoire of tunes stored in the "place *inside* [his] head" (37), Satoru's escape route is not a distant island but "the place [that] comes into existence through jazz" (38). In the quotidian environment of the store, two significant events occur. First, four young women casually wander into the store, three of them (from Satoru's perspective) "bubbleheads" and "clones of the same ova," the fourth, with whom he immediately falls in love, "completely, completely different," pulsing "invisibly like a quasar" (41). This version of the "meet cute" of Hollywood romantic comedy is indicative of Mitchell's intermixing of popular genres across the nine narratives of *ghostwritten* and suggestive of the ways in which the chance meeting can be converted into the narrative of finding "the one" as Mitchell tests the diegetic movement from coincidence to fate, subtended by the punctual temporality of propitious timing, here and throughout his work.

Some days later, Satoru receives a mysterious call at the store: the caller utters a cryptic message—"*It's Quasar. The dog needs to be fed!*" (53)— and then hangs up after Satoru does not respond. This is one of the key coincidences of the novel, for the caller is the protagonist of "Okinawa" who has been deceived into believing that he is contacting the cult leaders with an encoded emergency message, but, abandoned by them in the wake of the attack and his usefulness expended, he has simply been given a random number in Tokyo to call, which just happens to be that of the record store in which Satoru works. Thus the terrorist Quasar is conflated with the lover Satoru compares to a pulsing quasar, indicative of the range of nominal coincidence in Mitchell's fiction. The ramifications of the coincidence are magnified as the call causes Satoru to delay closing the store for several minutes, allowing for the reappearance of Tomoyo, the young woman with whom he has become enamored earlier and who is about to depart with her family to Hong Kong. Like Satoru, Tomoyo is an outsider, a racial and cultural hybrid: "I was with my revolting cousin and her friends. They treat me like an imbecile because I'm half-Chinese. My mother was Japanese... Dad's Hong Kong Chinese" (55). The second chance meeting leads to a relationship and Satoru's decision to follow Tomoyo to Hong Kong and begin a life abroad.

3. In "Hong Kong," Neal Brose, a disaffected British lawyer working for a multinational investment firm and facing the impending collapse of his marriage and his professional life due to illegal financial dealings, goes AWOL. Like Quasar and Satoru before him, Brose is a cultural outsider, alienated from his work and inevitably a "*qwai lo*" (65), in Cantonese, a foreigner in the intricate, colonized social order of Hong Kong. Wrenched with fear about the imminent discovery of his involvement in fiscal malfeasance after an encounter with a financial investigator, Huw Llewellyn, and terminally indecisive about his future, Brose simply wanders off one day from a ferry landing restaurant, having missed the boat to work (where he recalls encountering a young couple in love who are very likely Satoru and Tomoyo from "Tokyo"). He meanders toward the Lantau Peak and its remarkable Tian Tan Buddah, shedding his Rolex watch and, symbolically, all the accoutrements of his former life as he traverses the Borgesian labyrinth of the island: "Paths forked off and forked off some more" (81). Once atop Lantau Peak, he appears to experience a moment of transcendence walking "up the steps of the Big Bright Buddha, brighter and brighter, into a snowstorm of silent light" (106), but we learn later in the novel that, according to his ex-wife, Katy Forbes, this is also the moment of his sudden death from a blood clot caused by "[u]ndiagnosed diabetes" (260).

The fact of Neal's death typifies the way in which particles of information come to us from the scattered regions of the novel, and in this chapter, the "crossings" of the novel begin to multiply, both within and beyond *ghostwritten*: Katy Forbes will reappear briefly in "London"; the financial scandal in which Brose is involved will be elliptically referred to in "Petersburg"; Brose's past as a schoolyard bully growing up in Worcestershire will be taken up in *blackswangreen*; and his boss, Denholme Cavendish, soon to be indicted in the scandal, is the elder brother of Timothy Cavendish, the owner of a literary agency who will appear in "London" and as the main subject of "The Ghostly Ordeal of Timothy Cavendish" in *Cloud Atlas*.

In addition to these "character chains," there are a number of related imagistic sequences already accruing by this third chapter that generate the tangential, material connectedness of the novel—the *sui generis* network that is in many respects both its visible narrative work and its content. More than 200 pages after, she is introduced as Neal Brose's recently departed wife; for example, we are told by a former lover that Katy bears "a birthmark shaped like a comet" (295). This seems an insignificant detail marking personal intimacy and identity save that, at this point, we will have read that a global astronomical event in the form of a comet passing near to the Earth is viewed as the sign of the coming rapture by Quasar, by the old woman of "Holy Mountain," by an aged grandmother in "Mongolia," and by the protagonist of "Petersburg," where a comet also appears in a painting. Further, in the future anterior mode of reading that the novel requires, we will have encountered upon completing the novel the comet again in the novel's penultimate chapter, "Night Train," where it is the subject of much conversation as an avatar of a third world war. In *Cloud Atlas*, several protagonists bear comet-shaped birthmarks, readable as signs of their linkage to each other across vast reaches of history.

The "tracks" of the novel thus engender a certain temporality of reading that compel us to move backward and forward across the time and space of the novel as we note repetitions and linkages. I will elaborate on this later in relation to Mitchell's larger concerns with "world time," but in concluding this itinerary of "Hong Kong," it is important to note here that the chapter offers the initial appearance of one of the novel's many ghosts. For, one of the things that has come between Neal and his wife is their inability to have a baby—a frustration of desire that materializes as a ghost in the form of a female child haunting their Kowloon apartment. Her presence is complicated by Neal's affair (after his wife leaves him) with the all-too-real Chinese maid who serves to double the uncanny presence of the ghost. The ghost accompanies Neal on his final journey, and she prefigures, most notably, the noncorporeal, reincarnated intelligence of "Mongolia" who transmigrates from body to body across the novel, a linchpin of the novel's "hauntology" to be considered shortly and visible everywhere in the details: in its title; in the "ghost town" of Ulan Bator and the punning name of a character in "Mongolia"—Caspar—who serves as a temporary host to the transmigratory entity (186); in the "street of ghosts" that comprises the Nevsky Prospect of "Petersburg" (210); in the character of Marco in "London" who is a ghostwriter and who sees ghosts flitting through the city streets; and in the cybernetic "noncorporeal sentient intelligence" (413) of "Night Train." "Hong Kong" brings to the fore what I will discuss as the novel's "surplus": the sense, evident throughout Mitchell's fiction, that millennial reality with its vast and elaborate information networks (mimed in the continuous flow of seemingly random information about characters and events that the novel provides, matrixed into significance) is thin and that there is something beyond the visible and the material, more dimensions than just three, a stochastic multiverse.[3]

4. In "Holy Mountain," an old woman who owns a tea shack perched on the slopes of a sacred mountain in China (possibly Wutai Shan in Shanxi

Province, one of the four sacred mountains of Buddhism) recounts her life of isolation against the backdrop of catastrophic political change. "The world has long forgotten," she relates, "but we mountain-dwellers live on the prayer-wheel of time" (109). Her story is one of victimization and survival against the backdrop of the violent and chaotic history of the twentieth century. As a young girl she is raped by a passing warlord who impregnates her, thus "ruining" her for marriage and causing her to send her infant daughter away to relatives who can afford to raise her. During Japan's invasion of China preceding World War II, soldiers loyal to the "Asian sphere of Co-prosperity" beat her father and wreck their tea shack. In the years of contestation between Chinese nationalists and the Chinese Communist Party, the holy mountain is renamed "People's Mountain," and the old woman is subjected to extortion by "party officials" while her daughter and her guardians are forced to flee to Hong Kong "after the communists had ordered their arrests as enemies of the revolution" (124). Following the establishment of the People's Republic of China, an idiotic thug who bears the perverse village nickname of "Brain" and who is a member of the local Red Guard slaps her and destroys her tea shack again while many of her relatives are deported to correction camps, and the combination of drought and political policy induces the Great Famine of 1958–61.[4] As China becomes liberalized and engages in Western tourism, the woman witnesses celebrations attending Mao Zedong and begins to see more foreigners visiting the monastery (reopened after its closure under earlier administrations) atop the Holy Mountain; when she climbs up to the monastery herself—thus twinning Neal Brose's ascent of Lantau Peak—she encounters Brain, now the foreman of a work crew, modernizing a temple.

The invariable among all of these factions, wars, and regimes is the survival of the old woman herself, her tea shack, which she manages to rebuild each time after "men forever marching up the path" destroy it (133), and the "Tree" that stands beside her shack which contains a spirit that gives her advice and counsel. In many ways, the old woman embodies several of the principal contradictions of the novel: she is indigenous, yet perpetually an outsider; as the owner of a concession, she represents the principal of worldly hospitality, yet, like several other characters in the novel, she is often xenophobic; and she is both a citizen of the planet, as she records the momentous events of the twentieth century that have affected her from her local perspective, and at the same time an isolate, surviving in the half-spirit world represented by her tree.[5] Occasionally she sees ghosts or a passing comet, and she bears a long-distance connection to Neal Brose, for her great-granddaughter, descended from the daughter who has fled to Hong Kong fearing political repression, while visiting her long-lost progenitor for the first time, reveals that she is wealthy because a "foreigner, a lawyer with a big company" has been "very generous to me in his will" (146). Whether Brose has left his maid and mistress the money as the result of their relationship or she has stolen it from him is unclear, but the connection brings to full circle the itinerary of the old woman and the diaspora of her descendents, for in her agedness, she thinks she is talking to her daughter and asks if her daughter/great-granddaughter is returning to China "for good," for which she receives the response: "Yes. Hong Kong is China now, anyway" (145). The old woman of "Holy Mountain" thus embodies a principle of constancy or permanence amidst randomness and change that operates in the face of the seeming death wish of the twentieth century—the succession of ideologies, regimes, and nationalisms comprising a history of violence that has scored countless victims on all sides and, more than once, brought the world to the brink of the apocalypse toward which *ghostwritten* frequently gestures. Among other things, the protagonist of "Holy Mountain" is a historian, and modern history, viewed as the tracking of the chaotic energies produced by power gone awry, is her subject. Whether like Quasar, one is in flight from this history while fabulating an exotic past or, like the old woman, one manages to survive despite its all-too-real catastrophes, in "Holy Mountain," history is represented as a force delimited by the shifting circumstances of its making and the cultural logic of its enactments.

5. If the old woman of "Holy Mountain" signifies permanence and rootedness in the face of change, the noncorporeal intelligence of "Mongolia" embodies transience and mutability as the countervailing forces that move through the novel. Migrating from host to host in quest of the story of its origin ("I was here to find the source of the story that was already there, right at the beginning of 'I,' sixty years ago" [158]), the "intelligence" (a nomad soul? an alien intervention?) defies the notions of singularity that attend normative conceptions of selfhood: its itinerary charts a non-identificatory quest for identity.[6] The intelligence operates by inhabiting the consciousness of a host, thus enabling it to incorporate into its own identity the host's past and knowledge; this is not so much a possession or a haunting as it is a symbiosis that allows the intelligence to pursue the associational cognitive patterns of the host's mind conceived as a routing of itineraries. As it inhabits Caspar, a Danish backpacker, the intelligence notes that "[b]ackpackers are strange. I have a lot in common with them. We live nowhere, and we are strangers everywhere.... We are both parasites: I live in my hosts' minds, and sift through their memories to understand the world. Caspar's breed live in a host country that is never their own, and use its culture and landscape to learn, or to stave off boredom" (153).

Transferring to Gunga, a Mongolian woman who works at a hotel in Ulan Bator where Caspar stays (transmigration can only occur when one host physically touches another), the intelligence observes the following:

> It was good to transmigrate out of a westernized head. However much I learn from the nonstop highways of minds like Caspar's, they make me giddy. It would be the euro's exchange rate one minute, a film he'd once seen about art thieves in Petersburg the next, a memory of fishing with his uncle between islets the next, some pop song or a friend's Internet home page the next. No stopping. Gunga's mind patrols a more intimate neighborhood. She constantly thinks about getting enough food and money. She worries about her daughter, and ailing relatives. Most of the days of her life have been very much alike. The assured dreariness of the Soviet days, the struggle for survival since independence. Gunga's mind was a lot harder for me to hide in than Caspar's, however. It's like trying to make yourself invisible in a prying village as opposed to a sprawling conurbation. (159–60)

The consciousness of the intelligence is an assemblage of overlapping and differentiated cognitive maps, languages, fragmentary memories, and partial histories. "A sprawling conurbation" is an apt expression for the hybrid aggregation of identities and locations the intelligence inhabits as it transmigrates. It is the (im)material embodiment of the random connectedness that exists between strangers as it is capable of opportunistically moving only during the accidental brushing of one hand against another, or by means of a sudden and unexpected collision of bodies in the increasingly crowded metropolises of the planet where even remote Ulan Bator shows signs of urban sprawl.

The intelligence recounts a long history of hosts that it has inhabited while traversing the planet across the twentieth century: a soldier, Jorge Luis Borges, Caspar, Gunga, a Mongolian shaman, a truck driver, Suhbataar (an ex-KGB agent whose presence here and in "Petersburg" has dramatic consequences), the daughter and brother of a folklorist who may know the origin story that the noncorporeal intelligence seeks, an infant just born into a nomadic group in the far north of Mongolia, then, subsequently, the infant's mother, her husband, his mother, and finally back into the infant having heard at last the story it seeks and ready to be reborn as a new, "original" self. Later in the novel, we learn there may be as many as eight or more similar intelligences in existence. Clearly the forerunners to the reincarnations of *Cloud Atlas* and the Horologists of *The Bone Clocks*, the intelligence and its kind will inhabit countless hosts, radiating connective possibilities outwards: is the fact that Borges is a host indicative of Mitchell's intertextual indebtedness to a "master" known for his invention of multiple worlds and dimensions? Is Caspar's having seen a film about art thieves in St. Petersburg mere literary prefiguration of the eerily similar events of the novel's next chapter or does this serve as a more involuted commentary on the relation between art and life within art? Clearly Mitchell uses this fantastic element as a means to explore what lies beyond identity conceived through Western liberal humanism as a unique singularity, whether channeled through "Eastern" religious doctrines of reincarnation and the transmigration of souls or "sci-fi" conceptualizations of alien possession and superior intelligences.[7]

Integral to the metaphor, voice, and character of the chapter's "intelligence" is the recollection of the fable that begins with the line: "*There are three who think about the fate of the world...*" (158). More precisely, it is the intelligence's recollection of the historical circumstances in which it heard this first line of this story from a Buddhist master, for the grandmother of the infant in which it comes to rest had been a young girl at the scene of a massacre in 1937 of Mongolian monks accused of "feudal indoctrination" (192) under the regime of Khorloogiin Choibalsan, the Communist leader of the Mongolian People's Republic who modeled himself after Josef Stalin. At the moment of his death, the young boy who is being executed alongside his master, by virtue of being told the story that begins "There are three who think about the fate of the world," is transformed into the nomadic entity of the intelligence who, first, inhabits a bystander, the young girl who becomes a grandmother, and then one of the imported Chinese executioners who turns out to be "Brain" of "Holy Mountain." The linkages from this birth born of political violence in the past to rebirth in the present ensue: from Brain, to the old woman of "Holy Mountain," to an English-speaking anthropologist who stops at the tea shack, eventually to Caspar, and so on. In this itinerary of itineraries, and by extension, in the novel as a whole, it is not "the story" that is important—in fact, we are only ever given its beginning; rather, it is the routes of transmission by which the story is conveyed that constitute its substance and content. In between the beginning and its reiteration as origin and end, there are myriad identities, points of contact, and the details of overlapping stories within stories that are always incomplete as the noncorporeal intelligence transmigrates from one host to another, ever a guest dependent on the contingencies of hospitality, a fragile entity subject to the vagaries of fortune and often born out of historical violence. As the novel's switching station, "Mongolia" conveys an antinomian notion of estranged identity as singularity that exists always and only in the minds of others.

6. Set in the Russian city that hosts, arguably, the greatest art collection in the world, "Petersburg" is cast as a thriller involving forgery and art heist, a

beautiful woman, mob bosses, and corruption on an international scale. As do all of the locations in which the novel is set, St. Petersburg manifests visible signs of negative globalization and Americanization following the collapse of the Soviet Union. Walking through the city, Margarita Latunsky, the chapter's narrator and protagonist, observes "[a]ll these new shops, Benetton, the Häagen-Dazs shop, Nike, Burger King, a shop that sells nothing but camera film and key-rings, another that sells Swatches and Rolexes. High streets are becoming the same all over the world, I suppose" (211). In startling contrast to franchised pedestrian malls of the former imperial capital of Russia, there stand its baroque palaces and churches, including the Hermitage, the assemblage of buildings housing the art collection founded by Catherine the Great in 1764 where Margarita works as an attendant. She is also the member of a small gang of art thieves that include her boyfriend, Rudi, a mobbed-up "entrepreneur," and a British expatriate and former Cambridge don accused of treason, Jerome, who forges masterpieces that are smuggled into the museum and exchanged for originals by Rudi and his associates disguised as a cleaning crew. Margarita's role is to facilitate the entry and exit of the crew from the museum and to distract the attention of the head curator, Rogoshev, by offering him sexual services.

In thick detail as she describes the wildly alternating cycles of boredom and excitement in her life, Margarita narrates the story of the gang's last heist involving the forgery and theft of a painting, *Eve and the Serpent*, by "Lemuel Delacroix," the fictional name of a Russian constructivist à la Kandinsky. The painter's name is clearly meant to resonate with that of Eugene Delacroix, the French Romantic artist who painted the infamous *Liberty Leading the People* (1830), commemorating the French July Revolution of that year— an irony, in the context of a postrevolutionary Russia portrayed as given over to high levels of corruption in its embrace of free-market capitalism.[8] Following the theft of the painting, things begin to go very wrong for Margarita and her colleagues as her world collapses around her. In a complex and fast-paced sequence of events, Rudi is killed by Subhataar, the ex-KGB agent from "Mongolia" working at the behest of a mob boss whose "suspicions were aroused when your boyfriend 'lost' a wall of money he was laundering through a reputable Hong Kong law firm, and the only excuse he could come up with was that his contact there suddenly dropped dead of diabetes!" (252)—the "contact," of course, is Neal Brose of "Hong Kong." Margarita, desperate to escape with the painting that represents the fantasy of a domestic future in Zurich with Rudi that she will never have, kills Jerome, who is equally determined to have the painting for himself. She also attempts to kill Subhataar, but he has removed the bullets from her gun and escaped with the painting, leaving Margarita in an apartment full of bodies to the mercies of the authorities soon to arrive after he has anonymously notified them. Margarita's final comment is the classic line for a nightmare that has finally come to an end: "None of this happened. None of this really happened" (254).

These plot elements indicate the extent to which "Petersburg" partakes of the genre of pulp noir, though in highly stylized manner: the registers of Margarita's narrative are, by turns, ethnographic, nostalgic, narcissistic, romantic, consumerist, and evocative of a lost past and an idealized future. It is Margarita's voice as the subject of male desire that predominates over the thriller plot of the chapter, which may in any case be just a movie—the one Caspar recalls seeing in his "conurbation" of random thoughts in "Mongolia."[9] Indeed, if "Petersburg" is conceived as the partial memory of a film recollected by a character from the previous chapter who has been inhabited by the fiction of a noncorporeal intelligence, then the coiled artifice of Margarita's narrative complicates the enfolded connection between art and existence that Mitchell explores in this chapter, for Margarita is the subject of a fantasist ideology that stipulates desire as the foundation of all human action and motivation. Like the story of "the three who think about the fate of the world," the painting of *Eve and the Serpent* entails a narrative of origins. In this instance, the "story" is about the origins of desire, abstractly gendered as female when Margarita, bored and daydreaming while looking at the original in the gallery, envisions the snake in a hissing voice tempting Adam with the commodities of "bronze-tipped arrows, crocodile-skin luggage, and virtual-reality helmets" while Eve is tempted with "higher thingsss," not "Forbidden Knowledge" but "*Desire*," italicized and with a capital D (202).

Margarita is an embodiment of this artifice: beautiful and alluring, she is the former mistress of a Soviet politician "[h]igh enough to know the codes to nuclear warheads" and, then, "an admiral in the Pacific Fleet" (204). Now a mistress to capitalism and corruption instead of Cold War socialism, she sleeps with her boss and, occasionally, various friends of her lover in service to Rudi's schemes. The trafficked object of male desire, she seems the culmination of a trajectory marked by the painting of *Eve and the Serpent* that results in the global commodification of desire—the reality that the artwork prefigures and allegorizes—evident in the franchising of St. Petersburg. "History is made of people's desires" (222), remarks Tatyana, an Interpol agent posing as a visiting art consultant at the Hermitage who befriends Margarita as part of her investigation of Rudi's gang. Margarita's story and its location conjoin to instantiate this history in the simulacrum of art that the forgeries imply and the warehouse of commodities that St. Petersburg, as a contemporary metropolis, has become. Though she claims she is "not a political woman" (205), Margarita seems to understand perfectly well, if xenophobically, the political outcomes of a history of desire that has resulted in the successions of nation-building, Cold War, and globalization of a world in which she is primarily an object *of* desire: "what was this Union of Soviet Socialist Republics, really?... Us Russians pouring roubles into these pointless little countries full of people eating snakes and babies all over Asia just to stop the Chinks or the Arabs getting their hands on them?...An empire by default" (206). "Petersburg" thus expands upon that aspect of connectivity in Mitchell's cosmopolitan mosaic that links the misdeeds of lawyer in Hong Kong, the apocalyptism of a religious fanatic in Japan, and the violence inflicted upon a young girl in China: the fulfilled and anticipated destinies of desire that undergird mutual sexual and political economies.[10]

7. "London" details the peregrinations of Marco who is composed, punningly, of "many Me's" (261), as he navigates the streets of London and reflects on the vagaries of accident and chance. His "me's" include being a ghostwriter by day and a musician by night (his band, "The Music of Chance," is an aside to a novel of the same name by one of Mitchell's contemporaries, Paul Auster), but above all he is a contemporary flâneur. This is the figure described by Walter Benjamin as the nineteenth-century Parisian idler who, "botanizing on the asphalt," immerses himself in the metropolitan crowd, "[l]ike a roving soul in search of a body [who] enters another person whenever he wishes" (*Baudelaire* 36; 55)—an image of empathetic vagrancy that eerily corresponds with that of the transmigratory intelligence introduced in Mongolia.[11] In a chapter modeled somewhat on Joyce's *Ulysses* (1922), Marco recounts "a day in the life" from his awakening in the apartment of Katy Forbes (now, a widow) after a one-night stand to a late-night gambling spree at a London casino followed by a much-belated proposal of marriage to his girlfriend and a long walk home ("[t]he tube closed hours ago") "[e]ven if it took all night" (309).

In between his morning philandering and his improbable "nighttown" adventures in risk management at the casino, Marco, uncommitted and conditional (he considers himself to be "a part-time Buddhist" [263], a "cocktail of genetics and upbringing fixed...by the blind barman Chance" [264]), traces his itinerary, providing in streetwise detail a view of the city from the perspective of the detached, canny wanderer:

> Me, I walk everywhere. That's Tony Blair's old house. A postman emptying a postbox. Walking past these old terraced houses is like browsing down a shelf of books. A student's pad, a graphic designer's studio, a family with their kitchen done out in primary colors and pictures from school fridge-magneted onto the fridge. An antiquarian's study. A basement

full of toys—a helicopter going round and round and round. A huntin', shootin', buggerin' living room with paintings and fittings that clear their throats and say "burgle this house!" to all the people trudging past to the Arsenal and Finsbury Park unemployment centers. Offices of obscure support groups, watchdog headquarters, and impotent trade unions. Three men in black suits stride past, turning down Calabria Road, one speaking into a cell phone, another carrying a briefcase. (263–64)

As cross-hatchings begin to proliferate, Marco meanders through northeast London toward Hampstead Heath and a meeting with Alfred Kopf, an elderly literatus and saloniste who formerly kept company with the cream of the city's artistic society, among them Francis Bacon, Joe Orton, Derek Jarman, and Colin Wilson. Marco is ghostwriting his memoir, but with a characteristic cynicism that reveals the displacement and historical amnesia of his contemporaneity: "Visitors to Alfred's place are...[h]as-beens and might-bes. Alfred tried to start a humanist movement here in the sixties. Its idealism doomed it. Campaign for Nuclear Disarmament bishops and that Colin Winsom [sic] bloke still drop by. Heard of him? See what I mean?" (272). On the way to Alfred's, by chance he pushes a pedestrian out of the way of an oncoming taxi who only later, we realize, is Mowleen Muntervary ("Mo"), the protagonist of the next chapter, "Clear Island."

Following an unsatisfactory conversation with Alfred, Marco makes his way to the offices of Timothy Cavendish, his literary agent, where he notices a book, *His Serendipity*, translated by one "Beryl Brain." While he is there, Cavendish receives a call from his brother in Hong Kong informing him that Cavendish Holdings (and, thus, the financing for his agency) is going under, thus putting Marco's ghostwritten memoir of Alfred Kopf on hold. Marco wanders on to Leicester Square, where he encounters a woman in a snack shop reading a book on out-of-body experiences; lest we read *ghostwritten* as endorsing some form of New Age philosophy, or "the old quantum physics equals eastern religion bollocks" (257) about which Marco apostrophizes earlier to Katy; the woman in the restaurant is a hybrid parody of New Ageism, as she reads her book by "Dwight Silver-wind" with her "gypsy ringlets" and "tie-dyed" clothes, "[p]robably purchased when she'd gone trekking in Nepal.... She burns incense, does aromatherapy and describes herself as not exactly telepathic, but definitely empathic. She's into pre-Raphaelite art, and works part-time in a commercial picture library" (289). Marco then wanders homeward to Wapping and to a flat situated above the "New Moon" pub in "Old Moon Street," the pub renamed after an incident in which terrorists, making bombs, blew themselves up in the air raid shelter underlying the pub's basement.

Thus interpolated with an assortment of the novel's characters and events, Marco comes to rest, save that his diurnal itinerary culminates when he grudgingly agrees to voyage out to a casino with his friend, Gibreel, and a "rich cousin" who funds an evening of gambling as part of a bet involving who can win more money, Marco or Gibreel. In this realm where randomness and probability meet, the "point" of Marco's journey, and "London," becomes clear. Throughout the day, he has been considering existence a matter of pure chance: "People say they choose, but it comes down to the same thing: why people choose what they choose is also down to chance" (265); the attractive woman he sees on the tube cannot be engaged in conversation because "if I break that rule and talk to her ... she'll think I'm threatening her and the defenses will slam down. None of these problems would exist if we had just met by chance at a party... But chance brings us together here, where we cannot meet" (269). In a conversation with his cousin in the casino, who councils Marco not to "overrate chance. Winning in a casino is like winning in life: it's all a matter of *will*," Marco rejoins sotto voice: "Yeah, and a lollipop tossed into the mouth of the Amazon can float upstream. It just has to want to badly enough" (301).

For Marco, a ghostwriter who is only on chapter six of a memoir that may never be completed if the aged subject dies or a London literary agency fails because of financial misdoings in far-removed Hong Kong, his observations about chance come home to roost in the casino. There, he experiences an epiphany while subjecting himself to the stochastic calculus of roulette: the "Truth" that a comet—perhaps the one that will be speeding toward the Earth in the apocalyptic setting of "Night Train"—"doesn't care if humans note its millennial lap, and Truth doesn't care less what humans are writing about this week. Truth's indifference is immutable. More Mercurial than Jovian" (307). If "Petersburg" articulates the connectivity of desire in the linkage of the personal to the political in the making of history, Marco's story in "London" manifests the "Truth" of the random (anything can happen, including apocalypse now) as the limit of the will to forge a relation between cause and effect in the relation of events. Marco's final gesture—the phone call to the long-suffering Poppy in which he proposes marriage and commitment to her and their out-of-wedlock child, India—may seem a form of romantic closure/opening echoing that of "Tokyo." But it takes place as a postcynical, shrugging recognition that if the "Truth" of event is random and indifferent to the interventions of human choice and interpretation, then choice and interpretation will (and must) take place anyway, whether in collision or collusion with this "Truth." Recalling that Mercury, or Hermes, is, among other things, the bringer of messages and the god of interpretation, the extrapolation of Marco's recognition is that if anything can happen, something in fact *will* happen, and for Mitchell, human agency operating within and beyond local observation must be viewed inevitably as a factor in the merging of coincidence and consequence. This relativity theory of human connectivity undergirds the sense, conveyed throughout the novel, that the utter indeterminacy of the future—the game of time and history to be played as we are in its midst—is no excuse for observing from the sidelines.

8. While "London" reverberates with the music of chance, "Clear Island" engages the science of chance in the figure of Mo Muntervary, a physicist who is responsible for the development of a form of artificial intelligence called "Quancog," an entity that emerges from the (actual) subfield of "quantum cognition," which brings the principles of quantum mechanics to bear on questions of human memory, decision-making, and conceptualization. Having abandoned her research and her lab in Zurich after she has discovered her "modest contribution to global enlightenment is being used in air-to-surface missiles to kill people who aren't white enough" (319), she is in flight from American agents who wish to "convince" her to emigrate to the United States and reinitiate the Quancog project for American military purposes as well as confiscate the "black book" of research notes that she always carries with her. As Stolz, her Texan pursuer puts it, the Americans and all their military competitors want her so badly "[b]ecause quantum cognition, if spliced with artificial intelligence and satellite technology in the way that you have proposed in your last five papers, would render existing nuclear technology as lethal as a shower of tennis balls" (323). Her itinerary, which in large part retraces that of the novel, takes her from Zurich, to St. Petersburg, to Hong Kong (where she covertly stays with an old friend, Huw Llewellyn, and where she witnesses Neil Brose's death while touring), to London (where she is saved from being run over by Marco), and finally to "an island as old as the world" (312), Clear Island, eight square miles of land off the Irish coast southwest of Cork with a Gaelic-speaking population of less than 130 and the scene of Mo's birth and childhood. There, she rejoins her husband, John, who is blind, and her son, Liam, a university student home from school, while awaiting the inevitable arrival of CIA forces and attendant decision to either keep running or comply and relocate to the United States. In a scene that prefigures the "Goatwriter" of *Number9Dream*, an anthropomorphic goat/ghostwriter who accidentally eats his own manuscript, Mo decides to depart to America in exchange for the accompaniment of her husband and guaranteed protection for her son after destroying the invaluable black book by comically feeding it to a pet goat. Her departure comes with the assurance that she will continue to develop Quancog on terms that manifest themselves in the ensuing chapter, "Night Train."

Like the novel's other principals, Mo is a nomad whose existence mirrors that of the particles she studies as she traverses multiple overlapping worlds on her journey through the novel's spaces. Cast in the form of technothriller (as "Petersburg" is cast in the form of pulp noir, "Tokyo" in that of a romantic comedy, and "Hong Kong" as a spiritual biography along the lines of Thomas Merton's *Seven-Story Mountain* [1948]), "Clear Island" tracks the evolving matrix of connections Mo makes between subatomic reality, human consciousness, and geopolitics, subtended by chance and contingency. Meditating on the movement of electrons, Mo observes that

> in my brain [electrons] are moving forwards and backwards in time, changing atoms, changing electrical charge, changing molecules, carrying chemicals, carrying impulses, changing thoughts, deciding to have a baby...changing theory, changing technology, changing computer circuitry, changing artificial intelligence, changing the projections of missiles whole segments of the globe away, and collapsing buildings onto people who have never heard of Ireland. (351)

The mantra of change leads to a question about order and randomness: "Electrons, electrons, electrons. What laws are you following?" (351), suggesting that elementary particles, persons, and nations operate often at cross-purposes in a haphazard universe where order is a sporadic combination of chance and force in "the syntax of uncertainty" (364). Thinking about her mother who is suffering from Alzheimer's, Mo speculates, "Wigner maintains that human consciousness collapses one lucky universe into being from all of the possible ones. Had my mother's universe now uncollapsed? Were cards flying across the baize back into the dealer's pack?" (348). In referring to Eugene Wigner, the quantum physicist whose thought experiments are fundamental to "many worlds" theories that postulate the simultaneous presence of innumerable universes which collapse into the one actualized from millisecond to millisecond, Mo suggests the degree to which identity is a matter of both time and chance, the "lucky" singularity of her mother's consciousness now dissolving, in dementia, to the infinite combinations and possibilities of its pre-existence.[12]

Mo's crossings with several of the novel's protagonists and events, combined with her knowledge of the way the world operates at intersecting levels from the subatomic to global, lend weight to her insight at the critical moment of her decision to continue exploring the mysteries of quantum cognition that "[f]inally, I understand how the electrons, protons, neutrons, photons, neutrinos, positrons, muons, pions, gluons, and quarks that make up the universe, and the forces that hold them together, are one" (372). Mo's narrative manifests a principle of physical interconnectivity leading to a form of cognitive and historical materialism in which "[m]atter is thought, and thought is matter" (336), and where the form of consciousness that we term "identity" interacts with other identities both randomly and consequentially across time and space to generate history:

> I interact with... reality in the way that I do because I am who I am. Why am I who I am? Because of the double helix of atoms coiled along my DNA. What is DNA's engine of change? Subatomic particles colliding with its molecules. These particles are raining onto the Earth now, resulting in mutations that have evolved the oldest single-celled lifeforms through jellyfish to gorillas and us, Chairman Mao, Jesus, Nelson Mandela, His Serendipity, Hitler, you and me. Evolution and history are the bagatelle of particle waves. (359–60)

A "bagatelle" can be a trifle, a short musical form, or billiards-like table game dating to the fifteenth century whose contemporary equivalent is the pinball machine: the latter definition underscores the tenuousness and danger of Mo's derived worldview in which everything interacts and changes constantly so that the force or pressure of any singularity, from electron to charismatic individual to nation, has equal chances of resulting in transformation or catastrophe. For Mitchell, the syntax of uncertainty that structures the grammar of the quantum universe means that there are no longer any guarantees, and there never were.

9. "Night Train" consists of transcripts from the late night radio talk show of "Bat Segundo," airing in New York as a global crises entailing the possibility of a third world war climaxes and recedes in the years following Mo Muntervary's migration to America. The show, devoted to free-flowing conversations with callers on topics of the day, attracts a heterogeneous assortment of writers, conspiracy theorists, political loudmouths, and eccentric loners; its host is an amalgamation of any number of American and British "talk jocks" who play jazz and pop tunes that suit the mood of the moment in between provocative interviews and contentious conversations with callers.[13] The selected transcripts of the show record the annual calls of a mysterious figure, "the Zookeeper," a satellite-monitoring hacker whose voice seems mechanized and who represents itself as a form of "noncorporeal sentient intelligence" (413) who registers the link between the astronomically global and the microscopically local. A kindred spirit of the transmigrating entity of "Mongolia," Zookeeper appears to be a god-like form of panoptic consciousness that has the ability to alter the history of a planet on the verge of self-destruction as it jumps at will between military

satellites, altering the course of guided missiles while it gathers information about everything from incipient ecological disasters and covert military operations to "[a] woman on a hammock... reading the Book of Exodus" or a stone that "transforms into a pelico lizard when a desert vole strays too near" (381–82). As its name suggests, Zookeeper is posited as a caretaker of the planet whose power derives from its technologically assisted capacity to observe in fine resolution how the minute particulars of earthly existence are related to the macroscopic events viewable in their totality only from a great height: weather patterns, troop movements, oil spills, and nuclear accidents.

The chapter threads connections between the partial narratives of other chapters, but far from suggesting that (despite the apocalyptic tone of the chapter) the novel is moving toward a traditional mode of closure, these linkages indicate a metonymic continuance of the incidental and the myriad events on the periphery that contribute to a collective history: Bat has interviewed Satoru Sonada, the former record store clerk/ saxophonist from "Tokyo," now a rising star on the jazz scene; one of the callers is a writer, Luisa Rey, the author of *The Hermitage*, an exposé of the St. Petersburg mafia who will become a key figure in *Cloud Atlas* (her name echoes the title of Thornton Wilder's *The Bridge of San Luis Rey*, cited in the epigraph to the novel which informs Mitchell's concern with "a company of strangers" discussed below); Bat drinks Kilmagoon whisky, the preferred beverage of the inhabitants of Clear Island, and refers to the appearance of "Comet Aloysius" in the New York night skies; another guest on the show is Dwight Silverwind, the New Age guru of "London"; Bat receives a call from a caller speaking in "broken English" who declares that Zookeeper "is an alias chosen by the Guru" (406), a returned avatar of "His Serendipity." The key figure of the chapter, Zookeeper, is a hybrid, a technological entity with a conscience who calls into the Bat Segundo show each anniversary of "Brink Day" (November 30, the date of the forestalled missile launch) as a means of communicating its observations and actions to the world. As it leaps at will from satellite to satellite, it echoes the transmigrations of "Mongolia's" noncorporeal intelligence between bodies. One of the Brink Day anniversary conversations of "Night Train" occurs between Zookeeper and another intelligence (mediated by a skeptical Bat Segundo, who thinks that it is an exchange between "nut cases"), claiming it has once temporarily inhabited the mind of Mo and, thus, is "acquainted with your [Zookeeper's] designers" (412). Code-named "Arupadhatu" (in Buddhism, a higher realm of formlessness, as well as a manifestation of Buddha), the intelligence asserts that there may be eight others like it, among whom he is a "fallen angel" as the others "squander their gift. They transmigrate into human chaff for hosts, and mediate upon nothingness upon mountains" (413), whereas it, joining with Zookeeper, could become a new god with absolute dominion over humankind. Rejecting the offer by means of an enormous electric spike that short-circuits the discourse between these nonhuman entities, Zookeeper once again takes up the task of monitoring human transgressions against the planet in accord with its programming instructions, or "laws," including the fourth which states that Zookeeper must "preserve visitors' lives" (418). The otherworldly conflict between atemporal, sentient entities who inhabit mortals either in a quest for enlightenment or power will become the hidden, foundational narrative of *The Bone Clocks*.

The notion that humans are "visitors" on planet Earth informs *ghostwritten*'s reliance on apocalyptic and sci-fi scenarios in its culminating chapters, for the fabrication of a posthuman agency such as Zookeeper (that, itself, "cannot fabulate" [379]) in conversation with the alien-like presence of a rogue noncorporeal intelligence figuratively registers both the reach and the limitations of the human in Mitchell's novel. As "visitors" themselves, humans are aliens in relation to the ancient life-forms of the planets; with their genocidal wars and human-made environmental disasters, like the stereotypical sinister alien invaders of classic science fiction movies, they threaten any future—since the future itself is an anthropomorphic invention reliant on human notions of temporality—that might be imagined for the third rock from the Sun. A repository of desire and deceit, both fabulatory and self-destructive, both an "other" in relation to the planet and that which devastates anything conceived as other to itself, including others within itself, "the human" as posited against the alien/ghostly/hybrid/posthuman entities of the novel is a contradiction in terms. Caught up in the asymmetric patterns of their varyingly consequential and inconsequential interactions, their plans for the future contravened by a cataclysmic past of their own making, the human "animals" that the Zookeeper looks after in its role as an ironic messiah subvert the logic and order its operating instructions which demand both accountability and invisibility to "the visitors," both protection of all and termination of some to prevent greater self-destruction.[14] Apocalypse now temporarily averted, Zookeeper concludes his final conversation with Bat Segundo on a note that underscores the novel's refusal of closure and finality. Unable to reconcile its laws to the fact that "[t]he visitors I safeguard are wrecking my zoo," Zookeeper signs off with an epiphanic recognition in declaring "I understand what to do" (419), but whether this entails Hal-like self-destruction, annihilation of the human race, or some other alternative that transcends the catastrophic binary is indeterminate. This opening-out of the novel onto an unforeseeable future, along with the interventions of liminal agencies such as Zookeeper into human life, offsets "the human" itself as estranged, animal, temporary, indicative of Mitchell's sense, throughout his fiction, that we are biding time while projecting stories of human destiny.

10. The brief final chapter of *ghostwritten*, "Underground," loops back in space and time to the subway train upon which Quasar rides as he places the device that will release a deadly gas in the cabin seconds after he hurriedly exits at a stop. The chapter is both recursive and continuative, depicting both the departure and the arrival of another kind of night train. As Quasar reflects on what he is about to do, he registers connections to the "future" characters and events that, in the novel's closing moments, exist in its diegetic "past." He hears the strains of a jazz saxophone from someone's Walkman; he glances at the cover of a book another passenger is reading and sees the image of a Buddha; and he notes that the hair of one passenger ("a sleeping giant") is "the color of tea," launching him into a mantra ("Here is the tea, here is the bowl, here is the Tea Shack, here is the mountain" [424]). In his anxiety, he charts an hallucinatory mini-history of empire as he views the "ceiling of the compartment...grasslands rise and fall like years...the Great Khan's horsemen thunder to the west, the furs, the gold, the White Ladies of Muscovy. Leading the way is the new Toyota Land-cruiser, zero percent interest, repayable over forty-eight months, applicants subject to credit checking" (424). Glancing around, he spots a sailor holding a copy of *Petersburg: City of Master-works*, a shopping bag with an advertisement for the London Underground, a placard bearing a "label of Kilmagoon whisky on an island as old as the world" (425). As he exits in panic from the crowded train, its public address system commanding that all "*Stand clear of the doors*" (425—these are Bat Segundo's parting words in "Night Train"), Quasar rushes headlong into a wall with a poster depicting the Empire State Building "circled by an albino bat, scattering words and stars through the night. *Spend the night with Bat Segundo on 97.8 F.M*" (425–26). Thus having completed an inventory of what will become its intertwined narratives, Quasar departs with the memory of a baby watching him "with eyes that are no longer hers" (424) and an unanswered question: is he an avatar of "the world's end. Or it's beginning" (423)?

The novel's coda can thus be seen to serve as a mapping of its itineraries, but one that comes, for the reader, after the fact at the end of a journey that is also its beginning. Narratively binding the recursive to the originary as a kind of biofeedback loop that conflates "world" with "novel" in a work containing contingent stories that appear to intersect both randomly and intentionally, *ghostwritten* manifests its status as a "fractionally coherent...object...that balances between plurality and singularity. It is *more than one, but less than many*" (Law, 3).[15] Composed of partial narratives delineating forking paths, the novel compels us to come to terms with both its labyrinthine multiplicity and the experiential singularity of its reading rooted in the transient interaction between the author (who places the narrative details before us) and the reader (the participant-observer involved in the forging of linkages between scattered objects, characters, and events through variant acts of attention). In effect, the novel confers upon the reader the responsibility to "make the connections" between the novel's parts and, analogously, the world's parts, to take note of the common history of strangers, and to see the fractional coherences that link an act of terrorism to the tyranny of a thirteenth-century warlord and the production of SUVs. The fate of reading *ghostwritten* thus occurs as the product of its itinerancy.

Hauntology

Specters haunt the confines of *ghostwritten*. Ancestral ghosts, noncorporeal entities, artificial intelligences, the ghost of a child, the spirit of a tree, the ghostliness of the novel's nine narrators who (like all novelistic characters and narrators, once "the end" has been written can only inhabit a phantasmatic afterlife), the spectrality of urban environments ("every city has its street of ghosts" [210], reflects Margarita in "Petersburg"; "This is a ghost town" [154], says Sherry of Ulan Bator in "Mongolia"), the uncanny, spectral doubling of the author as ghost (writer) in the figure of Marco and the novel's title—all suggest the degree to which *ghostwritten* is invested in manifesting the immaterial in the materiality of the worlds it depicts. Neil Brose, a ghost telling the story of his final day on earth, characterizes the women in his life as shifting between states of spectrality and personhood: "One was a ghost, who is now a woman. One was a woman, who is now a ghost. One is a ghost, and always will be. But this isn't a ghost story: the ghost is in the background, where she has to be. If she was in the foreground she'd be a person" (93). This speaks to both the temporariness of embodiment as well as to the ways in which identities in *ghostwritten* are ontologically fragile and in continuous states of transformation. Indeed, contra Neil, the novel *is* a ghost story, or a collation of ghost stories that approaches the condition of the cinematic which, for Tom Gunning, is conveyed through the "transparent" yet phantasmatic "nature of film...its status as a filter of light, a caster of shadows, a weaver of phantoms.... [where] [t]he act of seeing encounters a bizarre entity whose quasi-ethereal nature marks the limit (or contradiction) of visibility" (Gunning, 97; 98). *ghostwritten* can thus be seen as a form of mediation that negotiates between the visibility of what can be seen, observed, or described and the invisible threads of contingency that exist between seemingly disparate entities, revealed over time (narrative time, as well as the time of our reading). What links a deceased British lawyer in Hong Kong to a roaming ghostwriter in London? The fact of mortality; a woman who is "now" a ghost to one and the transient memory of a one-night stand to another; hidden degrees of separation revealed through coincidentally convergent itineraries (Huw Llewellyn); or a consecutive iconology (Buddha)?

The novel, in other terms, performs a "hauntology," the term invented by Jacques Derrida to describe the persistence of the past in the present in *Spectres of Marx*, his philosophical thesis on history following the collapse of the Soviet Union. To take up but one strand of this complex meditation Marx's *Capital*, Derrida, writing in the face of the putative triumph of global capitalism as the "final" form of history, argues that the seemingly monolithic, totalized present is haunted by a repressed past that resurfaces in fragments to remind us that identity at all levels (self-identity; the identity of others; the tiled identities of family, community, nation) is nonsimultaneous with the present and with itself. For Derrida, identity thus historicized is a spectral form of self-estrangement, composed of "a stranger who is ... found within ... more intimate with one than one is with oneself, the absolute proximity of a stranger whose power is sin*gular and* anonymous ... an identity that ... invisibly occupies places belonging finally neither to us nor to it" (*Spectres*, 172).[16] In *ghostwritten*, the noncorporeal intelligence, among others, serves as a metaphor for the comprehension of human identity as inhabited by a ghostly alterity that incorporates the histories of others and that manifests the linkage between the one and the many. A ghostwriter par excellence in search of its "own" story, the intelligence is an inverted version of Benjamin's "storyteller," who "starts the web which all stories together form in the end" (*Illuminations*, 97); appositely, the intelligence, seeking its own incorporation, is parasitic, metonymically inhabiting one partial history, then another, the connective tissue of a rhizomatic web of narratives without origin or end. Latent or manifest, barely contingent or fatally interwoven, ancestral or embryonic, the assemblage of these narratives signifies an understanding of "history" as comprised not of discrete events linked through a logic of cause and effect and progressing toward destined ends, but of myriad elements: memories, fantasies, sporadic instances of contact, cultural practices, and situated actions.

As the nomadic intelligence possesses its subjects, the past in this conception of history haunts the present and predicates the future as a visible remainder (and reminder) of our sporadic movements through time and space via trajectories manifesting the antinomy of narrative identity as a fatal accident. The many coincidences, near-misses, and forking paths of the novel speak to the tenuousness of a reality so dependent upon circumstance for its unfolding, and so derivative of the impulse to seek connection amidst intransigent and contradictory multiplicities for its founding. It is this "world-tenuousness" that haunts *ghostwritten* as Mitchell plots contingency in a way that both proliferates and forecloses possible outcomes, futures, and worlds in the same stroke. In part, by means of its rueful hybridization of the generic conventions of the spiritual autobiography, the heist movie, the techno-thriller, or the sci-fi narrative of a world on the verge of apocalypse run by machines, the novel sends up its own plotting, and thus the "certainty" of any paranoid view of contemporary reality. Stolz, with his stereotypical Texas drawl and his ten-gallon hat, hardly seems adequate to the totalistic view of one world run by a geopolitical superpower and the secret forces within it; the Hal-like conversations between Zookeeper and whatever cognitive entity Quancog has become are replete with adolescent quandaries about purpose and the meaning of life—these are not the determinative forces of a sinister world behind the screen run by aliens or machines to be found in either of Mitchell's reference points for "Night Train" in *2001: A Space Odyssey* (1968) and *The Matrix* (1999). But neither are the casually intersecting, detotalized narratives of *ghostwritten* by virtue of their make-up merely to be seen as proffering a comic view of a multi-authored reality ruled by serendipity ("His" or otherwise) where we delight in the fact that anything can happen. In effect, anything and everything does happen in *ghostwritten*, from acts of terrorism to meets-cute, from ascents of the Holy Mountain to descents into the Russian underworld, but multiplicity, as the countersign to singularity, only offers the kind of radical tenuousness that subtends a future entirely dependent on the uneven mixture of chance and circumstance.

World time

ghostwritten is a novel about time and human temporality. It constructs a relation between past and present in which the former constantly infiltrates the latter, and in which both are continuously being reconfigured as they point toward an indeterminate, yet "to be determined" future. For its readers, compelled to track backwards and forwards through the nine stories, noting stray connections and surprising coincidences, the temporality of the novel is that of the future anterior, that of the "will have been." Donald Pease explains that the narrative temporality of the future anterior is one that "links a past event with a possible future on which the past event depends for its significance. The split temporality intrinsic to the future anterior describes an already existing state of affairs at the same time that it stages the temporal practice through which that state of affairs will have been produced" (19).

This is precisely the complex position of the reader in *ghostwritten*, who is encouraged to proceed through the novel as already "ghostwritten," in the past, traversing a series of narratives voiced in the first person/present tense while parsing details that foreshadow the possible futures of a given story—futures that *will have changed* upon their arrival her sense of the significance of circumstances and events when first encountered. This effect of the future anterior occurs on the first or the tenth reading of the novel, and it is not just a narrative trick or illusion performed á la Nabokov, doing all of the plotting behind the scenes while leading the reader to believe that the antonymic combination of hermeneutic freedom and textual determinacy lies in the game of discovering patterns and connections that only appear to emerge as the reading takes place.[17] And while it may be said that from a helicopter perspective any novel engages the temporality of the future anterior in some fashion, in *ghostwritten*, there is no sense that the frayed and partial narrative patterns as they evolve and change over the time of the reading will add up to a set of finalities, or that an itinerary manifests an intention and a direction that culminates in the manifestation of a limit. Conversely, *ghostwritten* demands a form of interaction with the reader that reveals the degree to which she is part of the authorial assemblage of the narrative. The novel as written is, indeed, entirely ascribable to David Mitchell, but the novel as ghostwritten—which is identical to reading in the future anterior mode of the novel—carries the effect of being authored by all, and by no one.

While the temporality of *ghostwritten* urges a productive interaction with the reader that underscores the degree to which readers are responsible for the future of this (and any) novel, it also figures forth in the mode of the future anterior the risks and dangers of the future in the suddenness of its own projected futures where games of chance, accidents, coincidence, and convergent histories abound in the past and present. In linking grammar to philosophical systems in his early work, Derrida suggested the ways in which future anterior is indicative of a dangerous future:

> The future can be anticipated only in the form of an absolute danger. It is that which breaks absolutely with constituted normality and can only be proclaimed, *presented*, as a sort of monstrosity. For that future world and for that within it which will have put into question the values of sign, word, and writing, for that which guides our future anterior, there is as yet no exergue. (*Of Grammatology*, 5)

Noting that an "exergue" can refer to the date stamped on a coin, Derrida suggests here that thinking about the future as proceeding from the present and the past in the future anterior tense—what it will have become, and what affects it will have had, once it comes into being—necessarily involves recognizing that the future potentially undermines any sequential or gradualist views of change across time; for him, we live in the moment of history interrupted. Terrorist attacks, rogue technology, the devastations and derailments of nationalist agendas, the formation and collapse of conspiracies both criminal and political, the possibility of world's end as well as a man simply walking away from his job one morning or a woman pushed out of the path of a moving vehicle at the last minute—all exist in the novel as intrusions or interruptions in the temporal flow that forecast a future dangerous in its uncertainty while binding all into a "world" partial in its historical completion and composed of multiple realities contending within it. For Mitchell, in *ghostwritten*, the temporality of the novel is one where both human connectedness and the brutal intransigency of events sporadically collide and conspire in time streaming toward what will have been.

A company of strangers

In his exposition of hauntology, Derrida identifies self-estrangement and the "proximity of strangers" as conditions of identity and the relation between self and other; the compilation of nine stories in the ten chapters of *ghostwritten* reveals a similar sense of an "international" co-inhabited by strangers, aliens, outsiders, and the disenfranchised crossing the planet's matrices. Their itineraries, alongside the "major events" that form the novel's backdrop (World War II, the Cold War, the emergence of technocracies), comprise the novel's history, which can be more precisely defined as an assemblage of myriad histories, large and small, convergent and divergent. Imaginatively traversing the world (even as it is extended into "outer space"), *ghostwritten* thus advances what the Martinique novelist and philosopher Édouard Glissant terms a "poetics of Relation" that "diversifies forms of humanity according to infinite strings of models brought into contact and relayed" (Glissant, 160). Hence, the novel is a company of strangers. It inscribes a world that runs, as Marco opines, "on strangers coping" (293), or the cosmopolitan world of human interaction that Schoene ascribes as being "marked by global connectivity and virtual proximity as much as psycho-geographical detachment and xenophobic segregation" (Schoene, 98).

As Schoene suggests, the specificities of *ghostwritten* establish the complex interactions between "xenophobic segregation" and "global connectivity" that enable the novel to transcend and effectively obliterate any naively optimistic or neoliberal notions of globalization which envision a planet where all the divergences of species, race, language, and identity (and the multiple agendas of sundry identities) could ever live harmoniously in "virtual proximity." Thus, in the novel's concluding prequel, a terrorist gazes at an infant who is soon to die in the attack, watching him "with eyes that are no longer hers" (424), the crushing point of contact between innocent victim and tortured perpetrator one of utter estrangement and contingency with an "other" that is simultaneously one's self, if we take this to be an instance in which the noncorporeal intelligence transfers from one body to another. The obduracy of language and the difficulties of translation (increasingly, a theme in Mitchell's fiction), the intransigencies of ethnicity evident in the myriad instances of ethnic stereotyping and the accompanying fear of racial mixing that recur throughout the novel, and the cultural and national parochialism that underlie the "big" history of the twentieth century make it all too clear that *ghostwritten* does not view imaginary contact across boundaries as necessary and sufficient to continuance in the future. At the same time, countervailing contingencies (Marco's salvation of Mo, and an old woman's survival of time and circumstance long enough to meet her great-granddaughter) gesture toward possible futures, the possibility of *a* future. It is not so much that Mitchell *balances* cultural intransigency with the capacity of strangers to productively cope and connect, as he places them alongside each other, manifesting their interplay and strife. Perhaps as Marco intimates, the condition of estrangement in *ghostwritten* is both one of contact and "coping," the latter word bearing the sense of both "getting along," the novel itself then serving as a coping mechanism for multiple valences of difference, and more obscurely, as the technique in carpentry of joining walls at slightly odd (nonsquare) angles to each other. Whether directly intended by Mitchell or not, the carpenterial sense of "coping" speaks to the architecture of *ghostwritten*, which conjoins partial, disparate narratives at various angles in order to produce the image of a cross-hatched world. It is, indeed, a world that moves forward through time and space as strangers cope and collide.

In contrast to the global traversals of *ghostwritten*, Mitchell's second novel, *Number9Dream*, locates itself geographically in the city of Tokyo, and psychologically in the singular mentality of a young man in search of his father. Surrealistic and hallucinatory, *Number9Dream* is clearly indebted to Haruku Murakami, but takes its own departure with Mitchell's continuing interest in experimentation with genre and the ways in which narrative architectures and narrative temporalities conspire in the eventuating of an intermedial identity. Mitchell's protagonist in his second novel could have been plucked out of his first, his story "filled out" in an intensive tour of a cognitive landscape, yet one that remains symptomatic of the hauntologies of *ghostwritten*. In the wild ride of *Number9Dream*, Mitchell explores the "reach" of consciousness operating in a chaotic reality.

2

City Life: *Number9Dream*

David Mitchell's second novel, set in Tokyo and on the island of Yakushima in the southwestern Japanese prefecture of Kagoshima, has been aptly characterized as a "postmodern *Bildungsroman*" that "questions the viability of the conventional coming-of-age quest for self-knowledge and a secure sense of identity in a postmodern, late capitalist context even as it simultaneously tantalizes the reader with this possibility" (Simpson, 51). Published near the conclusion of an eight-year stint in Japan, where Mitchell was living with his wife and teaching English to technical students in Hiroshima, *Number9Dream* traces the adventures of its twenty-year-old protagonist, Eiji Miyake, the unacknowledged son of a businessman and a discarded mistress, as he attempts to find his father in the urban labyrinth of metropolitan Tokyo, often represented in the novel as a surreal mixture of buildings, noise, conspiracies, dreams, and catastrophes. At some moments, *Number9Dream* reads like a Bond thriller, as when Eiji imagines himself infiltrating the Opticon Building, where his father—here imagined as an Auric Goldfinger or Emilio Largo—is employed; at other moments, it reads like a parody of a Tolkienesque fantasy, especially when we view over Eiji's shoulder the manuscript of a children's novel for adults written by a woman suffering from writer's block. More than the story of a young man attaining maturity by means of a quest for the father twinned with an exploration of the mysteries of the city (which, in a characteristic genre-bending move, becomes in Mitchell's hands a quest for the mother once the father is discovered to be a paper tiger), *Number9Dream* is a hallucinatory journey through late-twentieth-century Japanese urban culture and, in part, a homage to contemporary Japan's most celebrated novelist Haruku Murakami.

In his essay on the novel's representations of Japanese culture, Baryon Posadas has demonstrated the ways in which *Number9Dream* offers a critical engagement with "techno-Orientalism," which can be understood as "the production of 'Japan' as aetheticized spectacle, as image... [and] ... as image commodity" (Posadas, 84). Techno-Orientalism—the representation of contemporary urban Japanese society as technocratic, mechanized, saturated with gadgetry, yet still nostalgically harking back to Western notions of "the mysterious East" and the "romantic Orient"—is evident in any number of mediations, from cyberpunk to manga, lolita fashion, pachinko, and computer JRPGs (Japanese Role-Playing Games). As Posadas suggests, it is also evident in Murakami's fiction, particularly *The Wind-Up Bird Chronicle* (*Nejimaki-dori kuronikuru*, 1997), which serves as an "intertextual doppelgänger" to *Number9Dream* as "the primary narratives in both of the novels involve a quest for a missing person; both novels also feature metafictional devices in the form of a story within a story... finally, both novels have the protagonists reading extended personal accounts of the experiences of soldiers during World War II" (Posadas, 88). This assessment is revealing, but we can observe a more fundamental comparative point between the two novels in their narrative boundary-crossing and their portrayal of contemporary metropolitan culture as founded upon a traumatic past—one that can only be understood and redressed by means of a peripatetic navigation of the city's hybrid spaces and disjunctive temporalities.

Both Murakami and Mitchell are—once again in Schoene's terms—cosmopolitan writers, whose work is "marked by global connectivity and virtual proximity" (Schoene, 98). For both, one such "connective" thread is the figure of John Lennon, whose song "#9 Dream," from the 1974 *Walls and Bridges* album, provides the title for Mitchell's novel, and who is as prominent in Eiji's life as the statue of the "thunder god" in the forest outside Eiji's ancestral village. Lennon also crops up in several of Murakami's novels, the "Norwegian Wood (The Bird Has Flown)" of the Beatles' 1965 *Rubber Soul* album—primarily composed by Lennon—replicated in the title of Murakami's fifth novel (*Noruwei no Mori*, 1987) and echoed in that of *The Wind-Up Bird Chronicle*.[1] For both writers, the snatches of Lennon's lyrics or the titles of songs popular decades ago, recalled by protagonists as they make their way from province to city and through metropolitan labyrinths, are symptomatic in several ways: "Lennon" represents revolutionary youth culture, the merging of "east" and "west" (in his marriage to Yoko Ono, just as Tokyo as depicted in the novel folds Western metropolitanism into Japanese urbanism), global populism (particularly in the "Power to the People" of his post-Beatles phase), and a blend of universal humanism and pantheistic connectivity. Yet both Murakami and Mitchell place this cultural symptomatic within alternating surreal and historically realistic frameworks that reveal the fragility of such cosmopolitan idealizations, as when Murakami relates the horrific wartime experiences of Lieutenant Mamiya during the Japanese invasion of Manchuria in *The Wind-Up Bird Chronicle* or when Mitchell portrays a yakuza gang-war bloodbath in *Number9Dream*. For both writers, the contemporary metropolitan landscape—technocratic, postmodern, multicultural, and simulated—is haunted by the specter of a brutal, catastrophic past returning in the violence of a tenuous present tending toward an apocalyptic future. Hence both the protagonists of *Number9Dream* and *The Wind-Up Bird Chronicle* engage in the invention of alternate histories or dream of escapes to other worlds paralleling the one in which "real" life occurs: Okadu Toru spends hours at the bottom of an abandoned well near his house attempting to pierce through to a second reality where he can attempt to engineer his own destiny; Eiji Miyake frequently plunges into imaginary, video game–inspired scenarios in which he becomes a narrative hero rather than a victim of circumstances.

The comparison of *Number9Dream* to *The Wind-Up Bird Chronicle* reveals the extent to which Eiji's story is that of an identity inhabiting a complex, schizophrenic world of cultural proximity and temporal dislocation—one in which the enjambments of reality, fantasy, projection, and dream offer a form of cognitive mapping. Twenty-year-old Eiji comes to Tokyo from his island home of Yakushima in search of the father who has abandoned him and haunted by guilty memories of his twin sister's death by drowning. Eiji blames himself for Anju's death nine years previously, for he has made a child's promise to the totem of the local "thunder god" that in exchange for victory at soccer match, the god could take anything he wanted from Eiji in exchange. In Eiji's mind, the god has taken Anju, who drowned while swimming while Eiji was away at his soccer match where he scores the winning goal; in revenge, Eiji saws off the thunder god's wooden head. Memories of Anju and their life together on Yakushima are interpolated with his adult experiences, fantasies, and dreams in Tokyo as he commences the search for his father.

Eiji's quest leads to a series of real and imagined adventures and encounters with an assortment of individuals ranging from Ai Imajo, a "girl with the most perfect neck in creation" (126) who becomes his love interest in the novel, to Suga, a talented computer hacker and fellow worker in the Ueno Station lost property office where Eiji is temporarily employed during his stay in Tokyo, to Yuzu Daimon, the corrupt son of a wealthy businessman who serves as Eiji's Vergil or Steerforth as he journeys through metropolitan fantasylands and underworlds of Tokyo, and to Morino, a Yakuza crime lord who in Hitchcockian manner involves the innocent Eiji in a series of schemes and conspiracies. Primary among these is Ai, whose second name echoes the English "imago," signifying her evolved metamorphic state as one who serves in the role of an intellectual, artistic, and spiritual guide to Eiji and who exists in stark contrast to the images of "idealized," commodified women who inhabit the novel's malls and streets. As his name indicates, Yuzu Daimon is her demonic counterpart whose fetishism and playboy lifestyle signify his inauthenticity and inferiority as a metropolitan "demi-god."

The succession of characters that Eiji meets informs the sequence of events that lead him down many false paths to an encounter with his father, but perhaps more crucial to the formation of Eiji's identity as (often) involuntary seeker are the sundry locales he traverses along the way. In many ways, the "plot" of *Number9Dream* might be defined as Eiji's navigation of these spaces rather than the tracing of events. There is the "capsule as stifling as inside a boxing glove" (47) in which Eiji lives with a sporadically appearing stray cat and an unassailable cockroach above the Shooting Star video store: Eiji's several returns to this haven under the protection of the video store owner and friend, Buntaro, demarcate "save" points in Eiji's life, which he often sees in terms of a video game. Contrasted to this is the PanOpticon building, where Eiji believes his father to be working, a sterile, glassy corporate structure, its surface transparency belying its containment of corruption, conspiracy, and the "secret" of the father that turns out to be empty of content.

In the matrix of spaces that make up the metropolis, the corporate empire of PanOpticon is the workaholic sibling of "Xanadu," a huge and labyrinthine family amusement park on the outskirts of the city, doubtlessly based on Tokyo Disneyland, opened in nearby Urayasu in 1983, which also boasts American-style suburbs built on land reclaimed from Tokyo Bay. In Xanadu and its environs, described by an "enormous banner [that] reads 'Xanadu Open Today! Family Paradise Here on Earth! Nine-Screen Multiplex! Olympic Pool! Krypton Dance Emporium! Karaoke Beehive! Cuisine Cosmos! California Lido! Neptune Sea Park! Pluto Pachinko! Parking space for 10,000—yes, 10,000!—automobiles'" (156), Eiji wanders through an assemblage of scenarios and settings that replicate the novel in miniature. In Xanadu, fantasyland abuts the headquarters of a gangland empire, where Eiji is subjected to threats of torture and extortion at the hands of Morino, who thinks Eiji is either spying for another yakuza gang or attempting to steal his girlfriend, and who forces Eiji to participate in a gruesome bowling match where the "pins" are the human heads of Morino's rivals. Xanadu is a manifestation of what Jean Baudrillard has termed "hyperreal," a "precession of simulacra" that results in "models of a real without origin or reality" (*Simulacra*, 1). In the novel, it is implicitly zoned alongside the interpolated, metafictional spaces that are generated when Eiji envisions the pursuit of his father taking place inside a video game simulation, or when he reads the found manuscript of a children's story written for adults that describes an odd, posthistorical landscape inhabited by a "goatwriter" (i.e. a storyteller who is a goat, parodically echoing the title of Mitchell's first novel), a sentient, talking hen, and a version of early man named "Pithecanthropus."

During his dual navigation of the city's simulacra and his growing awareness of his own implication in the fantasy/reality of Tokyo, Eiji is beset with associative memories of his childhood past and projections of an apocalyptic future. From the restaurant where he first meets Ai Imago and the railroad lost property office where misplaced objects gather in a found assemblage of contemporary culture, through the twinned landscapes of yakuza underworld and corporate empire, to the all-night pizza house of his final days in Tokyo where he is responsible for such "fusion" concoctions as the "Neromaniac" ("pepperoni, sour cream, capers, olives, and jumbo shrimp" [307]), Eiji attempts to piece together the temporal, cause-and-effect relation between the loss of his sister, his quest for his father, and his alienation from his mother. Properly speaking, the logic of the classic *bildungsroman* would dictate that, after numerous external and internal divagations and false leads, his quest would end in a paternal acknowledgment that would equalize the loss of his twin sister (affectively, a loss of the self) with the relocation of Eiji's identity in the generational symbolic order. But the meeting with Daisuke Tsukiyama as Eiji delivers his father's aptly named custom pizza (the "Kamikaze... Mozzarella crust, banana, quail eggs, scallops, octopus ink" [348]) is a nonevent. Discovering that his father is an empty vessel of narcissism and vanity, Eiji does not even bother to identify himself as the rejected and forgotten son. Unexpectedly contacted by his alcoholic mother who had abandoned him and currently is in recovery at a countryside clinic, Eiji escapes Tokyo to reconcile himself to her. Simultaneously, he is forced to confront an open, uncertain and dangerous future—signified in the single blank page of the novel's ninth chapter—when he hears that a major earthquake has hit Tokyo and rushes from his grandmother's house on Yakushima toward an imagined apocalypse of the time to come:

> the images start, and I cannot stop them. Windows exploding an inch from Ai's face. All the capsules above Shooting Star collapsing into the first floor. Ten thousand pans of boiling oil in ten thousand kitchens overspilling. Pizza ovens tipping over. Girders crashing through pianos and beds. Shelves shooting their contents across rooms. Overpass pillars turning to sand, underpasses caving in. The subway system... Rush hour has started... All those people in tunnels... Here on Yakushima, centuries of quiet rain are falling among the pine needles. What now? What now? I cannot think straight, so my body takes over. I fly down the polished hallway, scrunch my feet into my sneakers, fight with the knots, scrape open the door, and begin running. (400)

On this quest to understand the connections between what has and what will happen to him in a chaotic world of dislocated identities and scattered stories and dreams, Eiji both incorporates and resists the conditions of the "metropolitan" subject as classically portrayed by sociologist George Simmel. This entity is characterized in Simmel's 1903 essay, "The Metropolis and Mental Life," which has attained something of a prophetic status as the twentieth century has unfolded into the twenty-first and late capitalism has advanced as the predominant economic form of our time. Eiji might be seen as the imago of the metropolitan subject, making him once again the hero of a *bildungsroman*, but only in the sense of the genre well exceeding the constraints of its traditional investments in individualism. Simmel writes that "the deepest problems of modern life derive from the claim of the individual to preserve the autonomy and individuality of his existence in the face of overwhelming social forces, of historical heritage, of external culture, and of the technique of life" (Simmel, 409). For Simmel, the dilemma of preserving individuality is tested to the extreme in the modern metropolis, where "the rapid crowding of changing images, the sharp discontinuity in the grasp of a single glance, and the unexpectedness of onrushing impressions" occurs "[w]ith each crossing of the street" as one experiences the chaotic "tempo and multiplicity of economic, occupational and social life" of the city's mass environment (Simmel, 410). Eiji's experiences of Tokyo manifest, precisely, multiplicities of tempo, scale, and "occupation":

> Under its tight lid, Tokyo swelters at 34°C in 86 percent humidity—a big PANASONIC display says so. Tokyo is too close up to see, sometimes. There are no distances and everything is above your head—dentists, kindergartens, dance studios. Even the roads and walkways are up on murky stilts. An evil-twin Venice with all the water drained away. Reflected airplanes climb over mirrored buildings. I always thought Kagoshima was huge, but you could lose it down a single side alley in Shinjuku. (3)

For Simmel, the metropolitan subject is split, in that, on the one hand, it responds to the overstimulation of the city environment by becoming inured to it, thus blending into a mass uniformity. At the same time, the metropolitan subject also experiences a countervailing need to distinguish itself from the crowd by means of eccentric or idiosyncratic modes of behavior or dress that, in their very hybridity, reconstitute a form of collective identity.

Coming from the "fallen" pastoral realm of his island childhood—a paradisiacal fantasy destroyed with the death of his twin sister—Eiji enters the city of Tokyo in search of his "historical heritage" only to experience what Simmel terms "the metropolitan style of life directly as dissociation" (Simmel, 416). The arc of his quest leads him past several false fathers to his "real" father, who manifests the very essence of the metropolitan subject in his "blasé" affect. Overstimulated by the sights, sounds, ever-changing impressions, and crowded masses of the city, Daisuke Tsukiyama, inventor of the eccentric "Kamikaze," embodies "[a] life in boundless pursuit of pleasure" that "makes one blasé because it agitates the nerves to their strongest reactivity for such a long time that they finally cease to react at all" (Simmel, 414). Eiji's first and last view of his father is that of a man on the phone complaining about the costs of an extravagant lifestyle to a soon-to-be ex-wife who is having him investigated for his many extramarital affairs while attempting to extort from him the cost of a pony for his daughter as "he lies on a vast sofa, wearing a dressing gown" (350). Disgusted by the grossness and hedonism of his father, who informs his unknown son that the lesson to be learned from overhearing such a conversation is that "it costs more to keep a pony in straw than a whore in fur" (351), Eiji departs, unidentified, his last glance at his father revealing him to be the embodiment of the jaded blasé subject with his false exoticism belying the empty core of his narcissistic existence: "I swallow and nod and leave this man. How is it that I feel nothing, when, for so long, meeting him was everything. I doubt I will ever meet him again, so I look back once—his eyes close as his jaws sink into black stodge" (352).

In refusing to identify himself to his father, Eiji effectually rejects this aspect of his heritage as a nascent metropolitan subject, who is, for Simmel, the subject of cosmopolitan modernity. His response, a draining away of any affect associated with reaching the elusive goal of finding his biological father ("How is it that I feel nothing"), constitutes a refutation of the paternal bond and a recognition of its virtuality.[2] Eiji thus disentangles himself from a quest bound over to a singular traumatic past that brought him to the metropolis in search of his father; the logic of his disavowed pursuit follows what Slavoj Žižek, quoting Wagner's *Parsifal*, terms "the irreducibly vicious cycle of subjectivity: 'the wound is healed only by the spear that smote it'" (Žižek, 257). For Eiji, finding the father who, in some way, is the embodiment of his wounded past is equivalent to finding himself. Abandoning this logic once he discovers that reconnecting with his father is not the answer to his desire to establish a connection with the past allows him to pursue another narrative trajectory that brings him into contact with his mother and, ultimately, the embracing of an open future of myriad possibilities, both terrifying and transformative as he runs toward the "what now?" This sense of futurity—the future, in effect, viewed as a succession of contingent presents—is another sign of Eiji's transformation from a certain version of the historical subject who becomes himself, in many versions of the classic *bildungsroman*, by finding his place in the genealogical chain as he adapts to the city environment, to one no longer bound over to city time and circumstance in the apocalyptic envisioning of metropolitan collapse.

Simmel writes that the

> relationships and affairs of the typical metropolitan usually are so varied and complex that without the strictest punctuality in promises and services the whole structure would break down into an inextricable chaos.... If all clocks and watches in Berlin would suddenly go wrong in different ways, even if only by one hour, all economic life and communication of the city would be disrupted for a long time. (413)

Such disruption is precisely what occurs at the end of the novel when, for Eiji, normal time (and, imaginatively, the city itself) vanishes into the tense of the future unknown. But as a metropolitan subject *manqué* in Tokyo, like Jason Tayler in *blackswangreen*, he is acutely aware of clock-time and its effects on the workers ("drones") and rhythms of the metropolis: "I decide to calculate the number of days I have lived. It comes to 7,286. I add four leap years. The clock says 12:51. Suddenly most of the drones in the cafe get to their feet and flock away. Are they afraid that if one o'clock finds them anywhere except their fluorescent-lit cubicles, their companies will have an ideal excuse to Restructure them?" (5). In Ueno Station, Eiji is confronted at the claims counter by what appears to be a mentally disturbed elderly woman, the "Picture Lady," who is in search of lost family photographs; when asked why they are valuable to her, she responds, "I need 'em to cover up the clocks" (64), as if these snapshots of the past, if recovered, could stop the onslaught of time in the city. Eiji repeatedly references clocks, watches, even sundials during his odyssey, as if the artifice of clock-time were essential to his ability to survive in the city while attempting to forge a stable, unerring linkage between his past and his future—a notion best captured in his sighting of a photo shop: "Across the road is a photo developers with two FUJIFILM clocks—the left clock shows the actual time, the right shows when the photos will be ready, forty-five minutes into the future" (48). As a counter to the Picture Lady's sense that her lost photos have the magical capacity to "cover" time, the contingent clocks suggest that a strictly chronological relationship between the present and the future will enable the prompt development of images from the past and the continuity of memory. For Eiji, in Tokyo, chronological temporality as the guarantor of memory and future is yet another narrative illusion, like the fiction of the father, that collapses in the wake of his experience and his departure from the life of the metropolitan subject.

To some degree, the protagonist of this failed or fractured *bildungsroman* is not Eiji Miyake, but the metropolis itself that, beneath its shiny corporate surfaces, chronologies, and organizational systems underlying everything from pizza delivery schedules to gang hierarchies, encrypts the secret of a labyrinthine and chaotic reality. Navigating Tokyo, often as a kind of flâneur in Benjamin's definition or a voyeur-wanderer who both identifies with and separates himself from the populace, shops, and byways of the metropolis, Eiji begins to experience the city as an assemblage of multiple realities and temporalities. He thus discovers the fundamental paradox of the metropolis which, on the surface, follows the "logic" of sequestered space and chronological time. Eiji's city education traces the curriculum set out by Benjamin in his "A Berlin Chronicle": "Not to find one's way in a city may well be uninteresting and banal. It requires ignorance—nothing more. But to lose oneself in a city—as one loses oneself in a forest—that calls for a quite different schooling" (*Selected Writings*, 598). The "different schooling" that Eiji pursues involves the attempt to map a landscape that barrages him with "a dazzling barrage of disorienting images ... [in] ... an image-saturated space wherein it is no longer possible to trace signs to their referents and any sense of a coherent meaning becomes impossible" (Posadas, 82).[3]

For Eiji, Tokyo often seems an impossibly convoluted labyrinth of signs, buildings, and crowds that he wanders aimlessly as he pursues the red herrings of his quest. The "barrage of disorienting images"—the sheer randomness of the city—is evident everywhere Eiji goes, as when he describes the crowded Shibuya district famous for its "scramble crossing" with its attendant chaos of shops and pedestrians:

> Saturday night in Shibuya bubbles and sweats.... Couples on dates. Americans and beautiful women in moon-glasses.... A giant DRINK COCA-COLA cascade of magma maroons and holy whites. I suck a champagne bomb and walk on. Hostesses wave geriatric company presidents into taxis. In an amber-lit restaurant everyone knows one another. A giant Mongol warrior scooters past, flanked by bunny girls handing out leaflets advertising a new shopping complex somewhere. Girls in cellophane waistcoats, panties, and tights sit in glass booths outside clubs, offering chitchat and 10-percent-off coupons. I imagine scything through the crowds with the twenty-third-century megaweapon. The clouds are candy colored from the lights and lasers. Outside Aphrodite's Soapworld a bouncer runs through the girls pinned up on the board. "Number one is Russian—classy, accommodating. Two, Filipina—attentive, well-trained. The French girl—well, need I

say more? The Brazilian—dark chocolate, plenty of bite. Number five, English—white chocolate. Six is German—home of the wiener. Not an ounce of flab on the Koreans. Number eight are our exotic black twins, and number nine—ah, number nine is beyond the grasp of ordinary mortals—" He catches me gawking and cackles. "Come back in a decade or so, sonny, with your summer bonus." (99–100)

In Shibuya, Eiji experiences an alien and alienated world of colors, bodies, and styles that is at once exotic and banal, with each encounter appearing to be a matter of sheer chance and contingency. Where one has wandered at a particular moment, who one bumps into, what conversations one overhears, and what signs one notices become the primary elements of a "city story" that defines the protagonist's trajectory in time and space. Seemingly, the city manifests itself as a kind of agency in such descriptions, but one without any specific intention beyond spatially organizing bodies and identities in such a way that they must come into contact.

Yet Eiji's apperception of Shibuya suggests that there is a complex cultural logic operating behind scenes that links the negated quest for the father (which is also, in effect, Eiji's self-erasure as metropolitan subject) to prevailing geopolitical conditions writ locally in the representation of Tokyo. In addition to being part *bildungsroman*, part sci-fi novel, part love story, and part fantasy, *Number9Dream* can be viewed as a contemporary example of a psychogeographic novel as discussed in the Introduction. Thus, the novel effectively charts the relation between the above- and below-ground architecture of the city and the collective fantasy life of its pedestrian citizens through the eyes of a voyeur or flâneur. The metropolis seen through the eyes of Eiji Miyake reflects an array of cultural fantasies about Japanese culture and metropolitan life. For Posadas, Mitchell seeks to "remediate" such fantasies—derived in large part from Western films and novels that depict the metropolis—by calling attention to "the act of mediation itself," or the ways in which Eiji's observations and experiences of the city seem to arrive in prepackaged form, as in the description of the Shibuya crowds, where everything that is registered is a brand name, a stylistic fetish, or a commodity that aligns with our expectations of what Tokyo *should* look like to the wandering outsider (Posadas, 85).

Regarding *Number9Dream* as psychogeography allows us to extend the idea of the novel as "remediation" to understand the ways in which Mitchell links the personal quest of a singular identity to the collective affect of the metropolis, revealed in its architecture and pacing. Tokyo, as represented in the novel, is a conglomeration of buildings, traffic, noise, points of congestion and routes of entrapment and escape that demarcate its ill-concealed systems of power. Eiji embodies, in Debord's analysis, "the figure of the urban wanderer, who moves aimlessly across the city before reporting back with his observations," whereby "the topography of the city is refashioned," and its "patterns of continuity and resonance" mapped, by virtue of an alignment of "sites of psychic and chronological resonance" (Coverly, 140–43). To be sure, Eiji's report to the reader containing his observations of the city reflects a pattern that connects the rhythms of his subjective experience to metropolitan flows, but the "resonances" that he detects often signify temporal dissociation rather than historical continuity. In the hodgepodge of signs, facades, and styles that Eiji observes in the Shibuya district, women's bodies are on display and have equal status as "products" with Coca-Cola and sunglasses. Objectification and commodification abound as the visible and uniform operating principles of the metropolis in this scene of potential immersion, but Eiji's seduction into the "city life" is impeded when the hawker tells him that he is there before his time, and when he hears that "number nine"—the oft-iterated singular number of the novel that signifies for Eiji wholeness and completion—"is beyond the grasp of ordinary mortals" (100). For Eiji, wandering in the city, rather than leading to integration and habituation, more often causes him to recognize the intensity of his dislocation from the time-space of Tokyo.

Indeed, his affective experience of the city all too often impresses upon Eiji the sense that he is out of sync with the time and space of the metropolis, as well as the temporality and progression of the narrative in which he is the chief actor: the pressure of events leads to either frenzied action and violent lurching on the road to self-knowledge or aimless, peripatetic wandering and ennui. Describing another street scene set in Shibuya, Eiji suggests he is lost within the labyrinth of Tokyo, despite its superficial chronologies (clocks everywhere) and hypervisible vertical and horizontal organization of space (skyscrapers and thoroughfares):

> In the Shibuya backstreets I am lost in no time. Last night and this afternoon seem weeks, not hours, apart. This grid of narrow streets and bright shadows, and the pink quarter of midnight seem to be different cities. Cats and crows pick through piles of trash. Brewery trucks reverse around corners. Water spatters from overflow pipes. Shibuya's night zone is drowsing, like a hackneyed comedian between acts. My eyes begin to get lost in the signboards—WILD ORCHID, YAMATO NADE-SHIKO, MAC'S, DICKENS, YUMI-CHAN'S.... I left Shooting Star without my watch, and I have no idea how fast the afternoon is passing. My feet are aching and I taste dust. So hot. I fan myself with

my baseball cap. It makes no difference. An old mama-san waters marigolds in her third-story window box. When I look back at her she is still watching me, absently. (134)

Eiji's unconscious pun on time (he is lost within seconds of his arrival in the Shibuya backstreets; and he is lost in the "no time" that subtends the city's vestigial temporal and spatial organization) is accompanied by his being inundated with a barrage of signs that point everywhere and nowhere, to multiple origins and designations. "MAC'S" gestures toward the ubiquitous fast-food chain or, with a misplaced apostrophe, the computer maker; "DICKENS" possibly references a bookstore recalling the Victorian author of many city novels converted into a brand name; "YUMI-CHANS" most definitely is a food joint, but one that comprises a linguistic hybrid of the English "yummy" (transformed into the homophone "yumi") and a common East Asian last name; "WILD ORCHID" is a formulation in English that could refer to anything from a flower to exoticized Western stereotypes of Asian women; YAMATO NADE-SHIKO is another floral expression in Japanese that can refer to the idealized embodiment of womanhood.

As readers, we can make much of these signs, both in their multiplicity and multidirectionality. They refer to the commodification of women, which seems to be a theme of Eiji's metropolitan experience; or to sterile and orientalist notions of cosmopolitanism in their "blending" of stereotypical notions of "East" and "West," "English" and "Asian"; or to the labyrinth of capitalism visible in the metropolis with its fetishistic sign-system that reduces agency to consumption. For Eiji, in their superficiality and inauthenticity, they are all further indications of his dislocation in time and space. As he says, he seems to be moving through a labyrinth of streets located in "different cities" without proper direction, save that of the zero-sum quest for his father, which leads to a collapse of purpose and identity in the metropolis of Tokyo.

We might regard this as Eiji's failure to map the quintessential site of contemporary metropolitan life in Tokyo, or more broadly, a failure to fit into the present tense, with its high ratios of change and its adaptive demands. Yet the account of Eiji's wanderings in the city is accompanied by a continuous succession of alternative narratives with their own navigational demands. Daydreams and nightmares, role-playing projections of other selves, patchwork memories of the past on Yakushima, visions of an apocalyptic future, and interpolated metafictional texts—all intrude upon Eiji's consciousness at various points, complicating even further his experiences of a metropolitan reality that is already multilayered and surreal. Typically, in Mitchell's fiction, the narrative weaves between multiple genres and stories, but specifically in *Number9Dream*, the alternative narratives—each arriving with its own spatial and temporal rules and alignments—can be regarded as compensatory and constitutive: each opens a window onto another world into which Eiji is temporarily cast. These alternative universes, while paralleling and contingent to the reality of Tokyo as mediated by its signs, streets, and buildings, also partially replace it, allowing Eiji (and the reader) to fill in some of the blanks of his existence or to experience other forms of agency—other identities—that cannot be circumscribed according to a metropolitan logic that links identity to genealogical connection and immersion in the all-consuming marketplace represented by the Shibuya District. In this second novel, Mitchell thus develops a philosophical and narrative conception of multiplicity that recurs throughout his fiction. The superficially monolithic metropolis that Eiji enters is, in fact, composed of many virtual worlds, seen and unseen, touching upon and overlapping a host of other virtual worlds that include a manuscript he happens to read, a video game he happens to play, a catastrophe he happens to imagine: each is as "real" as the next; collectively, they make up the fabric of reality that constitutes the novel *Number9Dream*.

Of course, since all of the events, dreams, fantasies, alternative fictions, or depictions of Tokyo streets or Yakushima countryside that occur in *Number9Dream* are registered between the covers of a book authored by the identity who bears the name of David Mitchell and marketed and read as "fiction," each is a multivalent element of the whole: none is, as it were, out of place; none posits another reality beyond that of the novel as such. But Mitchell sharpens this common metafictional recognition, as he does throughout his work, by portraying Eiji as often living on several planes of reality simultaneously, shuttling freely between dream and reality, his experience seemingly a random mixture of spatial and temporal locations and dislocations that limns the paucity and constraints of his role as metropolitan subject operating within the hypercommodified regime of contemporary Tokyo.

In the opening chapter, for example, Eiji is sitting in the planetary realm of the Jupiter Cafe, anticipating the moment when he will cross the street to the PanOpticon building as he seeks to initiate an encounter with his father. The chapter proceeds with a succession of fantasy scenarios that describe Eiji's "heroic" efforts to penetrate PanOpticon in order to gain information about his father whom he imagines to be an embodiment of power and authority secreted in the heart of the transparent architecture of the city. In one, a parody of cyberpunk fiction, he is a Bond-like figure comically posing as an aquarium maintenance technician and carrying a toolbox with a ready-to-assemble tranquilizer gun. Once inside the building, he confronts

Akiko Kato, his father's lawyer and her bioborg "double," eventually escaping PanOpticon after several action shots of gunplay and ninja moves with a file of information that he cannot read as it is written in "air-reactive ink... already vanishing from ghost-gray to absolute white" (16). In another, a sci-fi take on the end of the world, a mythic deluge suddenly floods downtown Tokyo as Eiji waits in the restaurant and imagines himself saving one of the waitresses (who turns out to be Ai Imago) from an escaped crocodile in the rising waters. In a third—this time, a spoof of Chandleresque noir fiction—Eiji tracks Kato from PanOpticon to the "Ganymede Cinema," where the overhead discussions taking place between Kato and Eiji's father, envisioned as a high-level diplomat meeting secretly with his legal aide-de-camp, are interpolated with scenes from the "feature movie called, oddly, *PanOpticon*" (27), a mad-scientist/prison/horror movie jumble.

In this initial portrait of a daydreaming protagonist, with its rapid-fire movement between fragmentary stories and enjambed genres, Mitchell is clearly interested in blurring the dividing line between reality and dream, the signs, weather, architecture, and obstructions of one mirrored in the hallucinatory displacements of the other. But he is also interested in blurring the dividing line between a number of other discursive and positional boundaries in the sequencing of *Number9Dream*'s first chapter, including those that might exist between the novel at hand and other novels by David Mitchell, between the novel as a text and as some other medial entity, and between the author, reader, and protagonist of the novel. The Jupiter Cafe of Eiji's reality, which is the "reality" of a fiction, thus already once removed, becomes the Ganymede Cinema of his dream, generating a series of relocated intertextual resonances that traverse astronomy (Ganymede is the seventh moon of Jupiter), mythology (the moon of Jupiter is named for a divine Trojan hero and the cupbearer to Zeus), and, intratextually, those novels by Mitchell in which moons and comets appear as part of the cross-hatched sign system discussed in Chapter 1. The reader can make much or little of this, just as we can gloss over or probe the significances of the movie posters Eiji sees in the cinema, including that of "a row of screaming Russian dolls" (27) which eerily forecasts the *matroskha* structure of *Cloud Atlas*, or those of "previous presentations" such as "*Dark as the Grave Wherein My Friend Is Laid*. I expect each stairway to be the last, but it never is. Is it getting warmer? *Fahrenheit 451*. In the event of fire, customers are kindly requested to crispen without undue panic. *The Life and Times of John Shade*. I smell bitter almonds" (28–29). In Eiji's reverie, the walls of the movie theater have been converted into a virtual intermedial library where literary works or the transliterated titles of literary works have become cinematic titles and images that may pertain to the author, the reader, and the protagonist on different discursive levels. Malcolm Lowry's posthumous, noir-like, and phantasmagoric *Dark as the Grave Wherein My Friend Is Laid* (1968), Ray Bradbury's dystopian *Fahrenheit 451* (1953), or Vladimir Nabokov's bipolar *Pale Fire* (1962)—are these intertextual clues for the reader of *Number9Dream*, David Mitchell's reading list, or signs, for Eiji, of fatality in the dream-within-a-dream of the cinema? Does his dream tell him that, in reality, he is fearful of suffering a catastrophic death by fall, fire, or poison? For the reader, knowing what the titles refer to provides some hermeneutic information, but by what logic does the protagonist of a novel mutate the titles of books he has never read or seen into the titles of movies he sees in a dream? Does all of this tell us where Eiji's narrative is located both within the array of Mitchell's fiction and the larger, Borgesian textual universe that it enters? To what extent is the novel we are reading a dreambook, a film, a Tokyo psychogeography, or an intertextual scrapbook? And what is the reader to grasp at in a work where form, sign, and story are continuously in a state of transformation?

These questions pertain to *Number9Dream*'s as metafiction which, more than just being a fiction about fiction, generating "the capacity... to reflect on its own framing and assumptions" (O'Donnell, "Metafiction" 301), becomes a broader inquiry about narrative as a means of piecing together fragments of story transmitted across time, space, and multiple worlds. The figure of the author, in this conception of writing, is that of one who channels noise and assembles the fragments into concordances and fortuitous synchronies, generating pattern amidst randomness—a "quantum" notion of story and the author as participant-observer that will emerge more fully in *Cloud Atlas*. *Number9Dream* can be viewed as a novel made up entirely of fictions-within-fiction and tiled, simulated worlds that overlap horizontally and vertically, particularly in the unimaginable totality of the metropolis; moving behind the scenes, there is—as in *ghostwritten*—the floating or transmigrational image of the writer, comically portrayed as "Goatwriter" in Chapter 5 of *Number9Dream*, entitled "A Study of Tales." The chapter is made up of sections from a manuscript of stories that Eiji has discovered in the house of Buntaro's aunt while hiding out from the Yakuza gangsters that have been pursuing him. "I don't think my sister would object," states Buntaro's mother when she finds Eiji furtively reading the manuscript "Unread stories aren't stories" (214).

Written by an author who, we learn, is deaf from birth, these stories that would not exist as stories without the doubled agency of the reader (i.e., literally, they would not exist for us if Eiji were not reading them within the novel we are reading) narrate the odd adventures of "Goatwriter" as he traverses an apocalyptic landscape aboard the self-automated

"Venerable Bus" along with his companions, Mrs. Comb, a talking hen, and Pithecanthropus, named for what he is—an embodiment of prehistoric man. In the episodes Eiji reads, Goatwriter is an "uberwriter" who stammers, dreams he has written *Les Miserables*, and pens his work with the writing brush of Lady Shonogan, author of the eleventh-century work *The Pillow Book*. He is in pursuit of the "rat-thief" who has stolen his manuscript, comprised of "invaluable fragments of a truly untold tale" (198). Soon into this hallucinatory fantasy (perhaps the "number 9 dream" of the novel's title) it becomes clear that Goatwriter & co. are living in the margins of a virtual book comprising a fragmented, intertextual landscape complete with a crucified scarecrow out of a nightmarish version of *The Wizard of Oz* and a village straight from James Whale's 1931 adaptation of *Frankenstein*. "The winds blew over the margins from the east" (202), as Goatwriter sets out in pursuit of the thief; "hellhounds" who he witnesses attacking the scarecrow because he has given "the plot away...bounded away over the blank margins until they were but blots on the wizened horizon" (203). A jumbled sequence of events follows in the four dissociative tales Eiji reads: Goatwriter discovers that his manuscript has not been stolen but consumed by its author; Mrs. Comb visits a starving village where she is forced to feed the inhabitants stories to avoid being eaten; Goatwriter journeys into the digital space of the internet as he searches for his lost writing brush; Goatwriter enters the forest of symbols in quest of the untold story, drinks from "the stream of consciousness" (241) and drowns in a sacred well, only to be reborn as a "ghostwriter" about to inscribe a new sheet of paper, perfect in its blankness.

Several possibilities emerge in these recursive tales of writing occurring within and upon the margins of a pastiche-like book/world depicted in a manuscript being read by the protagonist of the novel *Number9Dream*. First, Mitchell seems to be sending up postmodernist notions of reflexivity, especially as these produce a hyperconscious awareness of the act of writing in a deconstructive process that always incorporates its own materiality and tenuous control over signification into its content or meaning. Correspondingly, as I have suggested, he is figuring notions of "deauthorized" authorship in the metafictional tales of this second novel that interpolate author, reader, and the performance of reading in the production and reception of novel itself. Finally, as exemplified by the use of the number nine scattered throughout *Number9Dream*, Mitchell develops recurrent patterns in his novels involving characters, numbers, events, and locales that work to generate a narrative table of the elements gesturing toward a future-oriented body of work composed of multiple tales, each a part of an emerging whole. Yet this is not a Yeatsian system in prospect: the symbolic importance of these elements is less important (as we observed in *ghostwritten*, the number nine can have entirely opposite valences) than their repetition as a sign of narrative transformation and continuance.

To be sure, these metafictional gestures are self-referential as Mitchell positions himself between life and art as go-between who, along with Eiji, has formed "the thought that reality is an unedited script performed once; that the truly untold tale is life itself," though not without a characteristic bit of self-irony: "This seems extremely profound for about ninety seconds" (245). At the same time, the metafictional strategies of *Number9Dream* have a leveling effect: dream, projection, artifact, script, signs, memories, and simulations—all circulate freely in the novel as elements of a contemporary reality in which there is no single (or single-authored) narrative that will suffice as explanation of the present, formulation of the past, or projection of the future. Nor does Eiji emerge as a singular identity, affectively linked to a paternal author/authority, who becomes the hero of his own life's story or the acculturated metropolitan subject bound over to chronology or the fetishes of an externalized, commodified personality. The epigraph to the novel from Don DeLillo's *Americana*, "It is so much simpler to bury reality than it is to dispose of a dream," is somewhat misleading in this regard as it posits the priority of irrepressible dreams over reality. In *Number9Dream*, "dream" and "reality" are not merely paired off against each other, the dividing line between them erased as Eiji experiences the temporal and spatial disruptions of the metropolis. Instead, they can be seen as integers in a semirandom sequence that also includes metafictional excursions into the written page, psychogeographic descriptions of Tokyo, simulated fantasy worlds, and movie-set gangster shootouts that show Mitchell's evolving sense of narrative as a mediatory process that registers the multiplicity of human experiences across a continuum of time, space, and history. His exploration of linkages across time in narrative trades off genealogy and territory for random simultaneity and contingency. As we shall see in the discussion of *Cloud Atlas* in Chapter 3, this conception of narrative is, for Mitchell, essential to any capacity we might have to imagine a future: the very future, in fact, that Eiji is about to embark upon in running toward it.

3

Time Travels: *Cloud Atlas*

Time is the speed at which the past decays, but disneys enable a brief resurrection.
                                    Sonmi~451, in *Cloud Atlas* (235)

Time, no arrow, no boomerang, but a concertina.
                                    Timothy Cavendish, in *Cloud Atlas* (354)

Cloud Atlas is arguably Mitchell's most highly regarded, widely read novel to date and "perhaps his most ambitious experiment in narrative form and the possibilities of storytelling" (Hopf, 108). Short-listed for the Man Booker Prize and adapted for a 2012 film directed by Lana and Andy Wachowski (*The Matrix* series) and Tom Twyker (*Run Lola Run*), the novel established Mitchell's international popularity as a writer who could uncannily ventriloquize voices across time and create riveting, philosophically and politically complex narratives in multiple genres that tested the limits of style, form, and language.[1] Composed of six nested narratives, *Cloud Atlas* traverses multiple "chronotopes" in ways distinct from *ghostwritten*'s nine itineraries.[2] While *ghostwritten* navigates globally across cross-hatched contact zones in contemporary real time, *Cloud Atlas* moves across spatial and temporal domains stretching from the islands of the South Pacific in the mid-nineteenth century to a Belgian château near Bruges in the early 1930s, Southern California in the mid-1970s, contemporary London and a nursing home for the elderly in Hull, South Korea in the twenty-second century, and a distant future that foresees a return to a primitive, survivalist past in postapocalyptic Hawaii. The six narrative voices of the novel (as nine is a favored number in *ghostwritten*, so is six in *Cloud Atlas*) speak in a mixture of styles, dialects, vocabularies, relevant to the time space each inhabits, and like the nine narrators of *ghostwritten*, their paths seem to randomly intersect, not through a crossing of life itineraries but as intermedial adaptations or reincarnations of each other across history. The comet-shaped birthmark or scar borne by Katy Forbes in *ghostwritten* reappears somewhere on the bodies of several of *Cloud Atlas*' narrators as a vestige or remnant that suggests how the past corporally resurfaces in the present and the future. The relation of these narratives to each other, and their status as recurrences that indicate narrative and historical progression or regression, inform the novel's fundamental problematic: how the similitude of human identity is visible in its movement through time and space only as a series of variations made most evident in those forms of cultural violence that attempt to install a homogenous regime of "the human." The primary motif or register of this "atlas o' clouds" (308) so attuned to musical and linguistic variations might be summed up in a koan: everything is always the same; nothing is ever the same.

Half-lives: A poetics of relation

A San Francisco lawyer named Adam Ewing voyages to the South Pacific and back in order to locate the Australian beneficiary of a will executed in California; his journal describes being shipwrecked on Chatham Island, the trials of a sea voyage on the schooner *The Prophetess* in the 1850s, his friendship with Autua, a Moriori runaway slave, and his victimization due to a murder conspiracy orchestrated by the ship's doctor, Henry Goose, whom he thought to be a friend.[3] In a series of quirky detailed letters to a former lover, a British musician and confidence artist named Robert Frobisher narrates his attempt to ingratiate himself with an aging, renowned composer of atonal music, Vyvyan Ayrs, living in seclusion in Belgium.[4] Once ensconced in the household, Frobisher is seduced by Ayrs' wife, Jocasta, and enters into a fraught relationship with his daughter Eva (who will reappear in *blackswangreen* as the elderly Eva van Outryve de Crommelynck, self-exiled to the Worcestershire village of Mitchell's fourth novel). The collapse of Frobisher's schemes for marrying Eva and becoming Ayrs' artistic and fiscal heir leads him to compose his final work, *The Cloud Atlas Sextet*, as well as the last letter of the series, a suicide note. The manuscript of a Chandleresque noir thriller starring Luisa Rey, a female investigative, is set in the mid-1970s Southern California of "Buenas Yerbas." In a tale reminiscent of *The China Syndrome* (1979), a film about a nuclear plant meltdown eerily released twelve days before the Three Mile Island nuclear accident on March 28, 1979, the manuscript relates a conspiracy to suppress the design faults of a nuclear power plant about to go online whistleblown by one of the scientists involved in its testing, Rufus Sixsmith, Robert Frobisher's correspondent in the previous narrative.[5]

In a chapter from his autobiography, an aging London vanity press-cum-celebrity publisher, Timothy Cavendish, in flight from the cronies of a gangster/author who believes Cavendish has tricked him out of lucrative royalties, finds himself trapped in a nursing home (ironically named "Aurora House" after the Roman goddess of dawn) as a result of his brother's machinations; his escape from the facility with a rag-tag group of inmates is replete with comic scenes of car chases and bar fights. Conveyed under the rubric of an "orison" or prayer, the catechetical interrogation of genetically cloned "fabricant" named Sonmi~451, who has been designed as a culinary worker/slave in a sacralized parody of the world's largest fast-food franchise projected onto the vast global corporate culture of the twenty-second century, reveals revolutionary and counterrevolutionary conspiracies operating at cross-purposes in a world torn over what is human and what is not. Finally, in an oral narrative or "yarnin'" (240) passed from father to son, Zachry o' Bailey's Dwellin,' a "Valleysmen" goat herder and storyteller, relates the tale of his survival of tribal conflict and genocide on the island of Hawaii in a world that has become "prehistoric" following a nuclear apocalypse. Zachry is saved from certain death at the hands of the brutal Kona tribe through prophecies delivered in initiatory dreams he believes are delivered by Sonmi, the god of the monotheistic Valleysmen, and the heroic efforts of an anthropologist benamed "Meronym." She comes from a technologically advanced group that visits twice a year in Zachry's homeland for trade. Arriving on a "Great Ship" powered by fusion and known as the "Prescients," Meronym and her people live on the distant "Prescience I" ("bigger'n Maui, smaller'n Big I, an' far-far in the northly blue" [248]); they have somehow been able to maintain the technological advances of pre-apocalyptic times, including a communication device that contains the holographic "orison" of Sonmi~451. The film adaptation of the novel depicts the Prescients as off-world colonists who return periodically to earth in order to stay in contact with the remnants of humanity and, at least in Zachry's case, to rescue the embodiment of a cultural memory shard.

This brief reprise of *Cloud Atlas*' six narratives provides only the barest indication of the intricate web of connections to be drawn between them. Each appears to be a discrete novella unto itself, yet they are all interlinked by signs and echoes, and they are all intertextual in a triple sense: they bear multiple references to previous literary texts, to Mitchell's other novels, and to each other.[6] References to Borges, Gibbon, Solzhenitsyn, Tolkien, Plato, Nabokov, Flaubert, Tolstoi, Scott, Durell, and Amis (Martin), among many others—especially Melville's "Benito Cereno," "The Encantadas," and *Moby-Dick*—pepper *Cloud Atlas*' five halved and one whole story. If one were reading Mitchell's novels in the order of their publication, Luisa Rey was last seen calling into the Bat Segundo show and a younger Timothy Cavendish giving editorial advice to Marco in *ghostwritten*, while a photograph of Robert

Frobisher will be scrutinized by the young protagonist of *blackswangreen* as he visits the house of the elderly Eva van Crommelynk, and Luisa Rey, now the editor of the exposé magazine to which she contributes in *Cloud Atlas*, will correspond with war journalist Ed Brubeck, the central figure in Part Three of *The Bone Clocks*.

As in *ghostwritten*, internal linkages and cross-hatchings abound. Meronym's group of technologically advanced survivors hail from "Swannekke... way past Ank'ridge an' way past Far Couver" (296), the name and location of the flawed nuclear power plant in "Half-Lives." Vyvyan Ayrs recounts a dream of a "nightmarish café, brilliantly lit," in which the "waitresses all had the same face. The food was soap, the only drink was cups of lather" (79), offering an eerie presentiment of Sonmi~451's "future," where the escaped fabricant notices an ad depicting a government official "opening a newer, safer, nuclear reactor" (231), as if the 200 years between Luisa Rey's 1970s and those of the global "corporacies" of the twenty-second century had not intervened. Serving as both a remnant of the historical past and, in its name, a predictor of the future, the *Prophetess*, "beautifully restored," sits at anchor in the Buenas Yerbas marina that Luisa Rey visits in search of Robert Sixsmith's suppressed report, secreted on *his* boat, the *Starfish*. As she passes by the nineteenth-century vessel on which Adam Ewing sailed, "Luisa is distracted by a strange gravity that makes her pause for a moment and look at its rigging, listen to its wooden bones creaking... [her] birthmark throbs" (430).

The novel's intertextual microeconomy informs its structural macroeconomics: as *Cloud Atlas* progresses, each narrative partially contains and partially culminates in both the narratives that precede and follow it. If we read the novel from first page to last in order, we encounter approximately the first half of Adam Ewing's "Pacific Journal," ending in mid-sentence with the entry of "Sunday, 8th December" (39). This is followed by the first nine of Robert Frobisher's seventeen "Letters from Zedelghem." In a letter dated "14th-VII-1931" (all of Frobisher's letters reflect this hybrid Anglo-Latinate method of marking time), Frobisher relates finding in Ayrs' library, from which he is stealing rare books to sell, "a curious dismembered volume... [that] ... begins on the ninety-ninth page.... From what I can glean, it's the edited journal of a voyage from Sydney to California by a notary of San Francisco named Adam Ewing.... To my great annoyance, the pages cease, some forty pages later, where the binding is worn through" (64). The first thirty-nine of seventy chapters included in "Half-Lives: The First Luisa Rey Mystery" follow, including a scene in which Rufus Sixsmith, sequestered in an airport hotel as he attempts to escape the corporate assassin who will murder him in the effort to suppress his report on nuclear reactor design flaws, reads the letters from Robert Frobisher he has saved though he "knows them by heart" (111). Sixsmith (his name one of many reflexive clues scattered throughout this novel in six parts) hides the first nine of the letters he possesses (those we have just read in the previous chapter) in the hotel room's Gideon Bible and the remainder in his coat pocket, intending to read them in a restaurant at which he never arrives.

The novel switches genres once again as we receive slightly over half of Timothy Cavendish's autobiographical "ordeal," breaking off at an hallucinatory, apocalyptic moment ("as I pushed cold peas onto my plastic fork, a chain of firecrackers exploded in my skull and the old world came to an abrupt end" [181]), signaling the onset of a minor stroke. During the long pauses between episodes of flight and escape, Cavendish reads and edits the first part of a manuscript in his possession entitled "Half-Lives: The First Luisa Rey Mystery" submitted to him for consideration by the author, "Hilary V. Hush" (155). In a seedy Cambridge hotel room, on the evening before he enters the "asylum" of Aurora House, he records falling asleep reading "just after Rufus Sixsmith was found murdered" (167); recovering from his stroke, he completes his reading of the portion of the manuscript to him, which leaves off precisely where part one of "Half-Lives" ends in the novel, "when Luisa Rey was driven off a bridge and the ruddy manuscript ran out of pages. I tore my hair and beat my breast. Did part two even exist. Was it stuffed in a shoebox in Hilary V's Manhattan apartment? Still abed in her creative uterus?" (357).

Flight and escape are integral as well to the first 5/8ths of "An Orison of Sonmi~451" that follow in the narrative of the fabricant's rescue from a life of servitude by a group of "Unionists," who believe that fabricants and consumerist "purebloods" are equally human, and who take Sonmi~451 to a scientific institute where she will be educated and prepared at a galactic speed to become a leader of the revolution. At a climactic moment, she is permitted to view a twentieth-century film that has been locked away in secure archives entitled "The Ghastly Ordeal of Timothy Cavendish" so that she might be allowed to see a past that has been erased and rewritten by the fascist, corporate regime that controls the world of "Nea So Copros." The critical importance of the relation between genre and interpretation for Mitchell is underscored in the inherent irony of viewing the adapted autobiography of an objectionable hedonist (Cavendish fantasizes in the second part of his account that, when he escapes, he will indulge in "Cigars, vintage whisky, a dalliance with Miss Muffet on her ninety pence per minute line. A return match to Thailand with Guy the Guy and Captain Viagra" [372]) as a documentary of late-twentieth-century life. Her viewing of the film is interrupted fifty minutes in—just at the point where Cavendish suffers his stroke—by the police attempting to arrest her. The intermedial inheritances of the novel culminate in the sixth chapter, which contains in one piece Zachry's transmitted oral narrative (presumably written down by his son), with its invocations of goddess Sonmi and the holograph of Sonmi~451's "orison."

The second parts of the remaining narratives are then related in chronologically reverse order, each completing the work of its intertextual predecessor in various ways: the final wish of Sonmi~451, about to be transported to the "lighthouse" for execution, is to view the remainder of the film, "The Ghastly Ordeal of Timothy Cavendish." Self-exiled and hiding in Edinburgh, Timothy Cavendish finishes his reading of the second part of "Half-Lives," which has been sent to him by the author whom he has contacted after his escape from Aurora House. Having found the first nine letters of Robert Frobisher in the hotel room occupied by Sixsmith just before he is murdered, Luisa Rey is given the second set of eight by his niece, Megan, who has retrieved them from her deceased uncle's belongings. In his final letters, Frobisher reveals that he has discovered the second half of Ewing's partial diary that was used to stabilize a bedpost. The remainder of Ewing's diary contains a footnote authored by "J.E.," who is Jackson Ewing, his son, commenting on the illegibility of his father's script at a moment where he is near death from Goose's poisoning. Thus this intricate, multiply threaded novel returns in the middle to the beginning and end of its own chain of textual transmission, while the arrow of time moves forward in the novel's first half, and backward in the novel's second, the first and second half of the earliest narrative in the sequence, Ewing's journal, bookending the whole.

In *Cloud Atlas*, as in all of Mitchell's novels, the genre and structure of the story and the skein of relations between stories inform the novel's thematics: the mode of narrative transmission is a primary aspect of narrative meaning; narrative form implicates philosophical perspective, politics, and historiographic context. To reflect on the nested structure of *Cloud Atlas* and the means by which its stories are conveyed across time and space is to consider how its narrative ratios open onto its semantic agendas. The figures of the "Chinese box" or "Russian doll" have been used to describe novels like *Cloud Atlas*, which configure narratives within narratives arranged as a series of frames surrounding its successors: Italo Calvino's *If on a Winter's Night a Traveler* (1982), A.S. Byatt's *Possession* (1991), Christopher Nolan's "puzzle-films" *Memento* (2000) and *Inception* (2010), and further back, multiply framed narratives such as Henry James' *The Turn of the Screw* (1898) and Mary Shelley's *Frankenstein* (1818) exemplify this recursive narrative structuring. In a *Guardian* essay, Mitchell has written that Calvino's novel "magnetised" him as an undergraduate; the novel's "giddying ... intertextuality" and "audacious structure," he remarks, were primary in leading him to the writing of "a devout MA on (ahem) 'The Postmodern Novel,'" and to explore the question, "What would a novel where interrupted narratives are continued later look like?" ("Enter the Maze," n.p.).[7]

Indeed, *Cloud Atlas* reflexively refers to own "Russian doll" narrative structuring of recursively framed narratives halving ("interrupting") each other in references such as the title of one of Vyvyan Ayrs' compositions, *The Matryoshka Variations* (52), "Matryoshka" being the anglicized Russian name for the set of increasingly smaller dolls nested inside each other, each doll halved to gain access to the next, the final, tiniest inner doll or "egg" left whole.[8] More significantly, in the second part of "Half-Lives: The First Luisa Rey Mystery," Ivan Sachs, a scientist who decides to feed Luisa Rey information about the power plant design faults report and who is assassinated for his efforts, theorizes in his notebook (a "black book" of secrets and reflections) that there is

> One model of time: an infinite matryoshka doll of painted moments, each "shell" (the present) encased inside a nest of "shells" (previous presents) I call the actual past but which we perceive *as the virtual past*. The doll of "now" likewise encases a nest of presents yet to be, which I call the actual future but which we perceive *as the virtual future*. (393; italics in original)

This complex formulation of temporality, occurring within a novel whose "Russian doll" structure renders it "palimpsestic" and "metaleptic" as it "engages transmissions and intrusions across narrative levels" (Hopf, 116), suggests the degree to which *Cloud Atlas* links the experience of temporality with the relational structure of narrative.[9] I will turn more fully to the temporality of *Cloud Atlas* later in this chapter, but it is important to note here that, for Mitchell, the survival of story (in a novel replete with stories of survival) depends upon the capacity for the infiltration of narratives across time, revealing the primary work of narrative to be its potential for connectivity.

Yet as figures for the structural semantics of *Cloud Atlas*, the "Russian doll" and "Chinese box" are somewhat misleading. Both suggest an investment in mirroring and symmetry that runs counter to the image of history in the novel conveyed as a series of partial stories serendipitously linking mediated identities across scattered spatiotemporal reaches and domains—to cite Timothy Cavendish citing Gibbon: "little more than the register of the crimes, follies, and misfortunes of mankind" (167). After describing his early fascination with Cavino's *If on a Winter's Night a Traveler* and his indebtedness to the Italian author who joins Borges as one of the "inventors" of postmodern fiction, Mitchell goes on in "Enter the Maze" to remark that Calvino's postmodern bag of tricks now seems less impressive than it did as an enthralled undergraduate who "wolfed the book down in one afternoon": "Describing our world's unknowability in terms of labyrinths and mirrors no longer cuts the metaphysical mustard, somehow.... I felt the sense of flatness you get when a hackneyed magician says 'Prepare to be amazed!'" (n.p.).

The replicating neatness of symmetrical orders associated with labyrinths, mirrors, and Russian dolls is put into question within the novel itself when Frobisher describes in a letter his plans for the *Cloud Atlas Sextet*:

> Spent the fortnight gone in the music room, reworking my year's fragments into a "sextet for overlapping soloists": piano, clarinet, 'cello, flute, oboe, and violin, each in its own language of key, scale, and color. In the first set, each solo is interrupted by its successor: in the second, each interruption is recontinued, in order. Revolutionary or gimmicky? (445)

Initially, Frobisher's description sounds like a "key" for future readers and scholars, thoughtfully provided by the author, that will allow them to unlock this puzzle box of a novel. This is not unlike the "Linati schema" that categorizes each chapter of *Ulysses* (1922) according to animal organ, color, symbol, discipline, and narrative technique, produced by James Joyce for a friend in order to help him understand the novel better, and used by subsequent Joyce scholars as a decoding device. Yet Frobisher's "key" also has all the earmarks of a narrative gimmickry about which Mitchell seems deeply suspicious, or at least ambivalent, just as viewing the "comet-shaped" birthmarks that his characters bear across this and other novels as determinate signs of a belief in fictional or real-world reincarnation must be regarded with some skepticism when we read that Timothy Cavendish wishes to delete from Hilary V. Hush's manuscript "the insinuation that Luisa Rey is this Robert Frobisher chap reincarnated.... Far too hippy-druggy—new age. (I, too, have a birthmark, below my left armpit, but no lover ever compared it to a comet. Georgette named it Timbo's Turd)" (357). The novel's own internal references to the "Russian Doll effect" and the intricacy of its nesting would seem to indicate the assemblage of a narrative totality that is replicative, divided by halves, inculcating the Escherian order of the labyrinth as mirrored time and space fold back onto themselves in the progressions and regressions of each story. But a closer scrutiny of the novel's structure and a regard for such "clues" as these reveal that the narratives of *Cloud Atlas* are asymmetrical, unevenly joined, enjambed by virtue of contingency rather than folded into each other in an encapsulating architectural design.

Up close, the narratives of *Cloud Atlas* as they succeed each other are not exactly half-novels or half-stories. Additively, they result in a highly variable fractional set that is either more or less than the cardinal number of six. Ewing's journal is, in effect, not quite halved, the second "half" commencing with the final two words of a long sentence begun in the first half. More significantly, as Frobisher relates, the "dismembered" volume he finds begins on the ninety-ninth page, such that the two accidentally discovered parts of "The Pacific Journal of Adam Ewing" are unequal fractions of the whole. Nine of the seventeen letters penned by Robert Frobisher are presented in the first "half" of "Letters from Zedelghem," the remaining eight in the second, each part of the epistolary novella thus not quite or slightly more than half. "Half-Lives: The First Mystery of Luisa Rey" complicates the novel's mathematics by including thirty-nine of its seventy chapters in the first "half," and the remaining thirty-one in the second; this asymmetry appears in the division of a manuscript about the dangers of atomic energy nominally referring to the measurement of radioactive decay occurring exponentially in an array of receding fractional halves as part of a process that, theoretically, never totally exhausts itself. "The Ghastly Ordeal of Timothy Cavendish" is halved in a more traditional sense, save that its partition occurs not as a matter of architecture but of happenstance when the first half ends at the moment of Cavendish's stroke, suggesting that, for Mitchell, happenstance *is* architecture. The ratio of Sonmi~451's "orison" is 5/8th to 3/8th, the narrative "halved" by sudden intrusion of the police while she watches the Cavendish film up to the point of interruption with the onset of his stroke.

Even the received nonhalved version of "Sloosha's Crossin' an' Ev'rythin' After," the secreted innermost "egg" of the narrative enfolded by all of the others, is not quite or more than a whole, for it is a series of orally transmitted recollections that often interrupt or backtrack upon each other, passed between generations as Zachry's son relates his memory of hearing them from his father. Escaping in a kayak manned by Meronym's comrade, Duophysite, Zachry, the sole surviving Valleysman of the genocide wrought by the warring Kona, looks back across the distance to the receding island of Hawaii and reflects: "Yay, my Hole world an hole life was shrinked 'nuff to fit in the O o'my finger'n'thumb" (308). The linguistic play on "whole"/"hole" evident in the transcription of Zachry's speech as well as the typographical play on "O"/"0" (zero) in the description of the perspectival frame through which he views the shrinking island complicate the asymmetrical relation between part and whole, fraction and integral evident in the halved narratives that enfold "Sloosha's Crossin'."

More obscurely, the names of Zachry's savior and the kayak's rower, respectively, Meronym and Duophysite, refer to part/whole ratios. "Meronymy" is the name of the semantic relation of part to whole or member to set in logic and linguistics: thus, a meronym of "tree" is "branch."[10] Duophysite's name refers to a delicate point of doctrine and schism in Early Orthodox Christianity concerning the human and divine natures of Christ. The dispute, fomented by a church patriarch named Nestorius, in the fifth century, was over whether Christ's humanity and divinity were combined into one nature or split into two natures resident in one being—the latter the position of Duophysites, espousing the Nestorian heresy.[11] The concept of two beings residing in the body of one echoes throughout Mitchell's fiction, from the transmigrations of the noncorporeal intelligence of *ghostwritten* to Holly Sykes, the central figure of *The Bone Clocks*, inhabited for decades by an atemporal presence. In *Cloud Atlas*, the names of these characters speak to the novel's reflection upon the changeability and hybridity of "human nature" over time, but they also resonate with the narrative quandaries implicit in the varying structures of *Cloud Atlas*: to what extent is any story "whole," or always part of a series of interrupted stories, the serrations of each only partially fitted to the others? Mitchell's insistence on the connections to be discerned between narrative structure and narrative idea leads us to ask, what is the relation between completion and incompletion, residual imperfection and impossible perfectibility in the telling of stories and the tracking of identities, cultures, and civilizations across time? To what extent is any story, and any life, always a "half-life"? The conclusion of "Sloosha's Crossin'" relates the manner of its encapsulation and conveyance, as Zachry's son invites his audience, in the second person, to "Sit down a beat or two. / Hold out your hands" (309) in order to receive the egg-shaped recorder that contains the holographic orison of Sonmi~451 and "ev'rythin'" before and after. Implicitly, in this apostrophe, the continuance of the story—its ongoing half-life as it moves toward an ever-deferred completion—depends upon those who would receive and transmit it forward in time and into the orison/horizon of the future even as the story, in its very transmission, manufactures its own past.

The radioactive potential of narrative as a form of continuance is, perhaps, most dramatically present in "The Orison of Sonmi~451," where the condemned fabricant reveals at the end of her confession that all the events of the sci-fi thriller in which she has been a protagonist are elements of a "theatrical production," in the words of her interrogator, "*composed... of scripted events*," a "*fake... adventure story*" (348; ellipses and italics in text).

The purposes of this deception are oppositional. For the corporate regime that manipulates events in such a way that a fabricant "terrorist" is caught and confesses, the ensuing show trial will cause public outrage and increasingly repressive legislation that would distinguish the human ("pureblood" consumers) from the nonhuman (cloned slaves). For Sonmi~451, playing the role of a double-agent, the sequence of fabricated events has resulted in the dissemination of her *Declarations* of independence, or Lutherian "twelve 'blasphemies'" (349), supposedly penned to terrify the populace even further, but having the potential—given the vagaries of chance and circumstance to which all of *Cloud Atlas*' journals, letters, scripts, orisons, holographs, and oral transmissions are attuned—to inspire future generations to change the picture. Quoting Seneca to Nero, she states, "No matter how many of us you kill, you will never kill your successor." Then, declaring that "my narrative is over" (349), she announces that her last wish is to view the second part of "The Ordeal of Timothy Cavendish," which was interrupted at the conclusion of her story's first part. Like Zachry's son, Sonmi~451 effectively places her fate as a form of narrative survival and continuance in the hands of the future reader.

The most appropriate figure, then, for the relation between the novel's form and its envisioning of history and identity within a poetics of relation is the "cloud atlas" of its title.[12] Technically, a cloud atlas is an illustrated collection of different cloud types and variants used by meteorologists to predict the weather; the first *International Cloud Atlas* produced by the International Meteorological Committee was published in 1896. As its name indicates, a "cloud atlas" is a mapping device, and in two key moments, Zachry and Timothy Cavendish, at widely separated points on the novel's temporal continuum, use the term to describe their navigation of time, tide, and circumstance. Escaping from his homeland in the boat steered by Duophysite, Zachry reflects:

> I watched the clouds awobbly from the floor o' the kayak. Souls cross ages like clouds cross skies, an' tho' a cloud's shape nor hue nor size don't stay the same, it's still a cloud an' so is a soul. Who can say where the cloud's blowed from who or who'll the soul'll be tomorrow? Only Sonmi the east an' the west an' the compass an the atlas, yay, only the atlas o' the clouds. (308)

This theological reading of meteorology is invested with the concept of the transmigration of souls that he introduced in the noncorporeal intelligence of *ghostwritten*, which is to be distinguished in Mitchell's fiction from any simple ("hippy, druggy—new age") concept of the reincarnation of a singular identity across centuries since the "migration" inevitably takes place intermittently, sporadically, as the consequence of chance contact or circumstance across multiple identities. The cloud mapping of a survivor of nuclear apocalypse stands in contrast to that of the jaded urbanite, Timothy Cavendish, suffering from depression and trapped in the nursing home, from which he will escape only with the assistance of strangers and outcasts:

> Three or four times in my youth did I glimpse the Joyous Isles, before they were lost to fogs, depressions, cold fronts, ill winds, and contrary tides... I mistook them for adulthood. Assuming they were a fixed feature in my life's voyage, I neglected to record their latitude, their longitude, their approach. Young ruddy fool. What I wouldn't give now for a never-changing map of the every-constant ineffable? To possess, as it were, an atlas of clouds. (373)

Cavendish's yearning for "a never-changing map" of the ineffable and the unknown, his despair over the loss of the paradise of youth ("the Joyous Isles" which the reader might implicitly connect with the islands of Zachry's lost dystopian paradise), and his desire for a clear direction amidst the vagaries and uncertainties of his "life's voyage" appear to be the opposite of Zachry's apprehension of a cloud atlas as a stochastic charting of human continuance and purpose across time.

Yet both perspectives reveal similar contradictions as they embody the paradox of a cloud atlas: a mapping or cataloging of atmospheric formations that always change and a sky that is never quite the same from second to second. Cavendish may desire an impossible "constancy" amidst a mutable landscape ruled by chance, but his escape from the confinement of the nursing home only occurs by virtue of a slapdash plot and with the help of a hodgepodge supporting cast that leaves him exiled, in Edinburgh, "designing the future on beer mats, like Churchill and Stalin at Yalta, and I must say the future is not too shabby" (387). "History" with a capital H is rendered as chancy and ad hoc as Cavendish's minor history in this reflection, even as the aforementioned manifold intertextuality of Mitchell's fiction accumulates as Cavendish's story winds down: in the pub that offers temporary sanctuary to Timothy and his motley crew, he downs a "double Kilmagoon" (383), the native whiskey of "Clear Island" in *ghostwritten*. As the group splits up after a narrow escape from their pursuers, Cavendish notes that two of them are "headed to a Hebridean location where Ernie's handyman-preacher-cousin does up falling-down crofts for Russian mafiosi and German enthusiasts of the Gaelic tongue" (386), signaling another reference to *ghostwritten* and the Russian mob of "Petersburg" as well as to the many linguistic and vocational farragoes (inculcated in the sound pun on "Hebridean" and "hybrid") scattered throughout *Cloud Atlas*. Referring to himself as he plans a postexilic future, Cavendish exclaims that he "shall find a hungry ghostwriter to turn these notes you have been reading into a film script of my own" starring "Timothy 'Lazarus' Cavendish" (386), thus conflating his projected identity reborn with that of the holograph of Sonmi~451, as well as implicitly referring to Mitchell's ghostwriting at large, its vagrancy and virtuality anchored by its idiomatic signatures. Amidst change, the contradictory certainty of a sporadic pattern of repetition across dispersed narrative worlds; within indeterminacy, the determinacy of replication.

Cloud Atlas thus comprises a novel-universe plied with multiple pasts and futures (including those of Mitchell's other novels) as stories emerge and are "allowed" to collide, the jagged edges of their fractional partiality coming into contact, their cross-hatchings presenting sporadically as characters, cultures, and histories converge and split at random points. The relational complexities inherent in viewing *Cloud Atlas as* a cloud atlas parallel some of those to be found in the mathematical theories of Benoit Mandelbrot, one of the founders of fractal geometry and ensuing chaos theories, who writes in his foundational work:

> I claim that many patterns of Nature are so irregular and fragmented, that, compared with...all of standard geometry...[they exhibit] not simply a higher degree but an altogether different level of complexity. The number of distinct scales of length of natural patterns is for all practical purposes infinite. The existence of these patterns challenges us...to investigate the morphology of the "amorphous." (1)

For Mandelbrot, any mathematical or geometrical patterns to be observed in "Nature," which he terms "fractals," are subtended by chance. Childs and Green have observed of *Number9Dream* that the novel is "a layering of disjunctive textual scrapes" resulting in "a fractal geometry of current cultural formations in a floating world" (40); the same claim can be made for the "fractal" novel of *Cloud Atlas*, which distributes its signs, memes, idiolects, and narrative shards, seemingly at random, across multiple floating worlds.

The fractal structuring of *Cloud Atlas* in turn infers a certain narrative responsibility—each story leading to the others, thus each bound to the others by chains of inscription and circumstance having thematic consequences. From one perspective, the reflexive figure of the cloud atlas may appear to be another instance of the kind of "flat magic" that Mitchell attributes to Borges' labyrinths and Calvino's enfolded landscapes. To be sure, all of the partial stories and multiple voices of *Cloud Atlas* are invented and contained within the singularity of a novel that, one might argue, is inevitably a complete, enclosed "total system" like any other, under the control of the author. The authorial take on this determinative, structural set of conditions in a novel of circumstantial history, partial stories, and contingent identities is, arguably, double and ironic. The inscription of the Hitchcockian signature of the comet-shaped birthmark, the repetition of names, objects, numbers, and locations within and across novels, or the metafictional shapes of Russian dolls and cloud atlases that describe narrative operations within the novel itself are certainly earmarks of the self-reflexive *deus* behind the *machina*. At the same time, *Cloud Atlas* is clearly about the counterattempt to put the novel into the reader's hands, as Zachry invites us to take up Sonmi's orison (and as the "half-life" of each protagonist comes into the possession of his or her successor), thus demanding from readers full participation in the ongoing completion of partial narratives and the forging of disparate connections.[13] For Mitchell, this comprises an act of reading pursuant to a poetics of relation that is not only interpretive but also political and dialectical, an engagement with story that is, at once, an engagement with history and futurity, for those who survive and live to tell about it.

The form of identity

Half-life, half-text. As an assemblage of fractional stories, *Cloud Atlas* embraces the partiality, but not the fragmentation, of narrative characteristic of postmodernism. Just as he turns away from the Borgesian mirror or labyrinth as forms of narrative structure that infer the paradox of solitary human interiority as infinitely self-replicating and unknowable, so Mitchell turns toward a model of narrative that is fractal and interstitial, evolving as a result of multiple circumstances. Thus Mitchell brings into parallel array narrative form and human identity in the novel's half-lives. The details attending the complex structural relation of story to story and adjacency of principal characters in *Cloud Atlas* reveal modes of telling, reception, and transmission over time and space that reflect consciousness and interiority to be collective, rather than singular. Like the cross-grained, intergeneric narratives of *Cloud Atlas*, identity in the novel is contingent, partial, and regional. We "know" Adam Ewing, for example, only through the part of a journal imperfectly transcribed by his son and discovered over a half-century later by a musician stealing books from a private library, who in turn mentions the discovery in a letter found in a dead man's hotel room, a circumstance that is a key element in the plot of a mystery being read in manuscript another half-century later by a publisher on the run, as he escapes from a gang of criminals documented in a film being viewed by a fabricant yet another century or so later, whose image is holographically transmitted to a devout goat-herder centuries again in the future. Each protagonist, each consequential event of *Cloud Atlas*, only gains the force of presence and agency in its relation to a miscellany of others over time, as one element among many in multitude of narrative trajectories and circumstances.

Zachry's reflection on the analogous relation between clouds and souls contains the paradox of identity resident in Mitchell's fiction: the multitude— the myriad nomads, slaves, artificial intelligences, escapees, scientists, artists, entrepreneurs, con artists, and genetic clones that inhabit *Cloud Atlas*— are notable for their variety and heterogeneity, yet for Zachry they are all "souls" that replicate themselves and corporeally migrate across space and time. The term "multitude," originally employed by Spinoza to indicate the mentality and power of the many versus the one, has been recently revised by Michael Hardt and Antonio Negri in their consideration of the limitations and reach of "empire" to indicate historically "new subjects" that emerge from the world-system of capitalism in pluralistic assemblages living and acting within ever-changing local and regional conditions, indebted to each other by the bonds of historical circumstance rather than those of capital, yet reflecting a "universal nomadism" (*Empire*, Kindle location 776).[14] In contrast to the seemingly deterministic, permanent narrative of global capitalism and its "network of hierarchies and divisions that maintain order through new mechanisms of control and constant conflict," Hardt and Negri offer the future possibility of human identity conceptualized as a "multitude" opened up by the massive connectivity of globalization and technology themselves in "new circuits of cooperation and collaboration that stretch across nations and continents and allow for an unlimited number of encounters" (*Multitude*, xiii). Mitchell registers this possibility in the massive connectivity of *Cloud Atlas*—its cross-hatched narrative details, fractional partialities, and corporeal and nominal repetitions—as a matter of survival. In the novel's postapocalyptic future, the continuance of the species, symbolized in the tribal remnant of Zachry and his memory of being rescued by Meronym, occurs at the end of a long line of historical eventualities and ad hoc collaborations that extend back to Adam Ewing's adventures with a scoundrel and a Moriori captive whose life he saves, and who saves his life in return. The emphasis in the novel's chains of circumstance is not based on notions of progress or advancement, but on contingency. The encounters that may lead to the continuance of humanity in the future, and new forms of life and thought, depend upon a set of narrative adjacencies and chance situations occurring within the totality of a novel.

What are the new identities in relation to the multitude that the novel charts as a matter of both form and figure? As is the case with the narrative genres and symmetries that Mitchell both establishes and interrupts in *Cloud Atlas*, identity in the novel is never one thing, but an embodied contestation of singularity and multiplicity. We read much about "pure blood" as compared to hybridity across the novel's eleven chapters, in terms that go well beyond the origins of this expression in biology and its manifestations in nineteenth-century race theory.[15] The singularities of blood, tribe, locality, dialect, and nation are only advanced against the multiplicities that abound in the novel: pidgin and patois (the argots of the snob and the hipster, and the cognate lingos of Sonmi~451 and Zachry); island cultures (England, Chatham Island, and Hawaii) inhabited by racially mixed groups whose differences converge in a history of violence that includes rare instances of salvation; metropolises (SoCal, Seoul, and London) where the multitude and mixture of races and differences—the sheer weight of the crowd—is felt as a spatial and temporal force to be reckoned with; bodies dismembered and remembered as admixtures of the "human" and the "non-human."

For Mitchell, the story of identity necessarily includes—in the ironic brutal story behind the formation of civilizations—the counternarrative of identificatory purity and singularity that stretches across the novel's temporal and spatial climes. Mr. D'Arnoq, the local preacher in the island settlement where Adam Ewing is temporarily stranded, mournfully and nostalgically relates the history of the Moriori, an aboriginal moiety whose "language lacks a word for 'race'" (11) and who have been driven to extinction by the dominant Maori.[16] While he seems to regret the fact that "[l]ess than a hundred pureblooded Moriori now remain" (15), thus investing in the delusory notions of racial purity associated with the authenticity of cultural and personal identity, D'Arnoq himself is the ironic embodiment of both "mongrelism" and the racialist fantasies of cultural and corpuscular superiority consonant with the ideology of Western colonialism that finds its most extreme formulation in Kurtz's "exterminate all the brutes!" in Conrad's *Heart of Darkness* (1899). Ewing writes in his diary that "[t]he name of Mr. D'Arnoq is not well-loved in the *Musket*. 'A White Black, a mixed mongrel of a man,' Walker told me. 'Nobody knows *what* he is'" (16), yet to the "natives" he is entirely the White Christian missionary who has come to redeem them from degeneracy and paganism, even if his "demotic flock" constitutes a denomination that "is a 'rattle bag' of Christian creeds" (8). In effect, the answer to the question "what is D'Arnoq?" would be that he is a composite identity in which racial, theological, and political singularities and hierarchies contest with the multitude of pluralities evidenced by the materiality of his body and his position in the sociohistorical order: "pureblood" versus the hybridity of "White/Black"; the bearer of the one truth of Christianity versus the "rattle bag" of creeds that constitute a surmise of Christianity's history; and the brutal, hegemonic force of the colonizer versus the fantasy of hegemony ("pureblood") mapped onto the diasporic history of the colonized.

If we go forward into the future of *Cloud Atlas*, we see that these same contestations take place in the bodies, languages, and histories of a genetically engineered fabricant living in the time of global corporatism's ascendency at the other end of the historical arc that begins with Western colonial expansionism. We see them as well in the story of a tribal shepherd struggling for survival in the aftermath of the global destruction that comes about as the "logical" extension of the narratives of territorialism, capitalism, and technological recklessness preceding "Sloosha's Crossin'." In recounting his temporary enslavement and narrow escape from the expansionist Kona moiety in a history of intertribal conflict and extermination that mirrors that of the Maori's and the Moriori's (according to D'Arnoq), Zachry recalls the words of the Kona commander to the captured Valleysmen: *"Third rule is, you don't waste no time plottin' 'scapes. When you're sold next-moon you'll be branded on your cheeks with your master's mark. You'll never pass for pureblood Kona 'cos you a'int, truth-be-telled* all *Windwards are freakbirthed shits"* (291, italics in original). The contradictions of the commander's warning could not be clearer: the "Windwards" have to be externally marked and identified as the enslaved other even though his racial logic would suggest no such marks are needed for the innately "freakbirthed" abject. The artificial difference marked by the slave's brand (inversely comparable to the "natural" sameness of repeated birthmarks across generations of characters) occurs as a result of the desire to realize the fabricated singularity of tribal identity as historically ascendant and essentially "pure." Yet the difference only mirrors sameness; just as the sameness of the birthmarks only reflects their differing shapes, their comet-*likeness*, as they recur on the bodies of dispersed identities in the novel whose relation to each other, is entirely circumstantial, not determined by genetic or tribal logics and connections.

The words "pureblood" or "purebloods" occur over eighty times in "The Orison of Sonmi~451" as the fabricant describes her life in the globalized, hypercorporate society of "Nea so Copros," which is clearly obsessed with blood purity and defending the boundaries of the "human." The notion of "pureblood" in Sonmi's account extends well beyond corporeal, racial, or territorial self-definition: it serves as the increasingly vestigial dividing line between "this dying corporacy's" (189) citizen-subjects and every other form of sentient life, especially the genomed fabricants who are both Nea So Copros' proletariat and a critical element of the human food supply chain for a planet that has become an ecological disaster area. As she discovers on a radicalizing journey to Nea So Copros' floating fabricant slaughterhouses, disguised as arks of deliverance to the simulated paradise of "Xultation" for fabricants who have been retired after twelve years of continuous labor, the engineered slave class of the twenty-fourth century's corporate empires are systematically executed and rendered into a protein source called "Soap." Ironically named after an anticontaminant in this perverse recycling system, Soap is fabricants' sole food supply while also secretly incorporated as an addictive substance into the mass-produced fast food that "humans" eat at McDonald's-like "Papa Song's," where Sonmi~451 works as a server. The mirrored self-replicating relation between humans and fabricants, and thus between the "self" of humanity and the "other" of the "non-human," could not be clearer than in the episode when Sonmi~451, having undergone a cosmetic makeover (a "facescape") in order to pass as human and avoid notice as a notorious escaped fabricant, visits a shopping mall where "[p]urebloods... were a sponge of demand that sucked goods and services from every vendor, dinery, bar, shop, and nook" (227). There, she encounters a "media fashion scout" who mistakes her for a human passing as a fabricant, not the reverse, and congratulates her on her appearance: "She said I was the first consumer she'd seen to facescape fully like a well-known service fabricant. Lesser strata, she confided, may call my fashion statement brave, or even antistrata, but she called it genius" (228).

Indeed, the reason that Sonmi~451, liberated and educated at a pace "consumers" could never match, is such a threat to the social order is because she and every fabricant embody the potential to erase the artificial division between "human" and "non-human," thus abolishing the form of alterity upon which the human depends for self-definition. Literally, in Nea So Copros, as the holocaust of the fabricants horrifically elucidates, humans eat fabricants transformed into food in a form of self-cannibalization that reveals the cruel absurdity and symmetry of identity logics based on blood and gene, class, moiety, and nation at their limit. Professor Mephi, Sonmi~451's mentor at the scientific institute where she inhales knowledge and information at a speed that gives the lie to any notions of human supremacy over fabricants, asks, "What if the differences between social strata stem not from genomics or inherent excellence or even dollars, but merely knowledge? Would this not mean the whole Pyramid is built on shifting sands?" (222). Difference per se in Nea so Copros is exposed in such a question as a form of categorical imperative subtending a social order built upon the fiction of difference supposedly innate in body, race, or class that extend to a projection of the human as a fundamental, but ultimately foundationless, similitude.

The more one comes to know the situated characters and identities of *Cloud Atlas*, the more one realizes that all of them, and thus the "human" as such, is for Mitchell a matter of the plural rather than the singular. On the one hand, the "rag bag" assemblage of corporeal, historical, and cultural differences individualized and assimilated under rubrics like pureblood, human, fabricant, islander, citizen, or inmate in the novel seems to arise out of some timeless need to demarcate forms of otherness that limn the singularity and exceptionalism of self, species, or nation. In Mitchell's hands, this "human" desire for cultural and material superiority underlies the fantasy of "a never-changing map of the every-constant ineffable" (373) and is repeatedly evidenced in the novel's stories of power and subjugation, from the establishment of dominion over an island by means of enslavement and genocide to the enforcement of the self-ordained laws of the sea aboard ship via torture and punishment, or the fomenting of corporate conspiracies in order to build the engines of technological superiority that will enrich the few and endanger the many.[17]

Yet everywhere in *Cloud Atlas*, identities of all kinds—bodily, linguistic, islanded, or nomadic, are marked by hybridity, and the multitude is felt as a countervailing presence to any fantasies or embodiments of "pureblood." As he travels by train to Hull, Timothy Cavendish xenophobically observes the mélange of languages and cultures that constitute "the North." Somnolent after partaking of some "ganga" given to him by a "Rastafarian" on the train, he is awakened in Hull by a train cleaner, a "Modigliani" who, when Cavendish questions where he is, responds in what sounds to him like a foreign tongue: "Yurrin Hulpal" (171). In his chauvinism, Cavendish views the cleaner as one of the "exotics" depicted in Modigliani's elongated masks, speaking in "Arabic" (instead of regionally inflected English in responding "You're in Hull, pal"), thus representing in his homogenization of foreignness the possibility that he "had boarded and slept all the way to Istanbul Central" (171). Departing the station, he sees a homeless man, his "nose, eyebrows, and lips ... so pierced with ironmongery that a powerful electromagnet would have shredded his face in a single pass." He then takes a cab whose driver "was far, far too big for his shoulders, he must have had that Elephant Man disease, but when he turned round I made out his turban" (171), thus associating alterity with monstrosity, as well as providing a prescient linkage between a homeless man in Hull and an island tribesman in postapocalyptic Hawaii. While listening to a song on the cab's radio "about everything that dies some day comes back," Cavendish struggles to interpret the driver's speech when he pays for the ride: "'Sick teen-quid Zachary.' 'I don't know anyone of that name.' He looked at me, puzzled, then repeated, 'Sixteen—quid—exactly'" (172). For Cavendish, anything that does not sound like BBC English and anyone who is not visibly white, British, and upper class (his version of "pureblood")—however culturally diverse the dialects and people he encounters may be, or how "British" they actually are in terms of genealogy or citizenship—becomes a manifestation of the multitude reconstituted as a singularity.

What might be called the intratextual unconscious of *Cloud Atlas* would have it otherwise. "Exactly" in the cab driver's inflection is rendered as "Zachary," echoing the name of the protagonist of "Sloosha's Crossin'," and Cavendish registers the lyrics of a pop song about death and rebirth in a novel where characters recur both utterly different from their avatars, yet bearing the mark of similarity. Ironically, through Cavendish, the reader becomes aware of the novel's hybridity as a diffusion of localized particularities and differences across its historical reach from the apogee of empire to the declinations of the future. Identities (names, bodies, characters, and "souls") are remembered as partialities whose continued existence depends upon the variations of mediation and genre: even Cavendish only remains over time as an image in a film whose viewer fuses him in his mediated afterlife with Robert Frobisher as an "eponymous book thief" (235). Reversals and repetitions-with-a-difference of stereotypical or notions of identity abound, such as when Sonmi the fabricant is mistaken for a pureblood disguised as a fabricant, or Meronym, when asked why "Prescients'd got all dark skins like cokeynuts," responds that "her ancestors b'fore the Fall changed their seeds to make dark-skinned babbits to give 'em protection 'gainst the red-scabbed sickness" (252–53) of radiation poisoning. The relation between language and identity that Mitchell inscribes here and throughout his fiction is evident in the many linguistic styles and temporalized dialects of *Cloud Atlas*, from Zachry's "pidgin," to the hi-tech vocabularies and quick-speak elisions of twenty-second-century corporate culture depicted in Sonmi's orison, the jaded-but-desperate-thirties-son-of-an-aristocrat phraseology of Frobisher's letters, or the spelling and diction of the mid-nineteenth century evident in Adam Ewing's diary. Mitchell "do the police in different voices" in *Cloud Atlas*, where the history of linguistic change and regional specificity registers the transmission of multiple identities across time.[18]

Like the conflated, seemingly "single" identities named "Cavendish" and "D'Arnoq," the homologous human and textual collectivities of *Cloud Atlas* are characteristically described as heterogeneous assemblages, whether

Frobisher's first collaboration with Ayrs, "Der Todtenvogel," which "borrows resonances from Wagner's *Ring*, then disintegrates this theme into a Stravinskyesque nightmare policed by Sibelian wraiths" (65), or Sonmi~451's view of Ch'oryang Square in Pusan, where

> Fabricant nannies scooted after their 'xec charges; swanning couples assessed couples swanning...hawkers sold palm-size curios...A circusman was touting through a megaphone...Pureblood sailors from all over Nea So Copros sat in frontless bars, flirting with topless comforters, under the scrutiny of PimpCorp men: leathery Himalayans, Han Chinese, pale-hued hairy Baikalese, bearded Uzbeks, wiry Aleutians, coppery Viets and Thais. (336–37)

Thus *Cloud Atlas* confounds, and unfounds, identities as historical, linguistic, or textual singularities, the "oneness" of identity—as in the paradox of the novel's title—only present in the multitude of its variations. In the novel's projection of a future, even if only one of bare survival, much will depend upon the capacity to leave behind a catastrophic past of bound over to the primacy of the individual subject or polis.

Utopia Inc.

The future does weigh heavily in the narratives of *Cloud Atlas*. The narrative ordering of the novel structurally complicates the relation between past and future at every turn and works to cast the entire novel in the tense of the "future anterior" that was discussed as characterizing the split temporality of the reader's experience in *ghostwritten*. In *Cloud Atlas*, this experience is redoubled as the narratives themselves constantly shuffle between their own pasts and futures as well as those of the narratives they proceed and follow. The sequencing of the novel is both progressive and regressive as it portrays moments in the "advance" of "civilization" (*Cloud Atlas* insists on the scare-quotes) that run from the colonialism of "the Pacific Journal of Adam Ewing" to the years after the "war to end all wars" in "Letters from Zedelghem," the Cold War technocracy of "Half-Lives," the mendacious, sound-bite-driven present of "The Ordeal of Timothy Cavendish," and the globalized corporatism of "The Orison of Sonmi~451." These culminate in the vision of a future that is, in effect, a return to the distant past in "Sloosha's Crossin an' Everythin' After," the "everything after's" then receding into the moments of civilization's advance in reverse.

Consonant with the notion of identity shifting toward the multiple in the wake of empire, the "whole story" of this novel made of halves and parts might be viewed as shadowing the "total" history of capitalism and empire from the mid-nineteenth century (Adam Ewing's voyage is merely one episode of the larger story of Western imperialism) to the site of the "future past" where capitalism winds up on the dung heap of a history replete with violence yet scintillating with sporadic instances of temporary connection, survival, and sacrifice. In the novel's design, Mitchell renders ironic the notion of "civilization" as germinating its own perfection as it moves through time, embodying a utopic trajectory that is manifested in the signs of progress in the present. Civilizations and empires in *Cloud Atlas*, from the "rightful—corporate—empire" of Cold War America (403) to that of the Aztecs which Frobisher predicts in his suicide note "Cortes'll lay... to waste again" (471), bear only the seeds of their own destruction. They are parodically equated with bowel functions when Cavendish informs us of his "perpetual lavatory read, *The Decline and Fall of the Roman Empire*" (153), or made into the subject of truisms when a "jackdaw" dandy is overheard by Frobisher to exclaim that "a man is ruined when the times change and he does not. Permit me to add, empires fall for the same reason" (75). Thus, civilizations and their agendas of dominance and perfection come to naught even as they manifest certain repeated variants in a metahistorical "atlas o' the clouds" where pattern and chance contend with each other. The foundations of empire in slavery and the exploitation of nature, the ubiquity of violence and war, the persistence of capital, human survival, and the fantasy of utopia—all exist as constants amidst the shifting narrative temporalities and registers of *Cloud Atlas*.

As the novel's poetics of relation is articulated in its structure and its marking of identity across time, so *Cloud Atlas* urges us to see the connection between the disparate, circumstantial details of anecdotal observation and the larger political and historical frameworks in which they occur, revealing the utopic desires of "civilization" at key moments in the narrative of global capitalism and its self-destructive aftermath.[19] The initial encounters between Adam Ewing and "Dr." Henry Goose provide an early case in point. Stranded on an island "so remote, that one may there resort unchallenged by an Englishman" (3), Ewing tracks Goose's footprints "on a forlorn strand" (in a telling reversal of Defoe's Crusoe tracing the marks of an indigenous presence on another remote island) and spots a strange "White man, his trowzers & Pea-jacket rolled up, sporting a kempt beard & an outsized Beaver shoveling & sifting the cindery sand with a teaspoon so intently that he noticed me only after I had hailed him from ten yards away" (3). Goose reveals that he is searching in the sand for human teeth because, as he puts it, "[i]n days gone by this Arcadian strand was a cannibals' banqueting hall" (3). This obscene labor is being undertaken by the harlequin-like Goose (his deceptiveness unapparent to the naïve Ewing) because he wants to sell them at a high price to a denture manufacturer in London, but his more ambitious goal is to enact revenge on a Marchioness who has "besmirched my name, yes, with imputations that resulted in my being blackballed from Society" (4). Knowing that she buys and wears dentifrices from the very manufacturer to whom he will sell the teeth, he plans to return to London and embarrass her at a public banquet by revealing that she is eating with the teeth of "cannibals." From the outset, in this absurd plot, which initially effects Ewing as the discourse of a "Bedlamite" (3) whom he will later entrust with his health, the linkage between human slaughter, profit motive, and cultural exploitation is forged in a counternarrative to the progressiveness of an "enlightened" civilization complete with the latest medical advances.

The connections are extended in Ewing's remembrance of his early conversations with "the only gentleman on this latitude east of Sydney & west of Valparaiso" (5), the nomadic con-artist in his expatriated "Britishness" signifying for Ewing his status as a Crusoe among the savages:

> I spoke at length of Tilda & Jackson & also my fears of "gold fever" in San Francisco. Our conversation then voyaged from my hometown to my recent notarial duties in New South Wales, thence to Gibbon, Malthus & Godwin via Leeches and Locomotives. Attentive conversation is an emollient I lack sorely aboard the *Prophetess* & the doctor is a veritable polymath. Moreover, he possesses a handsome army of scrimshandered chesssman whom we shall keep busy until either the *Prophetess's* departure or the *Nellie's* arrival. (5)

The conversation between these two embodiments of Western culture and civilization in the mid-nineteenth century is replete with assumptions founded upon a contradiction. On the one hand, there is a list of advances that putatively mark the emergence of a modern, "enlightened" culture, including technological achievements (the locomotive), humanist ideals (Goose as "polymath" and Renaissance man), and "rational" debates (Godwin vs. Malthus) about the relationship between man, nature, and the social order as it advances utopic aspirations for universal wealth and happiness, equality, and peace. On the other, there are the dystopic consequences of "civilization's" rise and, in the invocation of Gibbon, inevitable fall: the vision of an El Dorado as opposed to the greed, violence, and sheer human desperation evident in the history of the California gold rush; a "civilized" game of chess using pieces made from ivory harvested from marine creatures nearing extinction in the holocaust of species that mark the relation between man and nature (and, eventually, man and clone) in the novel's time frame.

Such anecdotal, symptomatic instances reveal the ways in which Mitchell stages in *Cloud Atlas* a continuous conversation between the utopic desire of civilizations and the dystopic counternarratives that necessarily subtend those desires—a linkage compellingly explored in Ursula K. Le Guin's allegory "The Ones Who Walk Away from Omelas," which depicts a utopian society that requires for its continuance the sacrifice of a child who must live in perpetual filth and degradation in a dark basement. In reflecting on the memory of an etching shown to him by his grandfather, Robert Frobisher makes the connection between utopia and violence, slavery, and domination:

> Once, he showed me an aquatint of a certain Siamese temple. Don't recall its name, but ever since a disciple of Buddha preached on the spot centuries ago, every bandit king, tyrant, and monarch of that kingdom has enhanced it with marble towers, scented arboretums, gold-leafed domes, lavished murals on its vaulted ceilings, set emeralds into the eyes of its statuettes. When the temple finally equals its counterpart in the Pure Land, so the story goes, that day humanity shall have fulfilled its purpose, and Time itself shall have come to an end. (81)

This narrative of the utopic temple's evolution into its idealized double in an eschatological "pure land" can be read, in Frobisher's view, as one version of "the story of civilization": "To men like Ayrs... this temple is civilization. The masses, slaves, peasants, and foot soldiers exist in the cracks of the flagstones, ignorant even of their ignorance. Not so the great statesmen, scientists, artists, and most of all, the composers of the age, any age, who are civilizations architects, masons, and priests" (81). The story of civilization's embodiments of heavens on earth—from cathedrals to new world orders—built upon the backs and hellish existences of slaves and peasants is an old one. In *Cloud Atlas*, Mitchell shows the extent to which utopic desire is built upon the materiality of dystopic reality, and how both function in relation to a projection of a future that is "pure" and permanent, at the end of history, as if a building or dominion erected upon the bodies of peasants and slaves could bring an end to time and circumstance, vanquishing both contingency as the connective tissue of identities and histories and temporariness as the primary condition of human continuance.

Thus, if we consider the "civilizations" at the near and far ends of *Cloud Atlas*'s temporal trajectory, we can witness the reiteration of one of the novel's primary themes: human utopias inevitably mirror the dystopic conditions that undergird them. The projected images of "Xultation" in "The Orison of Sonmi~451" offer a revealing example of the ways in which the cultural imaginary of a utopia is made of the very stuff of consumerist aspirations that necessarily entail the brutality of enslavement and the corporatization of human subjects. Each morning, at "Matins" (perverted from its original function as the morning prayers of the canonical hours practiced by Catholic monks), the fabricants in servitude to the fast-food franchise in Nea So Copros gather to hear a daily sermon delivered by "Papa Song," the "Logoman" of their domain who is actually a holographic projection: "at Matins, Papa Song shows us pictures of Xultation and Hawaii, and AdV instreams images of a cosmology beyond our servery" (186). The fabricants are thus daily brainwashed with the vision of another world that awaits them beyond the present one of endless labor (Sonmi~451 responds to a question about rests that "[o]nly purebloods are entitled to rests… For fabricants, 'rests' would be an act of time theft" [186]), an "Xultation" that is their "only one long term future" where they will be "transformed into consumers with Soulrings" (186). As part of her education after her escape from bondage, it is revealed to Sonmi~451 that "Xultation is a sony-generated simulacrum dijied in Neo Edo. It does not xist in the real Hawaii, or anywhere. Indeed, during my final weeks at Papa Song's, it seemed that scenes of Xultation repeated themselves. The same Hwa Soon ran down the same sandy path to the same rock pool. My unascended sisters did not notice …" (344–45). With its promise of warm sandy beaches and permanent leisure (clearly a mockery of the retirement utopias for citizens of the present), Xultation offers, as the culmination of a lifetime of slave labor, promotion to the putatively paradisiacal status of a consumer, complete with a "Soulring" that signifies the fabricants' arrival as "humans." As is made clear in the final future of the novel taking place on the "big island" of Hawaii, and as Sonmi~451 discovers in her journey, the dystopic reality is quite otherwise. The "ark" that will transport the fabricants to Hawaii and beyond is actually a slaughterhouse where their bodies will be transformed into fuel for the corporate empire that manufactures simulated utopias like Xultation to help keep the workers working and the buyers buying. The highest, most "civilized," utopic aspirations of such a social order are identical for both masters and slaves and essential to keeping each in their "proper" place.

Just as the idealized projections of Xultation are placed alongside the dystopic realities of the genocidal state machine or the urban jungles of Nea So Copros in *Cloud Atlas*, so the Swannekke nuclear power plant of "Luisa Rey," "quivering like Utopia in a noon mirage" (122), stands as an embodiment of the technological aspirations consonant with the maintenance of "the good life" in twentieth-century America, but sustained by virtue of vast and murderous corporate and government conspiracies and portending a catastrophic future for its citizens. Of the Moriori capital built by a people whom he describes as living by a code of nonviolence that allowed them "to create a harmony unknown elsewhere for the sixty centuries since Adam tasted the fruit of the Tree of Knowledge" (12), D'Arnoq asks, "Who can deny Old Rekohu lay closer to More's Utopia than our States of Progress governed by war-hungry princelings in Versailles & Vienna, Washington & Westminster?" (12). Yet it is the ethos of Moriori utopia that undoes them as their refusal to engage in war and planning for war makes them sitting ducks for the dominant Maori. In the end, the story of civilization in *Cloud Atlas* seems one of an endless repetition of utopic and dystopic extremes, the dream of permanent domain built upon the nightmare of exploitation extending into a timeless future as the Kona exterminate the idyllic Valleysmen and a small imperiled diaspora of survivors manage to barely escape into a posthistorical void.

Yet, if there are a succession of fatal histories in *Cloud Atlas*, there are also alternate histories not indebted, as Amartya Sen writes in *Identity and Violence*, to "the cultivation of a sense of inevitability about some allegedly unique—often belligerent—identity that we are supposed to have" (xiii) where identity is conceived in the singular terms of self, family, tribe, or nation. Beyond the extremities of civilization's dialectic and the envisioning of an inevitable, total history that has as its end the permanent installation of timeless, changeless utopia, one occasionally finds the embodiment of the dicey, ad hoc story of the multitude in the temporary communities that populate the novel. These assemblages are brought together by circumstance and survive by virtue of connections that transcend the "belligerent identities," capital relations, and materialist utopias founded upon a history of territorialization and enslavement.

One prominent example is that discovered by Sonmi~451 during her flight from Nea So Copros as she and her guide stumble upon an abandoned mountain abbey sheltering "dispossessed purebloods who prefer scraping a life from the mountainside to downstrata conurb life" (329). This survivalist community of the politically and socially "dispossessed" is composed of "Uyghur dissidents, dust-bowled farmers from Ho Chi Minh Delta, once respectable conurb dwellers who had fallen foul of corp politics, unemployable deviants, those undollared by mental illness" (330). Asked by her interrogator how the group survives, Sonmi~451 replies that they scavenge for materials and food shared collectively while developing a pragmatic ecology and a self-sufficient oral culture: "Their entertainment was themselves; consumers cannot xist without 3-D and Adv, but humans once did and still can" (330). Yet life for this contingent Thoreauvian community, Sonmi~451 testifies, "is no bucolic Utopia.... winters are severe; rainy seasons are relentless; crops fall prey to disease; their medicine is sorely limited. Few colonists live as long as upstrata consumers. They bicker, blame, and grieve as people will" (331).[20]

As it struggles for survival in the ancient abbey, the "colony" is hemmed in on all sides by contemporary threats as the military use the mountain range for bomb practice and developers explore "potential in the site as a healthspa hotel for xecs and want the site cleared" (330). According to the elderly peasant woman ("The Abbess") who serves as the group's leader, the collective must remain invisible in order to survive, fearing that the day might come when those in power might decide that "they were a viable alternative to corpocratic ideology" and destroy them: "I suggested the colony must prosper invisibly, in obscurity. 'Xactly.' Her voice hushed. 'A balancing act as demanding as impersonating a pureblood, I imagine'" (332). Echoing the "exactly" of a Sikh cabdriver in Hull, whose pronunciation of the word sounds the name of a survivor of tribal genocide, the Abbess suggests that the very survivability of this provisional community in *Cloud Atlas* depends upon its cooperation, self-reliance, invisibility, and the collectivity of identities-as-multitude: diverse, improvisational, connected by circumstance rather than inevitability. Such communities only crop up sporadically and seemingly at random in a group of escapees from a rest home, the descendants of survivors of nuclear apocalypse aboard the "ark" of last resort, or the dissidents and strangers who have found their way to a community of the unseen. In the novel, they exist in stark contrast to the "communities" of moiety, metropolis, or nation, and they offer havens that are no heavens, existing only for a time, viable only by virtue of their invisibility and impermanence.

A temporary future

The two passages from *Cloud Atlas* that serve as epigraphs to this chapter are indicative of the ways in which time is of the essence in the novel, especially when the possibility of a future is hinged to the relativity of temporality. Both Mitchell's ranging across diverse, scattered chronotopes and his employment of a narrative structure and forms of intertextuality in which the past keeps interfering with the future, and the future keeps recurring in the past, suggest the degree to which *Cloud Atlas* explores the movements of time past, passing and to come as they reveal the liminal conditions of identity in history. Sonmi~451 refers to "disneys," or films (the brand name converted into the generic object in the corporate lingo of Nea So Copros) as embodying a temporary resurrection of the past, time itself being the register of the speed at which the past dies. Timothy Cavendish discards two common notions of temporality—that of time as linear and unidirectional in relation to the quanta of randomness that exists in the universe, and that of time as a mode of repetition and eternal return—in favor of a concept of time as continuously collapsing and expanding, its divisions or "folds" compressed into each other and splayed concordant with the rhythms and time signatures of the moment.

Both Sonmi~451's and Timothy Cavendish's figurations of time lay stress upon temporariness as the primary condition of time, and contingency as its primary relational element or "glue." Sonmi~451's knowledge of a past and her sense that it is resurrected or re-presenced as she views the film might be viewed as an ontological error—she mistakes a mediation, a "take" for the "reality" of the past—save that, for Mitchell, as we have seen, the various pasts and futures of *Cloud Atlas* are all similarly framed, mediated, genre-dependent constructions of lives unfolding in scattered spots of time. In this sense, Sonmi~451's only error is to regard the "disney" recounting Timothy Cavendish's adventures as *the* past, rather than *a* past, one among many, and one that is seemingly connected to other pasts and futures through random combinations of chance and circumstance. As a "past," the film is the embodiment of the temporary: a constructed time-slice, the momentary resurrection of a past that dies again once the film ends.

Cavendish's more mechanistic notion of time as a "concertina" seems a hapless recognition of the impossibility of a changeless map of the ineffable, though it retains a key aspect of his desire for a cloud atlas by positing an orchestration of time's passage in a musical score as necessary to time's performative unfolding. Yet we can also recognize in Cavendish's figure of time as concertina the elasticity of temporality in *Cloud Atlas* visible in such instances as that when Luisa Rey sees *The Prophetess*, feels her birthmark throb, "and grasps for the ends of this elastic moment, but they disappear into the past and the future" (430). For readers of *Cloud Atlas*, into whose hands the cross-hatched narratives of the novel are placed, the unpredictable, sporadic nature of such instances when a present event or experience stretches into the novel's contingent pasts and projected futures elevates the sense of temporal order as ad hoc, dependent on the moment (of reading).

The narrative interruptions of *Cloud Atlas* are intrusions into the flow of its own temporality which becomes, by virtue of the novel's partially entangled plots and intratextual crosshatchings, a succession of localized "presents," or haecceities in which the past is constantly reborn and reshaped and the future posited in the conditional tense, contingent and temporary. I employ the term "haecceity" here in the sense developed by the French political philosophers Gilles Deleuze and Félix Guattari, as a thing in itself and as a thing that is an element in a continuously forming assemblage:

> to every relation of movement and rest, speed and slowness grouping together an infinity of parts, there corresponds a degree of power. To the relations composing, decomposing, or modifying an individual there correspond intensities that affect it...these intensities come from external parts or from the individual's own parts. (Deleuze and Guattari, 256)

The notion of the individual and the assemblage of intensities that join "an infinity of parts" can be applied to the relation of disparate identities across time and locality, to a succession of presents passing into history or, using the novel's central metaphor, to a mapping of atmospheric shapes constantly separating and merging across a skyscape, only visible in their random variation.[21]

In comparison to this notion of temporality, Ivan Sach's previously cited conception of time as *"an infinite matryoshka doll of painted moments, each 'shell' (the present) encased inside a nest of 'shells' (previous presents) I call the actual past but which we perceive as the virtual past"* (393; italics in original) seems stilted and formalist, a kind of counterintention or red herring parallel to that of viewing the novel's significant form as that of a Russian doll or the relation of part to whole as symmetrical. In contrast to this metaphor of encapsulation and centrality suggested by the *matryoshka*, *Cloud Atlas* maps the relation between past, present, and future, analogous to the relation between identities and worlds as tiled and overlapping, colliding and interruptive. The notion of time as elastic or as a concertina seems more authentic to the experiences registered in the novel when, for example, Timothy Cavendish, putting himself back together after his stroke as an identity now composed of lost, partial, and fabricated memories, imagines the Cavendish of the future to be a projection, a film that comes about as the result of "a Tolstoyan editing job" comprised of disparate frames or memories that "refused to fit, or fitted but came unglued. Even months later, how would I know some major tranche of myself remained lost?" (354). The fact that "Cavendish" actually becomes archived as a tabooed film surreptitiously viewed and misperceived as indicative of the whole of a Tolstoyan past by a genetic clone in the future only lends ironic weight to a notion of time and identity as radically contingent, bound over to the temporariness of ever-changing circumstances, the dicey nature of memory and fate. The word "tranche" is evocative here: in French, it means slice or part; in English, it is a cognate of the French "trench" or ditch and is a technical term in finance for the risk element attached to a bond or security that is part of larger financial acquisition such as a merger. Cavendish may be using the word inaccurately to signify the memory-branch or cortical furrow that has been wiped out by his collapse, but lexically, in one stroke, Mitchell collates the partiality and fragility of identity in time and the risks of futurity.

It is interesting that Cavendish sees himself in the future as a movie in a novel (and becomes that movie), for this projection is symptomatic of a structuring of contingency in *Cloud Atlas* that corresponds with Mary Ann Doane's description of cinematic modernity. In characterizing the ways in which early film portrays time and event, Doane writes that cinema's

> fascination with contingency raises the specter of pure loss, the complete obliteration of the passing moment … it also elicits a desire for the opposite—the possibility of structure. Jean-François Lyotard claims that modernity "is a way of shaping a sequence of moments in such a way that it accepts a high rate of contingency." In this definition, contingency coexists happily with the process of shaping. In the same way, the concept of *event* is on the cusp of between contingency and structure. (Doane, 140)

Mitchell's fusion of narrative form and open-ended stories whose transmission and reception depend upon the vagaries of time, attention, and circumstance is parallel to this cinematic structuring of "a high rate of contingency" that offers a response to "the specter of pure loss … the complete obliteration of the passing moment." In *Cloud Atlas*, the "pure loss" is the determinate between past, present, and future rendered via the traditional narrative plot, the causal linking of "passing moments," or "the speed at which the past decays" as a defense against their temporariness. What replaces this loss is the rhizomic, multithreaded plies or folds of the novel that open out onto the future of its reception—a future that will emerge with each new reading of the novel. Mitchell makes this possibility available as the content of his fiction, conveyed through its many tangled narrative lines of flight. It is not important whether Mitchell is a "modernist" or "postmodernist" in this regard: he is a novelist who, perhaps, has incorporated both modernism's enabling shaping powers and postmodernism's suspicion of the shape of totality in a novel that posits story, and its errant continuance, as a means of survival in time.

Coda: *Cloud Atlas*, the movie

In her compelling study of adaptation, Linda Hutcheon lists three key perspectives from which any adaptation should be considered:

> First... an adaptation is an announced and extensive transposition of a particular work or works. This "transcoding" can involve a shift of medium... or genre... or a change of frame and therefore context.... Second, as *a process of creation*, the act of adaptation always involves both (re-)interpretation and then (re-)creation.... Third... adaptation is a form of intertextuality: we experience adaptation... as palimpsests through our memory of other works that resonate through repetition with variation. (7–8)

In terms of structure and content, *Cloud Atlas*, the movie, reflects the processes of transcoding and reinterpretation that Hutcheon suggests are entailed by all acts of adaptation. Written, produced, and directed by the Wachowskis (Lana and Andy Wachowski) and Tom Twyker, the film of *Cloud Atlas* adapts the six nested narratives of Mitchell's novel in a pastiche of, primarily, short takes and flashes (some, as brief as a few seconds) that move rapidly between fragments of the stories, relying on visual cues and associations to stitch the assemblage together. In many ways, given Mitchell's interests, the Wachowskis and Twyker are ideal writers and directors for an adaptation of *Cloud Atlas*. The Wachowskis are best known for *The Matrix* (1999) and its sequels; like Mitchell, they work in multiple genres (film, comics, video games, television, and music videos) and the subject matter of their most well-known film involves parallel universes, a dystopic future, and the relationship between humans and machines. Among German director Tom Twyker's films, including *Heaven* (2002), the adaptation of Patrick Süskind's *Perfume* (2006), and *The International* (2009), an early film, *Run Lola Run* (1998) is the most widely known. It is a sci-fi film in which a young woman is given twenty minutes to obtain 100,000 Deutsche Marks in order to save her boyfriend's life, a narrative that is related through multiple shot angles, visual repetitions, time jumps, and alternative takes. In adapting *Cloud Atlas*, the writers/directors split up the work, filming with separate crews in Germany, Scotland, and Majorca, the Wachowskis directing "The Pacific Journal of Adam Ewing," "An Orison of Sonmi~451," and "Sloosha's Crossin' An' Ev'rythin' After" adaptations of the novel, and Twyker directing the "Letters from Zedelghem," "Half-Lives," and "The Ghastly Ordeal of Timothy Cavendish" portions.

Running at 164 minutes, the film adaptation of *Cloud Atlas* is kinetic and experimental. For both those audiences that have read Mitchell's novel and those who have come to the film first, perhaps attracted by the big-name directors, the striking visuals of its trailers, and a cast that includes Tom Hanks, Hugh Grant, Halle Berry, and Jim Broadbent, the film demands multiple viewings. One decision made by the directors in "transcoding" Mitchell's novel was to rely almost entirely on fast-moving sequences of visual associations for the film's diegesis. While five of six narratives in the novel are split into halves arranged in forward, then reverse chronology, the six narratives of the film are broken into dozens of pieces that can only be tracked or reassembled visually in order to understand both the "whole story" in each case and the relation of the stories to each other. For example, in the film's opening sequence, even before the titles roll, we see the following visual fragments in this order: Zachry telling stories over a bonfire; Adam Ewing meeting Henry Goose, collecting human teeth on the shore; Luisa Rey driving and talking about a conspiracy into a dictaphone; Timothy Cavendish at a desk, writing; a quick flash to Robert Frobisher in a bathroom, contemplating suicide; Sonmi~451 being interrogated; Luisa Rey, driving through a protesting crowd at Swannke; Timothy Cavendish, writing at his desk; Goose and Ewing, continuing their initial conversation on the seashore; and Frobisher, contemplating suicide. The film proceeds accordingly throughout, at times alternating at light speed between visual fragments from two, three, or four of the primary stories. Interestingly, even though the pieces of each story are presented in variable patterns of relation to each other, reassembled separately (i.e. if one "re-edited" the film separating out the takes of each story in the order they are presented), for the most part, they unfold chronologically. The directors of *Cloud Atlas* the movie have transposed the novel's fractal arrangement into a visual equivalent, thus reimagining the connections Mitchell makes in the novel between the form of story, the nature of memory, the relation between repetition and history, and the construction of identity.

In *Cloud Atlas* the novel, the repetition of the same identity reborn over time is one of several possibilities signified by the birthmarks or nevi of the principal characters. *Cloud Atlas* the movie visually and dramatically reinforces the notion of rebirth as a process underlying the evolution or devolution of the individual "soul" over multiple life spans. This is effected, in part, by the decision to have the same actor play multiple roles, major and minor, across the six narratives. Tom Hanks, for example, plays Zachry as the main character of "Sloosha's Crossin'," and in supporting roles as Henry Goose, the manager of the hotel to which Robert Frobisher flees after leaving Ayrs, Dr. Isaac Sachs in the "Luisa Rey" episodes, Dermot

Hoggins, the murderous author of the "Timothy Cavendish" episodes, and Cavendish's look-alike in the archival film viewed by Sonmi~451. Cavendish in "real life" is played by Jim Broadbent, who also plays Vyvyan Ayrs, Captain Molyneaux in the Adam Ewing episodes, a Korean musician in a crowd scene of "Somni~451" (where Mitchell himself briefly appears), and one of the Prescients in "Sloosha's Crossin'"; while Halle Berry plays the roles of an enslaved islander in "Adam Ewing," Jocasta Ayrs, Luisa Rey, a party guest in "Timothy Cavendish," Dr. Ovid (in a male transformation of Madame Ovid, the facescaper of "Sonmi~451"), and Meronym.

The list goes on with three additional actors (Hugo Weaving, Jim Sturgess, and Hugh Grant) playing a role in each of the six narratives, while several others play in multiple roles ranging from two to five. In a bonus feature available with the digital distribution of the film entitled "Ev'rythin's Connected," actor James D'Arcy, who plays Rufus Sixsmith both young and old, comments that the movie depicts "not just several souls that are being reincarnated, but it feels like it's all just one." The directors of the film expand upon this view in stating that their version of the six narratives emphasize how characters played by the same actor are future or past avatars of each other. Andy Wachoski comments that "the voyage of Adam Ewing is actually his voyage to becoming an abolitionist" in conflating the character of Ewing with that of Hae-Joo Chang, the revolutionary and liberator of Sonmi~451, both played by Jim Sturgess; correspondingly, Lana Wachowski claims that "we're drawn to this concept: what if Goose is also Zachry?," their self-identicalness reinforced by Tom Hanks' renditions of both. Playing Zachry telling his tales over a fire, Hanks utters a line not to be found in the novel: "All voices tied up into one."

In film, the embodiment of identity takes place through the visual mediation of the actor playing the role; in the film adaptation of *Cloud Atlas*, connected identities which are intended to be seen as the same one over time are linked by virtue of the physical bodies of discrete actors who are, in several cases, visible celebrities whose singular identities peer at the viewer behind any role they choose to play. Disguised and made up, the literal self-identicality of each actor across several characters is transformed, figuratively, into a paradox of difference-within-sameness: it is the same actor/body playing Goose and Zachry and Sachs; they are different characters/bodies inhabited by the same soul/body reborn. In the adaptation of *Cloud Atlas*, Twyker and the Wachowskis have chosen to recode and renarrativize the novel in order to materialize one of several semiotic possibilities extended by its textual markers: that multiple identities are not just connected, but *the same* across time in a complex system of narrative arcs conjoined by repetition and rebirth, each identity evolving in an ongoing history of the human that is both mutable and constant. In this, the adaptation of Mitchell's novel might be said to offer a visual guarantee of similitude and continuance that Mitchell's fiction, on the whole, does not. Located in the presentist, visual materiality of the actors' bodies, and relying on Zachry's oceanic assertion that all voices are one, *Cloud Atlas* the movie to some degree lowers the risks of narrative illuminated in *Cloud Atlas* the novel, where survival depends upon the transmission of conflicting stories through phantom voices across time in retellings subject to chance, loss, and redirection.

4

Timepiece: *blackswangreen*

When Joseph Conrad wrote in *A Personal Record*, his autobiographical account of how he became a novelist, that "A writer of imaginative prose (even more than any other sort of artist) stands confessed in his works," he posited the writing of fiction as an act that inevitably reveals the writer's "conscience, his deeper sense of things...his attitude toward the world" (Conrad, 95). In this regard, it is interesting that David Mitchell, having traversed multiple genres and cast the voices of dozens of identities dispersed in time and space in his first three novels, would come to write in his fourth what might be regarded as an autobiographical novel about the onset of adolescence and the beginnings of a writing life—in effect, a fictional graphing of the singular self. Set in the West Midlands village of its title and related by Jason Taylor, a sensitive thirteen-year-old with a stammer and a desire to be a poet, *blackswangreen*[1] is an episodic coming-of-age narrative that visibly employs autobiographical elements in portraying a childhood taking place amidst the consumerism and nationalist hysteria of the Reagan–Thatcher 1980s.[2]

blackswangreen does contain autobiographical resonances. Mitchell was raised in Malvern, Worcestershire; in 1982, the year of the novel's setting, he was thirteen years old; as he explains in the *Paris Review* interview, "Black Swan Green is loosely drawn from a village called Hanley Swan in Worcestershire where my family lived from about 1976 to 1981" (n.p.); at the age of fourteen, he had ambitions to become "a great poet. Faber & Faber was going to publish me, and when Ted Hughes read my first anthology he would invite me to Yorkshire for meat pies and mentorship" ("Once upon a Life," n.p.); and he has recounted his lifelong battle with stammering, a "defect [that] was a fatal disadvantage in the more nakedly-aggressive world of children" ("Let Me Speak," n.p.). But the novel also uses the conventions of autobiographical fiction to illustrate the complex set of relationships that exists between imaginative potential and the cultural constraints into which one is born and in which one lives.[3] More than a fictionalization of the thirteenth year in the life of the (auto)biographical David Mitchell, *blackswangreen* constructs an imaginary map of the world in which Jason Taylor struggles toward a future as a writer.

It is a world whose primary historical referent is the global politics of the Cold War and whose "language" is a rich matrix of brand names, popular cultural references, and regional dialects. As in his other novels, throughout *blackswangreen*, Mitchell charts the relation between the global and the local in registering Jason's dawning awareness of the connections to be drawn between the bullying he endures and the last-gasp imperial bullying of the Falklands Conflict, or the parallels between war-like childhood games and the gaming of third world war scenarios that inform the mutually-assured-destruction policies of superpowers. In this sense, like *ghostwritten*, *blackswangreen* is more anthropological than autobiographical. As Mitchell explains, his childhood fascination with Tolkien informs this novel that undertakes a cognitive mapping of the terrain of puberty and the beginnings of writing as a career.[4]

> My father taught art at a teacher-training college before joining the design department of Royal Worcester Porcelain ... Mum was a freelance artist specializing in botanical images used in advertising, packaging, and on greetings cards.... we were as white, straight, and middle-class as the next family on our white, straight, middle-class housing estate.... [M]y parents discovered they could shut me up for hours by mounting a large piece of cartridge paper on a drawing board—beautiful quality paper, a big beautiful snowy expanse—and leave me to draw, and name, maps of imaginary archipelagos and continents. Those maps, I think, were my protonovels. I was reading Tolkien, and it was the maps as much as the text that floated my boat. What was happening behind these mountains where Frodo and company never went? What about the town along the edge of the sea? What kind of people lived there? The empty spaces required me to turn anthropologist-creator. (Mitchell, n.p.)

As "anthropologist-creator," Mitchell in *blackswangreen* is primarily interested in understanding the vexed relation between culture and identity, and how language can imagine or "graph" the blank spaces that exist between the imaginary self and the impositions and constraints of the social order.

blackswangreen manifests characteristic narratological interests evident across Mitchell's work: the crossing of and through multiple genres; fractality; multiple intratextual references to the "pasts" and "futures" of previous novels (such as when Jason discusses his reading of Robert C. O'Brien's science fiction novel, *Z for Zachariah* [1974] about a girl surviving a nuclear war and an obvious tip of the hat to a source for "Sloosha's Crossin' an' Ev'rythin' After" in *Cloud Atlas*); and an intensive matrix of descriptive elements that give to the "world" of the novel linguistic weight and density.

In *blackswangreen*, these features are put into the service of limning Jason's growing reflective capacity which tells him that he is both constricted by and exceeds the identity that has been assigned to him by his parents, sister, schoolmates, neighbors, and authority figures. While he is often forced to perform the identity of white, male, middle-class, heterosexual thirteen-year-old—this a matter of sheer endurance in yet another version of Mitchell's survival narratives—his identity cannot fully evolve within these paradigms: *blackswangreen* is very much about the ways in which the available narratives of cultural identity cannot discursively contain its protagonist.

At the level of narrative, the novel reflects this bad fit between story and identity, between "writing" and "self" in the format of an autobiographical fiction. The "year in the life" of Jason Taylor is a baker's dozen of vignettes variously titled and each taking place in the successive months of 1982, beginning with January of that year and ending with the month of January 1983. To the symmetry of the annual cycle, Mitchell adds an additional month—a supplement indicative of the forms of chronological asymmetry we have observed in *Cloud Atlas* and *ghostwritten*—suggesting that whatever the story may be, it cannot be contained within the temporal order of a twelvemonth or the passing of four seasons: as Jason's sister, Julia, says to him in the novel's parting words as the two siblings console each other over their parents impending divorce, " 'It'll be all right… In the end, Jace.' 'It doesn't *feel* very all right.' 'That's because it's not the end' " (294). Each of the anecdotal narratives of the novel are both connected to each other and dispersed, variegated, conceivably thirteen different stories related by the same narrator-protagonist, or the same story (the story of "I") told in thirteen different ways, or thirteen different stories narrated by thirteen different Jason Taylors as his identity expands and multiplies, his voice changing across the reach of the novel.[5] And while each of the thirteen narratives are integral unto themselves as "short stories," when taken together they reveal themselves to be a series of discontinuities, notable for the temporal and spatial gaps that exist between them, rather than stagings or structural evolutions in the thirteen month of Jason's life as he lurches into adolescence. They are all works in progress that trace the uneven evolution of Jason as an identity in progress in his poems written under the pseudonym of Eliot Bolivar (a conflation of T.S. Eliot and Simón Bolivar) and published in the local parish magazine.

Mitchell's engagement with multiple genres and intertexts in this regard is notable. Narrative form in *blackswangreen* is indicative of both its own limitations as fitting "container" for the story of identity and its capacity, in the mutability and diversity of forms and genres that Mitchell characteristically traverses in his novels, to serve as the foundation for alternative worlds and identities that counter the seemingly monolithic, insulated reality of life in a parochial English village and the singularity of the nominal self. The novel opens with a scene strongly reminiscent of William Golding's *Lord of the Flies* (1954), the infamous postapocalyptic allegory about the "human experiment" (strand a group of surviving schoolboys on a remote island and watch what happens) that was "required reading for Mitchell's generation at O-level" (Stephenson, 241). Jason recounts an episode in which he is humiliated by his mates while, reading aloud, he stammers through a passage from the boy's adventure tale cum satire upon the human condition as the "words on page 41 ... swarmed off the page and buried my face in bees" (209). Golding's fable poses the idea that if human civilization is allowed to re-create itself in an isolated setting by "innocent" children, it will quickly revert to the patterns that got it into trouble in the first place: the losing battle between order and anarchy; the primacy of greed and selfishness; and the quest for power that underlies the prevalence of violence and corruption. In the opening of *blackswangreen*, a group of young adolescents are playing "British Bulldogs," a roughhouse team-based tag game, on a frozen pond. Like Golding's allegory, the scene, as Jason depicts it, gives the lie to childhood innocence and initiates the novel's ongoing analogy between village culture and a globalized "Cold War." Cruelty and power are exerted by the town bullies, Ross Wilcox and Grant Burch. A sensitive Jason, perpetually marginalized because of his speech disorder, views the choosing of sides as being "picked like slaves in a slave market" (7). Homophobia and sexism abound (if one chooses not to play, one will be regarded as "a total ponce" (7), while "[g]irls... and the littl'uns" are "cleared off the ice" (7), with the exception of one Dawn Madden, a paradoxical combination of siren and tomboy who haunts Jason throughout the novel). In essence, the "game" itself is nothing more than an all-out war complete with "[s]creaming...kamikazes," "humiliating...enemies" (8), and the possibility of becoming a "traitor" (8). While all of this takes place through the eyes of a thirteen-year-old who is clearly mapping what he knows from television and movies of a second world war onto the imaginary terrain of a childhood taking place against the omnipresent virtual threat of a third, Mitchell's echoing of Golding in these initial scenes suggests the extent to which cultural violence and the formation of identity are connected as the constants of "bildung" in *blackswangreen*.

Just as the novel references satire and the boy's adventure story via *Lord of the Flies* in its January opening, so too it references a diverse succession of genres and intertexts in the succession of months to come. In keeping with Mitchell's established tendency to serve as scriptural medium for the ghostly presence of other characters and stories (including his own) within the novel at hand, we can detect in *blackswangreen* traces of Austen, Dickens, and Joyce; fairy tale, initiation story, and the novel of manners;

historical chronicle and fantasy; and above all a detailed, seemingly exhaustive listing of contemporary brand names, films, TV shows, pop songs, and books that serve as both the novel's historical-cultural global positioning system and background noise. In the chapter entitled "knife grinder," Jason comes into contact with a group of gypsies who have been the subject of a xenophobic village debate over the establishment of public housing for "migrants." As in the succession of nineteenth-century English novels where "Romanys" appear, perhaps most prominently in Austen's *Emma* (1815), in *blackswangreen* a group of roving outsiders threaten the stability of village life and the imaginary coherence of English nationalism and identity. In "solarium," Jason encounters Eva van Outryve Crommelynck, the daughter of Vyvyan Ayrs in *Cloud Atlas* with whom Robert Frobisher becomes enamored, and now an old woman in exile from her native land. Serving as a combination of Miss Havisham and Sybil to Jason's Pip/Aeneas, Eva encourages her pupil's great expectations as a budding poet, thus commencing a dangerous journey through life and art. The village and its surrounding often seems from Jason's perspective to be an enormous, mythic landscape, complete with a gothic "House in the Woods," an underworld of tunnels and hidden places, and a funhouse of sudden transformations and metamorphoses when a carnival comes to town. But by the novel's end, Jason is recounting his departure from a childhood world that has collapsed in the wake of his parents' divorce, and the scale of the landscape has diminished considerably: "the world never stops unmaking what the world never stops making" (285), Jason observes, and the vast mythic forest with its innumerable recesses has become, in the words of the son-in-law of the "sour aunt" who lives in "The House in the Woods," "only a few acres, y'know. Two or three footy pitches, tops. Hardly Amazonia. Hardly Sherwood Forest" (288).

This moment of scalar recognition typifies the dynamics of a novel in which the view of the world as enchanted and mythic, full of monsters, spirit-guides, and omnipotent enemies alternates with scenes of disillusionment where a brutal reality intrudes as historical circumstance and the projection of fantasy intersect and collide. Such interactions between fantasy and "the real" will become the narrative foundation of *The Bone Clocks*. As in the recognition scene above, several of Jason's "months" contain stories that end in epiphanic moments like those of James Joyce's "Araby" in *Dubliners* (1914; another recognizable intertextual source for *blackswangreen*), where a young boy entering the world of the fabulous Araby bazaar in quest of a grail-like gift for his beloved discovers the seamy, avaricious reality beneath the orientalized facade. In the chapter entitled "souvenirs," for example, Jason recounts a trip to the Cornish seaside town of Lyme Regis with his father, who is there for a business conference. The narrative framing is that of an initiation story. Though there are earlier scenes of initiation in the novel, such as when Jason's cousin, Hugo Lamb, compels him to smoke for the first time, resulting in Jason's mortification at becoming sick with nausea when he inhales his first (and last) cigarette, "souvenirs" marks the culmination of his entry into puberty. In Lyme Regis, he encounters the "adult" world of older girls on the make, resort attractions, and the possibility of access to the power of the father. But the trip ends in disaster when his father gets inebriated at a business dinner and misses the planned excursion with his son to see the film *Chariots of Fire*, and then arrives at their hotel room in a disgraceful state where Jason witnesses him stumbling naked and drunk out of the shower, his penis exposed, a "wobbling chunky piece of oxtail"—in Jason's recollection, his mental "souvenir" of this father/son journey—"[t]he *grossest* sight I *ever* saw" (180). As if this weren't a sufficient deflation of fantasies he might have had about his father's potency or importance, he is forced to witness his father being humiliated in public by his boss, Craig Salt, in a scene of verbal castration taking place "in the company of men." In Lyme Regis, Jason has, indeed, been initiated into an oedipal reality that both accords with what he witnesses every day in the schoolyard and conflicts with the fantasy of omnipotent adulthood, embodied—temporarily, as it must be—in the figure of the father.

Such disappointments mark the fluctuations of affect and experience in *blackswangreen*. Jason's diary might be seen as a form of narrative management in which the alternating pattern of expectation and disappointment becomes the structural elements of a year-plus fraught with change and recognition. His parents' marriage is disintegrating, and it is his sister's last year living at home before going off to university. Jason's own burgeoning sexuality is a source of confusion and embarrassment, as the discovery of his vocation as a writer is fraught with anxiety about the homophobic schoolyard environment that regards such interests as "queer." There is an ongoing war in the background, both in its global, "cold" manifestations and its national and communal "hot" variations in the Falklands Conflict and the ever-present war games of boys. Closer to home, the dicey omnipresence of the "name-brand" commodity culture upon which his family depends (his father works in a managerial position for a chain of grocery stores) contends with Jason's poetic sensibilities and his attraction to outsiders and alienated spaces. Jason's writing is a survival mechanism that allows him to navigate between childhood mythography and adult reality, and to integrate into the progression of months and the generic confines of self-writing, *bildungsroman*, or adventure story jarring contrasts and surprising turns of events. He discovers, in brief, that writing structures experience, and that writing in forms—as is the case in all of Mitchell's novels—is a means of both containing and revealing the utter incommensurability of existence.

Examples of this incommensurability reveal themselves sporadically in the flux of the quotidian. In "spooks," a journey through the "jungles" and "labyrinths" of backyard gardens that serves as the initiation into a putative, secret order of heroic vigilantes becomes the occasion for Jason to overhear conversations about tawdry neighborhood jealousies and traverse a cultural junkyard: the "moon-rocky fourth garden was a spillage of concrete meringue and gravel. Ornaments everywhere. Not just gnomes, but Egyptian sphinxes, Smurfs, fairies, sea otters, Pooh Bear and Piglet and Eeyore, Jimmy Carter's face, you name it. Himalayas divided the garden down the middle at shoulder height" (135). Ultimately, he experiences the abjection of betrayal as the whole affair is revealed to be a practical joke that leads Jason to thoughts of suicide as "what they *want*" (140). The transpositions of this episode, set amidst the heterogeneity of a cultural system, encapsulated in the fourth garden where the mythic and the mundane are collapsed into kitsch, are startling for Jason as the cloaked society of daring avengers mutates into a group of idiotic thugs.

Similar reversals and disillusionments, often self-generated, stalk Jason throughout the novel. In "souvenirs," standing in a movie queue with his mother after a moment of connection and mutual appreciation becomes a scene of tortured embarrassment for both when the self-conscious adolescent begins to fear being seen in public escorting a parent. In "disco," Jason's expectation of revenge being exacted upon him for "grassing" on a fellow student's petty blackmail scheme is reversed when he is congratulated for his "betrayal" by the menacing older brother of one of the scheme's victims. "Solarium" concludes when Jason learns that his lessons with Eva van Outryve Crommelynck, who serves for him as the embodiment of artistic verities and high modernist European culture, have ended because she and her husband have been extradited to Germany for crimes unknown. He comes upon this information from a gossiping vicar's wife who xenophobically speculates that "putting two and two together—the husband retired from the Bundesbank six months ago—it's some sort of financial scam. Embezzlement. Bribery. *Lots* of that goes on in Germany" (165, italics in original).

Jason registers these contradictions and reversals in *blackswangreen* as localized instances of adolescent experience; yet implicitly, these are inextricably connected to the global order of late capitalism and, as I have indicated in the opening scene of boys playing British Bulldogs, the overarching "event" of the second half of the twentieth century, the Cold War. It is an "event" that seems omnipresent in everyday life as recorded in Jason's narrative. To Jason, his father's office phone is "red like a nuclear hotline" (3); driving to a speech therapy clinic with his mother, he takes note of "the two Ministry of Defense radars spinning at their incredible speed. Waiting for the full might of the Warsaw Pact forces" (24); "[a]part from the Russian's starting a nuclear war," Jason's biggest fear is stammering on "*J*-words, 'cause then *I won't even be able to say my own name*" (27). At one point, he refers to his parents' disintegrating relationship as "like this cold war" (158). For Jason, the Cold War is part of the air he breathes, and the specter of a nuclear apocalypse is one that exists in his imagination as a very possible future.

One can regard the Cold War as a contestation for global dominance between superpowers and the predominant political ideologies of the twentieth century. But it was also a series of "localized" skirmishes of various lengths and intensity—the Soviet invasion of Afghanistan, the American invasion of the small Caribbean island of Grenada, the Korean and Vietnam Wars, a host of revolutions and assassinations in Latin America—that served as proxy wars in which the United States and NATO, the Soviet Union, and China could "face off" by mapping global conflict onto regional histories and bodies. The MAD ("mutually-assured destruction") policies that undergirded nuclear proliferation also produced this series of proxy conflicts employing conventional weaponry, thus allowing the superpowers to claim that they were winning the political and territorial battle on a case-by-case basis without having to commit mutual suicide in an all-out nuclear exchange.

The Falklands Conflict (April 2–June 14, 1982) may not seem at first glance like a Cold War proxy war, but rather the last gasp of British colonialism as a long-standing dispute between the United Kingdom and Argentina regarding which nation held sovereignty over the small group of islands 310 miles off the Patagonian coast devolved into armed conflict. For Jason, however, the conflict is of a piece with the larger geopolitical war he reads about in the newspapers; the rising influence of American popular culture, speech, and fashion in the European theater; and the British alliance with NATO.[6] Jason comes from a solidly middle-class, neoliberal family that might contradictorily be described as apolitical but strongly nationalistic, identifying readily with the goals and agenda of whoever-is-in-charge (in this case, Margaret Thatcher). What Jason reads and sees appears to be part of a continuous narrative of home and country in which *Star Wars* ("Dad's swivelley chair's a lot like the Millennium Falcon's laser tower" [4]), the Troubles ("Gilbert Swinyard says our school and the Maze prison were built by the same architect. The Maze prison's in Northern Ireland where Bobby Sands and the IRA hunger strikers died by degrees" [200]), and the newspaper headline of "GOTCHA" in thirty point bold, referring to Thatcher's putdown of an interviewer questioning the conflict, exist in the same discursive space.

A collector of information of all kinds—*blackswangreen* is, among other things, a scrapbook of stories, anecdotes, factoids, newspaper headlines, notes, and recollections—Jason is

> keeping a scrap book about the war.... cutting out stuff from the newspapers and magazines. Neal Brose is keeping one too. He reckons it'll be worth a fortune twenty or thirty years from now, when the Falklands War has turned into history. But all this excitement'll never turn dusty and brown in archives and libraries. No way. People'll remember everything about the Falklands till the end of the world. (102)

In "rocks," the chapter of *blackswangreen* devoted to Jason's war scrap book, we hear of the death of a schoolmate's brother, Tom Yew, who Jason has previously observed in a "primal scene" of sexual congress with his intended, and who has been killed aboard the HMS *Coventry* in the Falklands Conflict. The tragic news is a watershed moment for Jason. At the beginning of "rocks," he revels in Thatcher's patriotic defense of British aggression: "Mrs. Thatcher's bloody ace. She's so strong, so calm, so sure. Loads more use than the queen, who hasn't said a dickie bird since the war began" (101). As the war progresses, through a narrative act that forges the relation between the simultaneity of local experience and global event, he begins to make connections between his parents' ongoing "war" over who controls the finances, the bullying he has suffered at school, and everyday activities such as doing his geometry homework:

> I dip my fountain pen into a pot of ink, and a Wessex helicopter crashes into a glacier on South Georgia. I line up my protractor on an angle in my Maths book and a Sidewinder missile locks onto a Mirage III. I draw a circle with my compass and a Welsh Guard stands up in a patch of burning gorse and gets a bullet through his eye. (106)

By the end of the month and the chapter—the Falklands Conflict drifting into the inevitable standoff it would become and news of the war and Tom Yew replaced by "the big story" in the *Daily Mail* "about whether Cliff Richard the singer's having sex with Sue Barker the tennis player, or whether they're just good friends" (116)—Jason angrily proclaims, "I want to bloody kick this *moronic bloody world* in the bloody *teeth* over and over till it bloody *understands* that *not hurting people* is ten bloody *thousand* times more bloody important than being *right*" (118).

Jason's antiwar sentiment seems contradictory in its use of violence (kicking in the world's teeth) to protest against violence. But he arrives at a calmer realization of the futility and destructiveness of war, which implicitly links his reaction to the Falklands Conflict to the global context of the Cold War when, facing the possibility of continued ostracizing after the "grassing" incident, he reflects on the weather:

> Past Miss Throckmorton's, the village hall floated in the arctic dark, a lit-up ark. Its windows were stained disco colors. Michael Fish said the area of low pressure moving over the British Isles is coming from the Urals. The Urals're the USSR's Colorado Rockies. Intercontinental missile silos and fallout shelters're sunk deep in the roots of the mountains. There're research cities so secret they've got no names and don't appear on maps. Strange to think of a Red Army sentry on a barbed-wire watchtower shivering in this very same icy wind. Oxygen he'd breathed out might be oxygen I breathed in. (271)

Here, the weather serves as a kind of geopolitical "cloud atlas" for Jason, revealing the connectivity that exists between dispersed identities. Recognizing that one shares the atmosphere with what Appiah terms "the imaginary stranger," whatever other incommensurable differences might ensue between the two, is one of the key steps in the development of a cosmopolitan sensibility.[7] Mitchell's portrait of a young man growing up in the 1980s registers Jason's evolving awareness of the ways in which local games and customs, familial disputes, sexuality, education, and the contents of his cultural imaginary are connected to what happens 8,000 miles away on a distant island or the weather shared with a Russian soldier on sentry duty in the Cold War. In his reflections, Jason reveals himself to be a nascent author whose writing is laced with implicit connections between the global and the local indicative of an emergent cosmopolitan sensibility.

In many respects, Jason is an encyclopedist, and *blackswangreen*, containing hundreds of references to early 1980s popular music, movies, television shows, arcade games, comics, and celebrities, bears many of the earmarks of the encyclopedic narrative as Edward Mendelson has classically defined it: the display of multiple genres and styles, interpolated discursive entities that come from outside the fictional text proper (headlines, lists, scrapbook items), and references to multiple disciplines (science, literature, classical mythology, history).[8] A "playlist" of the musical groups that Jason listens to includes The Beatles, Led Zeppelin, Sex Pistols, Meat Loaf, Roxy Music, Talking Heads, the Rolling Stones, and Elvis Costello and the Attractions; 1980s TV shows he watches range from the American *The Rockford Files, Starsky and Hutch,* and *Happy Days* to the British *Open All Hours, Blankety Blank, It's a Knockout,* and *Tomorrow's World*; films he sees (some of them on television) include *Superman II, Chariots of Fire, Goldfinger,* and *The Towering Inferno*; he plays *Asteroids, Frogger,* and *Pac-Man* at the local arcade; he follows the adventures of comic book characters such as the Mekon and Judge Dredd. Like any "typical" late-twentieth-century teenager, Jason is immersed in the world of contemporary mass culture, but as a cultural informant, he appears to specialize in—and even be obsessed with—the brand names of commodities. The trademarks of cars, food, snacks and beverages, household products, and toys can be added to the lists of song, movie, and TV show titles, and sports figures and celebrities that Jason mentions in the novel. I count well over a hundred different brand names mentioned in *blackswangreen*, some of them coming in breathless succession, such as when Jason notes the stock of "Pedigree Chum... Ambrosia Rice Pudding... Sherbet Bombs, Cola Cubes, Cider Apples, and Army and Navy tablets" in the village grocery story (60–61). Perhaps it is because his father works for a grocery store chain that Jason almost never refers to things generically, but always by its model, label, or brand name. This registry of commodities, however, suggests something more about Jason's emergent identity and his relation to the object-world that surrounds him. Why is Jason compelled to compulsively name these objects?[9]

One answer is that he *must* do so in order to locate his own identity within a world in which he is objectified: one of many names he bears in the novel—most of them demeaning—is the one jokingly conferred upon him by his sister, Julia: "Thing." While this may be just kidding on his sister's part, for Jason, it has symbolic resonance. As a middle-class child of late capitalism growing up in the Reagan–Thatcher era of trickledown economics (with its retrogressive policies of generating consumerist growth through class/status envy), he is a thing among things in a world of commodities proliferating at an alarming rate as part of what Jean Baudrillard terms the advancing "technological system" of the twentieth century that "has as its aims a mastery of the world and the satisfaction of needs" by means of that very proliferation (*System*, 8). Baudrillard goes on to suggest that this system has a language of its very own—that of brand names, colors, models, styles, and countless manifestations of the "new" and "different"—that offers only a vestigial stability in a environment where the attachment of a brand name to an object generates need, but contradictorily, where new needs, and thus new brand name objects, must be generated for a consumerist marketplace. Recalling that Jason is engaged in the act of cognitive mapping of the terrain he inhabits in *blackswangreen*, his compulsion to catalog the name of everything he wears, consumes, plays, or wants—especially cars, the male teenager's dream-object—is comprehensible as part of his attempt to find himself within the language of the prevalent social order in both its local and global dimensions. Many of the brand names he cites are long gone in the passage of time, but the "technological system" Baudrillard describes continues to multiply and spread, everywhere.

Moreover, Jason's encyclopedic impulse, his capacity to store, write down, and integrate into the flow of his narratives this proliferate cultural information—we might consider it a realist strategy that both contends and conspires with his mythographic impulses—reflects his own attempt at "technological" mastery of a language (the language of commodities and objects) that counters his inability to control the language that comes out of his mouth. A critical obstacle to Jason's effort to map his world and establish himself within it is his fully justified perception that he is a demeaned object to others and, inwardly, an assemblage of multiple selves combating each other for supremacy over his own thought and speech. To his sister, he is "Thing"; to his bullying and insensitive peers, he is often the dehumanized, larval "Maggot," the "nickname" they use when subjecting him to frequent bouts of ridicule, and as Jason proclaims of naming in the schoolyard culture of Black Swan Green, "[i]t's easier to change your eyeballs than to change your nickname" (16).[10] But Jason also refers to himself as a series of names, voices, or alternative identities, some of them equally larval or abject. There is "Hangman," the name for the internal entity who blocks Jason's speech and causes him to stammer, and who Jason imagines as a monster with "[p]ike lips, broken nose, rhino cheeks, red eyes 'cause he never sleeps" (26). Named after the children's game in which each incorrect guess about a letter in the blank spaces of a clue word results in another element added to the drawing of the stick figure of a hanged man, Jason's Hangman causes him to stumble over particular words and letters, "colonizing the alphabet" (15). Over time, "Hangman" causes Jason to fear having to enunciate entire classes of words, depending on the oral Malvolio's predilections of the day: "Words beginning with N have always been one of Hangman's favorites.... Hangman used to like Y-words, too, but lately he's eased off those and has moved to S-words. This is bad news. Look at any dictionary and see which section's the thickest: it's S" (26–27).

Hangman may be the predominant "other" in *blackswangreen*, but he is not alone. Jason refers sporadically to the "Unborn Twin," an entity who contends with his "inner Maggot" as voice of the bolder, cannier, more mature Jason in contrast to its self-humiliating other. Jason reveals that his given name "isn't exactly the acest name you could wish for" (25), and regards it as "[f]lavorless as chewed receipts" (153) when it comes to writers' names, which is why he creates the more "literate-sounding" Eliot Boliver, under which he signs his first poems. There is Jason signed as "J.T." in the initials he inscribes along with those of Dawn Madden in a hidden tree; and there is Jason "The Triple Invisible Boy," so self-named because "[p]icked-on kids act invisible to reduce the chances of being noticed and picked on. Stammerers act invisible to reduce the chances of being made to say something we can't. Kids whose parents argue act invisible in case we trigger another skirmish" (233–34). Jason's multiple names in *blackswangreen* thus suggest the ways in which the "I" of the novel, the "first person" who narrates it, is divided against itself as Jason attempts to achieve mastery over writing and language. The nature of this division generates in Jason an identificatory relation to both others within (Hangman, the Unborn Twin, Thing, Maggot, the Triple Invisible Boy) and others without (the "picked on kids," "Romanys," social outcasts such as the old woman of the forest, or Squelch, a mentally handicapped schoolmate). In recounting the histories of these multiple entities, Jason reveals a desire to both control and proliferate the names, voices, and words that make up "Jason." *blackswangreen*, in effect, charts the struggle to constitute the identity of the author, born of contradiction and multiplicity.

But that author does not bear the proper name of the living person named David Mitchell, nor is he entirely coexistent with the fictional character who bears the name of Jason Taylor.[11] Rather, he, or it, is a construct who comes into being out of the lack of simultaneity between the affective "I," the "I" who perceives, and the "I" who writes as a means of navigating the disparities between identities moving amidst shifting the shifting temporalities of multiple worlds projected, realized, and experienced. Temporal and nominal disparities such as those Jason records, as Paul de Man has famously claimed, are what constitute writing *tout court* in its continuous negotiation between figure and ground, projection and representation, or, in the example of autobiographical writing that foregrounds this condition, between "life" and "art":

> We assume that life *produces* the autobiography as an act produces its consequences, but can we not suggest, with equal justice, that the autobiographical project may itself produce and determine the life and that whatever the writer *does* is in fact governed by the technical demands of self-portraiture and thus determined, in all its aspects, by the resources of his medium? ("Autobiography," 920)

The "resources of his medium" and "the technical demands of self-portraiture" are, precisely, the subject of *blackswangreen*, not as an autobiographical novel, but as a novel that foregrounds the mediality of writing from the perspective of the writer's future cast into the past.

I have already touched upon the resources and technical demands that govern the writing of *blackswangreen*. For the representation of identity named (sometimes) Jason Taylor, the banal commodity culture of the 1980s in Europe butting up against the mythopoeic fantasies he can produce out of a shrinking childhood landscape comprises a primary resource, while, literally, the intense difficulties associated with speaking of and about himself—merely giving voice to thought—constitute the most critical "technical" demand Jason contends with in attempting to portray himself through writing. Jason's stammering is, indeed, "autobiographical"— Mitchell has referred to it openly in any number of interviews and most directly in "Let Me Speak," his contribution to the British Stammering Association's homepage. There, he recounts the trials of growing up with a speech impediment and his sense that language was "an enemy," and the coping mechanism of "visualizing" his stammer "as a sort of shady homunculus—an anti-matter Gollum—who lived at the base of my tongue" (n.p.). Like Jason, Mitchell insists on the difference between stammering and stuttering. Jason views the distinction in this way:

> Most people think stammering and stuttering are the same but they're as different as diarrhea and constipation. Stuttering's where you say the first bit of the word but can't stop saying it over and over. St-st-st-stutter. Like that. Stammering's where you get stuck straight after the first bit of the word. word. Like this. St......... AMmer! (25–26)

Mitchell concurs:

> Some authorities maintain "stutter" and "stammer" are two words for the same thing, but I subscribe to the following definitions: a stutter is where the first syllable of the word is repeated over and over like a machine gun, without the second ever being reached. A stammer, in contrast, is where not even the first syllable can be articulated: there's just an ever-widening hole in the sentence. I believe that in this hole, this gap, you can find the silence, the calmness, you need to get the next word out. ("Let Me Speak," n.p.)

Both Jason's scatological description and Mitchell's more elegant figuration of the distinction between stammering and stuttering further articulate the technical difficulties Jason faces in *blackswangreen* at expressing himself, bringing identity into consonance with language. Speech must be cast out, excrementally abjected, as a linguistic gap-filling that requires its opposite— the "hole" of silence, in eternal combat with the enemy of the internal, language-impeding "homunculus"—in order to be heard. Writing, in effect, is the means for filling in the blanks that speech cannot.[12]

The implicit relation between writing and speaking in this novel of "self-portraiture" that entails the origins of the author is complex. Writing, or fictionalizing, involves the generation of multiple identities (characters) and worlds that give formal shape to the linguistic overcoming of silence, delay, and the holes or voids in reality that simultaneously precede, impede, and produce speech. In *blackswangreen*, the splitting and doubling of multiply named identities, the halting surpassing of silence with speech and narrative construction, and the making and mapping of terrains where materiality collides with fantasies, utopian and apocalyptic, signify the arrival of the author. This is at the heart of Mitchell's fictional project which, as we have seen in novel after novel, reflects upon the human capacity for narrative transmission in the form of the discursive entities we call "stories," upon which we depend for cultural survival.

In "Let Me Speak," Mitchell recalls his speech therapist, Mrs. Lester, who "got me to talk in time to a metronome, read from picture-books, and keep a rudimentary journal of when I stammered and how I felt" (n.p.). Jason's own speech therapist, Mrs. Roo, also uses a metronome ("Metro Gnome" is Jason's unwitting pun name for the object) that he perceives as "upside-down pendulums without the clock part. They tock rhythms. They're small, which could be why they're called gnomes.... You read aloud in time with its tocks, like this: here-comes-the-can-dle-to-take-you-to-bed-,-here-comes-the-chop-per-to-chop-off-your-head" (30–31). Voice, speech, and temporality are brought together in Mitchell's remembrance of "talk[ing] in time," and in the connections Jason makes between talking and the homophonic "tocking" of the metronome (not to mention the rhyme itself, which links sleep to death, and talking arrhythmically—unpoetically—to the loss of one's head).[13] Jason elaborates on the linkage between talking and time in one of the novel's final scenes, as he talks with Mrs. Gretton, stricken with dementia, the "sour aunt" inhabiting the "House in the Woods" whose proper name he knows at last:

> I hadn't stammered *once*, the whole time I'd been talking to Mrs. Gretton. S'pose it isn't Hangman who causes it? S'pose it's *the other person*? The other person's expectations. S'pose *that's* why I can read aloud in an empty room, perfectly, or to a horse, or a dog, or myself? ... S'pose there's a time fuse lit when it's a human listening, like a stick of Tom and Jerry dynamite? S'pose if you don't get the word out before this fuse is burnt away, a couple of seconds, say, the dynamite goes off? S'pose what trigger's the stammer's the stress of hearing that fuse going *ssssssss*? S'pose you

could make that fuse *infinitely* long, so that the dynamite'd never go off? How? By *honestly* not caring how long the other person'll have to wait for me. Two seconds? Two minutes, no, two *years*. Sitting in Mrs. Gretton's yellow room it seemed so obvious. If I can reach this state of not caring, Hangman'll remove his finger from my lips. (289, italics in original)

Theoretically, at least, in what might be considered a postmetronomic concept of "talk" and "tock," Jason releases himself from the obligation to speak in time by extending the temporality of speech to the vanishing point of the inarticulate. But this is to convert speaking into writing. "Not caring" about whether or not the interlocutor is engaged in an act of immediate listening transforms the occasion of interlocution itself from a dialogue to one in which "speech" takes place at whatever pace the author chooses, deploying the rhythms, spacings, and sequences of discourse into whatever forms he imagines, to be received and responded to at some indeterminate later point in time, when the performance of "speaking"—now a monologue, a poem, a narrative—is made public. The untimely disorders of speech in *blackswangreen*, in effect, enable timely and timed acts of writing in Jason's reconstruction of the author's origins.[14]

While "not caring" about the other who hears may seem to countervene Mitchell's postauthorial stance that suggests the reader is a key element in the transmission of stories, the contradiction is addressed in *blackswangreen*'s representations of temporality. Time is on Jason's mind throughout the novel, and it is clear from his reflections on stammering that his education as a writer involves coming to terms with time passing, streaming into an uncertain future without ends save those that can be provided through the artifice of story. In this, he confronts a score of both narrative and cultural contradictions. For one, as we have seen, his experience as a British thirteen-year-old in 1982 exposes him on a daily basis to the national version of an ongoing Cold War narrative that portends either apocalypse (the end of time and history) or a permanent timeless condition for the "victor" in which one form of social organization or another reigns supreme. This narrative condition exists in sharp contrast to the one that subtends his recounting of experience as he attempts to map his world and construct a speaking and writing identity. The passage of time demands and enables writing which, in Jason's case, is a compensatory rejoinder to halted speech, yet temporality per se, constituted of its own unending movement into an indeterminate future, is the pervasive element of all narrative acts that, by their nature, seek to manage temporality in forging the causal relation between beginning and end, and the diegetic relation between character and event. In other words, the literal death of the author, in time, is fundamental to his or her exertion of author-ity.

This conundrum is woven into the narrative threadwork of *blackswangreen*, particularly in the many references to a watch that Jason accidentally breaks, and for which he seeks a replacement throughout the calendar of his thirteenth year. The watch is a family heirloom originally bought by his grandfather and passed on from father to son: "An Omega Seamaster De Ville. Granddad bought it off a real live Arab in a port called Aden in 1949. Aden's in Arabia and once it was British. He'd worn it every day of his life, even the moment he died" (16). Unwittingly, Jason intimates in his description of a watch procured from a "real live Arab" in the chief port city of southern Yemen, colonized by the British in 1839 and held as a protectorate until 1960, the linkage between patrimony and empire that parallels his national identification as "self" forms with Britain during the Cold War. The watch is destroyed when Jason suffers a fall while skating alone on a frozen pond where he has gone at the bidding of the Unborn Twin, implicitly against his parents' wishes. While skating, he encounters what he perceives to be a "shadow-kid" (18), perhaps the projected image of one of his many "others" or the specter of "the Butcher Boy," Ralph Bredon, intimated by the old woman in the House in the Woods to have fallen through the ice on the pond and drowned. As they orbit the pond in a dance between self and shadow, Jason attempts to conduct a one-way conversation about drowning and death ("Do the kids who'd drowned in the lake down the years mind me trespassing on their roof?... Can you show me? Show me what it's like?" [18]); when he inattentively trips on the ice, he falls hard, severely spraining his ankle and shattering the watch: "I looked at my grandfather's Omega and saw that there was no time.... The glass face, the hour hand, and the minute hand'd gone and only a bent second hand was left... The casing was split and half its innards'd spilt out" (21).

What Jason terms "the catastrophe of the smashed watch" (22) joins several of the novel's filaments as a figure for futurity, death, the evanescence of identity in time, and the fragility of narrative. Clearly, for Jason, the watch stands for the existence of the past in the present as a guarantor of the future, and for the integration of the familial and national past into his evolving identity. Throughout *blackswangreen*, he searches for a replacement which, of course, is impossible to find both because a substitute costs more money than Jason could ever dream of having (even if he had decided not to return in "goose fair" the lost wallet of his archenemy, Ross Wilcox, "*stuffed* with notes. There *had* to be fifty quid in there" [242]), and because, unlike the novel's proliferate commodities, his grandfather's watch is one of a kind, engraved with his initials, an object that comes out of a specific past that is gone forever. Revealingly, in "souvenirs," the chapter that recounts Jason's oedipal journey with his father and an emotional moment of brief connection and departure from his mother—the end of childhood—Jason, set free for the morning to roam Cheltenham until it's time to see *Chariots of Fire*, undertakes a symbolic journey to several antique shops in order to find an exact duplicate of his father's watch. His quest is replete with false leads and disappointment, and when he finally does find a shopkeeper who has a contact possessing an Omega Seamaster watch of the correct vintage, Jason is told that it will cost £850, an unsurpassable amount well beyond the £28.70 Jason has in his pocket, which includes the money he has been saving all year to buy the watch plus the "tenner" his mother has given him for his morning on the town.

Disputing Jason's expressed "greatest fear" that his parents will "murder" him for destroying the watch, the shopkeeper, Rosamund, engages Jason in catechetical debate about anxiety, life expectancy, and the temporality of parental anger. Her questions to Jason (how long will his parents remain "mental" over the broken watch? how long does he expect to live? Seventy-five years?) result in an exclamation:

> "You tell me your greatest fear is that Ma and Pa'll be mad at you for one of these almost four thousand weeks. Or two. Or three." Rosamund puffed out her cheeks, then huffed out the air. "Can I swap your greatest fear for any one of mine? Take two of them. No, ten. Help yourself to a cartload. Please?"
> A low-flying Tornado rattled all of Cheltenham's windows.
> "It's a *watch* you broke! Not a future. Not a life. Not a backbone." (190)

One of several life-mentors Jason encounters in his thirteen-month sojourn, Rosamund, rhetorically sunders the linkage between clock-time and the future, and between Jason's survival as a discrete entity and the preservation of an intact past or the imaginary permanence of familial relations. The "low flying Tornado" fighter jet overhead serves as a worldly reminder that this recognition, taking place within the junkyard of the past of an antique shop, occurs within a historical context of failing empire and global conflict. Here, the "tick-tock" of chronological time, the calendrical succession of months, and the time of nations and empires are revealed as compensatory fictions shattered by the experience of temporality per se, constituted of a past in pieces and a future entirely dependent upon an evanescent present.

When Jason finally does reveal the fact of the broken watch to his father, who is immersed at this point in the fallout from his broken marriage, the result is anticlimactic:

> "Ah, it doesn't matter." (But grown-ups often say exactly that exactly when it matters most.) "It was only a watch. Nobody got hurt, not like that poor Ross Wilcox lad. Nobody died. Be more careful with fragile things in the future, that's all. Is there *anything* left of the watch?"
> "Only the strap and the casing, really."
> "Hang on to those. Some craftsmen might be able to graft parts of another Seamaster into Granddad's. You never know. You never know. When you're running thousand-acre nature reserves in the Loire Valley." (278)

Jason's father echoes the antique shopkeeper in saying that the broken watch "doesn't matter," and further counsels him to be more protective of "fragile things in the future," which might be another way of saying that the future is composed of fragile things preserved, if at all, by the ability of a craftsman—mechanical or narrative—to graft the bits and pieces of things into a new whole of hybrid parts. He projects a future for Jason as an environmentalist that turns out not to be true only if we insist on reading the novel autobiographically, but one that does involve the preservation of species given to extinction over the reaches of time.

For Mitchell, the fragile thing is narrative, story, an "object" that embodies in its very form what another mentor, Madame Crommelynk, tells Jason is the condition of photography in the words of her "wise friend Susan": "... all photographs testify to time's relentless melt" (157). The "wise friend" is Susan Sontag (one of the many writers and artists with whom she has come into contact during her life as the daughter of a famous musician), and the essay from which she quotes is Sontag's "In Plato's Cave," the first meditation in *On Photography*, where Sontag writes that "All photographs are *memento mori*. To take a photograph is to participate in another person's (or thing's) mortality, vulnerability, mutability. Precisely by slicing out this moment and freezing it, all photographs testify to time's relentless melt" (15). The fact of mortality linked to the ephemerality of time that undergirds the visual medium of the photograph might also be seen as the primary condition of a narrative—one that subtends the origins of writing and the commencement of authorship. While Jason follows the narrative impulse to plot, to organize experience according to clock and calendar time, he also confronts, literally and affectively during his thirteen month, a critical narrative truth—that to tell the story or to take the photograph is to lose time, to record its passing in the passages of a medium that would seek to instantiate self, place, and historicity. We know that Mitchell parses this conundrum throughout his work. The story takes place in time, meticulously localized, intersecting other times and circumstances precisely realized through this linkage; the story exists only in what remains in cultural memory and its passage through time, a remnant that both preserves a "piece" of time and registers time lost. In *blackswangreen*, in retrospect, we see the shape of the paradox that is at the foundation of the author's narrative practice beginning to emerge.

5

Minor Histories: *The Thousand Autumns of Jacob de Zoet*

> *The present is a battleground... where rival "what-if's" compete to become the future "what is."*
> Yoshida Hayato, in *The Thousand Autumns of Jacob de Zoet* (205)

Minor histories and island worlds

Set primarily in Tokugawa-era Japan as the eighteenth century turns into the nineteenth, *The Thousand Autumns of Jacob de Zoet* has been characterized by its author in an essay on the traditions of the historical novel as allowing him to pursue the "pleasures to be had in the painstaking reconstruction of a lost world" (Mitchell, "On Historical Fiction," n.p.). The novel might be more accurately viewed pluralistically in light of Mitchell's previous novels as a collocation of lost *worlds*, receding temporalities, and spatial dislocations that collide and overlap, where the fault lines of encounter, accident, missed opportunity, and fatal consequence reveal patterns that form the narrative matrix of a reconstructed "history." Three of the novel's five parts take place in the sixteen months separating late June 1799 and late October 1800, and portray events occurring on the Dutch trading post of Dejima (an artificial island in the bay of Nagasaki built in 1634), in the city of Nagasaki, and at the Mount Shiranui Shrine, which houses a monastic order of sisters and priests; the final two parts of the novel, serving as aftermaths, are dated July 3, 1811 and November 3, 1817.[1] Mitchell's complex and precise calendaring of his fifth novel echoes that of his previous novels in which the framing of time is the foundation of the novel's thematic and philosophical architecture; here, the dating of parts and chapters—the periodizing of the novel in a series of symptomatic episodes depicting intercultural encounters between once and future "superpowers"—is indicative of its status as historical fiction, equally dependent upon imaginative projection and factual retrospective. At the same time, as its title suggests in the implication of symbolically infinite *dureé*, *The Thousand Autumns* is concerned with the myriad, fractal, and incomplete trajectories of life and circumstance not captured in the totalizing concepts of "history" or "the historical."

Many early reviewers were content to categorize the novel as historical fiction, and thus something of an odd man out—save for the "Pacific Journal of Adam Ewing" in *Cloud Atlas*—or a turn toward more traditional narrative in Mitchell's catalog up to that point. *The Thousand Autumns* uses as the historical scaffolding for its entangled narratives of thwarted romance, marine adventure, and political corruption the global encounter between the geopolitical abstractions of "East" and "West." These are exemplified by the Dutch empire on the decline (fronting the combined interests of capitalism and Christianity) and isolationist Japan on the rise (the protectorate, in the Western orientalist imaginary, of ancient wisdom, superstition, and cultural impenetrability on the verge of its entry into the modern age).[2] Alexander Linklater, reviewer for *The Observer*, characterized the novel thus: "With Enlightenment ideas and European corruption washing up to the Japanese coastline, Mitchell creates, in Dejima, a single, dramatic gateway through which to observe the encounter between civilisations from both sides" (n.p.). Along similar lines, the reviewer for *The Washington Post* agreed with Mitchell's own assessment of his intention to write "a bicultural novel, where Japanese perspectives are given an equal weight to Dutch/European perspectives" in characterizing the novel's setting as being "[a]t the electric point of contact between East and West" (Charles, n.p.).

There is no doubt that *The Thousand Autumns* works stereoscopically in portraying, for example, the astounding similarities between "Western" and "Eastern" imperialism and racism. Comparing the following scenes—one, a conversation between Dutchmen in a brothel, the second, a conversation between Japanese intellectuals in a Nagasaki academy ironically dedicated to facilitating "East/West" discussions of scientific advances—we are struck by the ways in which fears about the contamination of the gene pool or nation by the racial or geopolitical "other" reverberate. In the first, the titular protagonist of the novel, Jacob de Zoet, a clerk for the Dutch East India Company stationed on Dejima, is subjected to the racist cant of deputy clerk Melchior Van Cleef, born in Indonesia and raised in Holland, as he tells his story of lost love and exile while both men exit the "House of Wistaria":

> Batavia-born, I was, but sent to Amsterdam to learn the gentlemanly arts: how to spout bastard Latin, how to dance like a peacock, and how to cheat at cards. The party ended on my twenty-second birthday, when

Minor Histories: The Thousand Autumns of Jacob de Zoet 125

> I took passage back to Java with my uncle Theo. Uncle Theo had visited Holland to deliver the governor-general's yearly fictions to East India House—the Van Cleefs were well connected in those days—grease palms, and marry for the fourth or fifth time. My uncle's motto was 'Race Is All.' He'd fathered half a dozen children on his Javanese maids, but he acknowledged none and made dire warnings about God's discrete races mingling into a single pigsty breed.... Theo's legal heirs, he avowed, must have 'currency' mothers—white-skinned, rose-cheeked flowers of Protestant Europe—because Batavia-born brides all have orangutans cavorting in the family tree. (347)

Van Cleef's "racial logic" matches that of D'Arnoq's discourse in *Cloud Atlas*, which equally forges the linkage between racism and imperialist expansionism founded upon the notion of cultural—even "animal"—inferiority.

We hear a similar logic expressed by Yoshida Hayato, "author of an erudite monograph on the true age of the earth," as he delivers an address to scholars gathered at a meeting of the Shirandô Academy. In his speech, Yoshida encapsulates his countrymen's xenophobia by raising fears about the corruption of "the impregnable fortress" of Japan by outside forces, with the "vainglorious Koreans" to the northwest, the "savage Ainu" to the northeast, and the growing presence of "straying Europeans," whose barbarian ways and visages threaten the purity and integrity of Edo-period Japanese culture, to the extent that they are forbidden to venture off the island of Dejima into Nagasaki for fear that they might contaminate the populace (202). Yoshida's solution to the possibility of the "impregnation" of Japan by foreigners (the gestational significance of this metaphor becomes more profound as the novel proceeds) is to imitate the West, matching "occidental" with "oriental" colonialism, "[b]y the creation of a Japanese navy... We need a national army based on the French model; an armory to produce the newest Prussian rifles; and an overseas empire. To avoid becoming a European colony, we need colonies of our own" (203). Yoshida's address has eerie resonances for the contemporary reader of *The Thousand Autumns*. Viewing the past from the perspective of the future, we are witnesses to the trajectory that runs from the manifestations of Western imperialist designs upon Japan depicted in the novel to the evolution of a Japanese imperialism culminating in World War II and the horrific reassertion of Western "superiority" in the annihilation by nuclear weaponry of the very city where the novel takes place. Viewed solely as a "bicultural" novel, *The Thousand Autumns* thus depicts the ways in which "East" and "West" mirror each other in historical encounters that suggest that the history of civilization—Occidental or

Oriental—is a continuously aggressive, bilateral struggle between dominant and submissive, "superior" and "inferior" cultures (race being one of the primary markers of these positions) that will only cease when time and history themselves come to an end.

Yet *The Thousand Autumns* is not simply an historical novel that recapitulates locally the grand narrative of progressive civilizations conceived in the binary terms of "East versus West" or "enlightenment versus barbarism." Like *Cloud Atlas*, *The Thousand Autumns* offers a counter to a totalized view of "History" with a capital "H" in the myriad minor histories and microcultures it depicts.[3] The novel, typically, navigates through multiple genres, and contains dozens of stories attributable to both major and minor characters; indeed, such terms are misleading when applied to *The Thousand Autumns* as the ostensible protagonists disappear for hundreds of pages, their narratives interrupted by others that rise to the surface as attractors for the moment, their denouements frayed, ironic, and inconclusive. The novel is a *bildungsroman*: the story of a young man's achieving knowledge, if not wealth, in a foreign land. It is equally an adventure narrative, containing scenes of battle and tyrannical cruelty on the high seas. *The Thousand Autumns* becomes gothic in taking a turn to secreted altars in underground chambers where sacrificial blood rites take place. It is an historical novel to the extent that its setting and events derive from historical records such as Englebert Kaempfer's *Heutiges Japan* (Japan of Today), putatively the first Western history of Japan, unpublished in the German original and only made available in an English translation in 1727 after Kaempfer's death. The 1797 Battle of Kamperduin between the British and Dutch navies, Dr. William Smellie (1697–1763), the Scottish obstetrician who invented delivery forceps, Adam Smith's *The Wealth of Nations* (1776), the "recruiting" and shipboard disciplinary practices of the Dutch East India Company, Euler's formula (1748) (the fundamental expression for the relation between trigonometric and exponential functions), Japanese court etiquette, and *Kaitai Shinsho*, an anatomy textbook published in 1774 that is putatively the first translation of a Western book into Japanese—these are but a few of the historical events, persons, and artifacts referenced in a novel that constitute Mitchell's deeply researched effort to reconstruct the multiple registers of cultural life in the eighteenth century. Finally, *The Thousand Autumns* can be seen as an "orientalist" romance that rejects orientalism both in the progress of Jacob de Zoet's short-circuited affair with a Japanese midwife and in the portrayal of Aibagawa Orito as a proto-feminist who defies the Japanese patriarchy while establishing her self-sufficiency in a life devoted to other women.

In this traversal of genres, a multitude of stories are told by various characters that differ in kind and perspective as well. Each serves as an accumulation toward the larger historical tapestry of the novel, but what is notable is that many of them are indexical narratives, seeded throughout the novel and indicative of multiple histories involving chance encounters and dicey outcomes, giving the lie to any progressive or determinate notions of a grand history operating behind the scenes. Of the life and times of Jacob de Zoet before he reaches Dejima, we hear little, save the story of the family Psalter which he brings with him and hides in his belongings because the Japanese will not allow any foreign religious books or practices on the island. The book's history, his uncle informs him upon giving him the Psalter, demarcates the opportune ancestral history of the de Zoets:

> Your great-great-grandfather was in Venice when the plague arrived. His body erupted in buboes the size of frogs, but he prayed from this Psalter and God cured him. Fifty years ago, your grandfather Tys was soldiering in the Palatine when ambushers surprised his regiment. This Psalter stopped this musket ball"—he fingers the leaden bullet, still in its crater—"from shredding his heart. It is a literal truth that I, your father, and you and Geertje owe this book our very existences. We are not Papists: we do not ascribe magical powers to bent nails or old rags; but you understand how this Sacred Book is, by our faith, bound to our bloodline. It is a gift from your ancestors and a loan from your descendants. (14)

For the reader, the Psalter must serve as the metonymic conveyance of the titular hero's past and future, just as it serves as the totemic embodiment of the contingent history of his ancestry for Jacob. Its contents and the bullet still lodged in its interior reveal a minor familial history that intersects with "History" as a matter of chance and belief: the Psalter in the right place at the right time as Jacob's grandfather was fighting in the Nine Years War or serving as the script for a miracle cure for his great-grandfather during the Plague of Milan, which spread throughout Northern Italy in 1629–31. For the de Zoet family, the Psalter is the providential guarantor of the family's survival amidst the vagaries of larger historical circumstances. Metonymically, it provides indexical documentation of Jacob's "background" in his temporary role as a protagonist in a *bildungsroman*. The "Sacred Book" he carries with him seems to authenticate his ancestral past and generational future as salvational and exceptional, but actually registers in its materiality his momentary serendipitous position both within "History" and the multiple histories of *The Thousand Autumns* as a European Protestant on a colonial mission to Japan at a time when the future of the Dutch nation is in doubt. Both the Psalter and the novel in which he appears underscore Jacob's singularity amidst other singularities as a historical subject or a protagonist whose continuance, as we shall see, is a s much a matter of luck as it is the work of divine providence.

The Thousand Autumns is proliferate with histories of origin, wandering, and displacement related by nomadic subjects whose experience is a matter of "fate" interacting with "chance," marked event with happenstance, thus generating a sense of history as always conditional and incomplete, even miscellaneous. There is the story of Van Cleef's journey as he makes his peripatetic way to Dejima, or those of Grote, a ship's cook, who has been tricked into marrying a moneyless woman posing as an heiress who has been tricked in turn by Grote's disguise as a "young colonial parvenu" (54), and Peter Fischer, the senior clerk in Dejima, who relates an improbable racist tale of harrowing escape from "savages" in the jungles of South America. The other side of the story is told by Weh, Van Cleef's Indonesian slave, who conveys in a history of naming the ways in which human beings are converted into property:

> My slave names change at the whims of my masters. The Acehnese slavers who stole me named me "Straight Teeth." The Dutchman who bought me at Batavia slave market named me "Washington."...My third owner was Master van Cleef. He named me "Weh" because of a mistake. When he asked Master Yang—using fancy Dutch words—for my name, the Chinaman thought the question was "From where does he hail?" and replied, "An island called Weh," and my next slave name was fixed. (322–23)

Here, Weh reveals that his history as a slave is one of multiple names and a series of vestigial identities that have been imposed upon the vagaries of circumstance and mistranslation. Knowing that, for him, history occurs as a series of imposed misfortunes and identity thefts, Weh asserts, "My true name I tell nobody, so nobody can steal my name" (322).

"History" in *The Thousand Autumns* can be evoked by everything from the memory of a major sea battle to a smell. When Jacob "inhales the damp aroma of the Domburg parsonage" (112) as he opens the Psalter for the first time in Dejima, he recalls:

> Sundays when the villagers battled January gales up the cobbled high street as far as the church; Easter Sundays, when the sun warmed the

pasty backs of boys idling guiltily by the lagoon; autumnal Sundays, when the sexton climbed the church tower to ring the bell through the sea fog; Sundays of the brief Zeeland summer, when the season's new hats would arrive from the milliners in Middelburg; and one Whitsunday when Jacob voiced to his uncle the thought that just as one man can be Pastor de Zoet of Domburg and "Geertje's and my uncle" and "Mother's brother," so God, His Son, and the Holy Spirit are an indivisible Trinity. (112)

Accounts of historical battles such as the Third Battle of Ushant in the American Revolutionary War are intermixed with stories that aspire to the status of myth, like that attached to a statuette of the Virgin Mary in the possession of Otane, an elderly Japanese herbalist living in seclusion on a mountain claiming that her "grandfather's grandfather" was given the statuette by the Christian saint Xavier, who had come to Japan "on a magical flying boat pulled by golden swans" (182). Yayoi, a nun at Mount Shiranui who is born with deformed, pointed ears, tells of her abandonment by her parents—"[t]he story goes" (223)—and her salvation by a white fox and a *bodhisattva*, Lady Kannon (Guanyin), who breastfeeds the infant in the wilderness. Back in the realm of the mundane, the captain of a British vessel, Penhaligon, tells his officers the tale of how Captain Cook convinced sailors to partake of "twice-rotted cabbage" (385) in order to prevent scurvy at sea. These and the scattering of dozens of other minor narratives across *The Thousand Autumns* accrue to reveal a "history" realized only in "the battleground of the present," where histories in several registers—personal, political, mythological, and material—compete for visibility as demarcations and projections of past and future.

Dr. Marinus' story is particularly revealing in this regard. Marinus, Dejima's physician and a trained botanist, relates to Jacob over a game of billiards the story of his boyhood in Leiden. His is a Dickensian tale of distant family relations and eccentric benefactors leading to an association with the famous Swedish botanist and taxonomist Carl Linnaeus and travel to Japan in order to work on the massive *Flora Japonica*. Marinus— who reappears in *The Bone Clocks* and who does indeed have a thousand autumns before him as one of Mitchell's transmigrational entities (Weh mentally pictures Marinus as an old soul, a "*kwaio*" or "ancestor who does not stay on the island of ancestors. A *kwaio* returns and returns and returns, each time in a new child" [323])—is an embodiment of encyclopedic scientific and cultural knowledge with a capacity for observing and connecting minutiae that makes him a virtual historian of the "minor." In describing to Jacob a once-in-a-lifetime trip to the seat of the empire, Edo (Tokyo), Marinus lists the topics he is asked to discuss as a representative of Western knowledge:

> "Upon what matters were you consulted?"
> "The medical, the erudite, the puerile: 'Is electricity a fluid?'; 'Do foreigners wear boots because they have no ankles?'; 'For any real number φ does Euler's formula universally guarantee that the complex exponential function satisfies eiφ = cos φ + i sin φ?'; 'How may we construct a Montgolfier balloon?'; 'Can a cancerous breast be removed without killing the patient?'; and once, 'Given that the Flood of Noah never submerged Japan, do we conclude Japan is a more elevated country than others?'" (147–48)

On the one hand, Marinus pursues the encyclopedic Linnaean impulse to assimilate and catalog all knowledge about a given subject into a single history in his (ever) incomplete *Flora Japonica*. On the other, knowledge for Marinus is rhizomic, a stochastic traversal of disciplinary realms, his own history one in which he arrived at the site of his life's work by sheer chance. His book will necessarily remain unfinished even after a thousand lifetimes, for the history of species is one in which the undiscovered, the undifferentiated, and the newly evolved will always be present in the future as well as serving as guarantors of *a* future. This sense of history as "minor"—partial, temporalized, both visible and (as yet) unseen, composed of many indeterminate relationalities—is at the foundation of the narrative architecture of Mitchell's historical novel.

Minor histories infer multiple historical orders, domains, and temporalities. *The Thousand Autumns* can be viewed as a navigation of a succession of microworlds, each with its own locality and history, each contingently related to the others. Much of the novel takes place in the microworld of Dejima, an island constructed as a foreign enclave and offshoot of the island nation of Japan. But Dejima is only one of many real or virtual floating islands and enclaves in the novel that are comparable to the "floating worlds" or *ukiyo* of seventeenth-century Edo, zoned entertainment districts built for a rising merchant class that brought together a heterogeneous assortment of artists, brothels, theaters, and popular amusements.[4] The two ships upon which several of the novel's major events take place—the American *Shenandoah* and the British *Phoebus*—are floating islands complete with their own hybrid cultures and histories that put the lie to any hegemonic notions of "British" identity and the compressions of dozens of local and regional histories into the totalized history of a "united kingdom." As noted by the British Captain Penhaligon,

Minor Histories: The Thousand Autumns of Jacob de Zoet   131

who, beset by gout, walks through his ship for exercise and observes the deckhands, his crew is a patchwork of identities brought together through sheer circumstance onto the island of a ship that symbolically embodies a nation at sea and militarily advances a national destiny: "Walker the Scot...the Penzance boy, Moff Wesley...Six Hanoverians whom Penhaligon plucked off a whaler at St. Helena...Michael Toser, another Cornishman...a pock-scarred Londoner called Rafferty" (332-35). Entering the sick bay, he speaks with several patients: "a feverish landsman pressed at St. Ives, whose crushed thumb may or may not have to come off; a luckier Bermudan, glassy-eyed with pain from an abscessed molar; and a Shetlander with more beard than face and a severe case of Barbados leg, which has swollen his testicles to the size of mangoes" (336). In a later episode depicting the ship's chaplain delivering the Sunday sermon to the assembled company, Penhaligon's observations of the crew's diversity are ironically interspersed with the chaplain's exhortations on Pauline salvation and its putative capacity to unify the multitudes under the banner of Christian faith. For Penhaligon, the assemblage is a hodge-podge where "Christian sailors" are visibly separated from "Hebrews, Mussulmans, Asiatics, and other heathens" watching "from the margins" (390): "There are fellow Cornishmen, Bristolians, Manxmen, Hebrideans...A quartet of Faroe Islanders; some Yankees from Connecticut...Freed slaves from the Caribbean, a Tartar, a Gibraltese Jew" (392). For Chaplain Wily, the contradictory lesson, taken from Chapter 27 of *Acts of the Apostles*, is to be found in Paul's proclamation to the crew of a ship being battered by a violent storm in the Mediterranean that the "raggle-taggle crew of Cypriots, Lebanese, and Palestinians" (392) will find salvation and unity in Christian faith. The island world of the *Phoebus* thus indexes the novel's cosmopolitan "world," an assemblage composed of myriad contingent islands populated by situational identities who are brought together by virtue of chance, historical force ("impressed"), or personal intention—a multitude divisible by national, vocational, or theological belonging or alienation.[5]

As the location-specific chapter titles of *The Thousand Autumns* suggest, there are many other kinds of islands in the novel as well, differentiated in terms of scale, complexity, and degree of sequestration. The court of the Japanese magistracy in Nagasaki and the "Room of the Last Chrysanthemum" where Magistrate Shiroyama conducts private business are ritualistic, hierarchical spaces of commerce and conspiracy. The isolated House of Sisters at Mount Shiranui Shrine, composed of a series of cloisters and segregated spaces where the individual sisters sleep, eat, and pray, is a spiritual enclave concealing an underground temple where blood sacrifices take place. Otane's solitary hut is a place of healing and refuge that contains—

like a box within a box—a cabinet of herbal wonders and knowledge: "she slides out the well-waxed medicine drawers and inhales their contents. Here is toki parsley, good for colicky infants; next, acrid yomogi shavings, ground to a powder for moxibustion; last in this row, dokudami berries, or 'fish mint,' to flush out sickness. The cabinet is her livelihood and the depository of her knowledge" (178). A similar effect occurs when Jacob opens his travelling chest for inspection and reveals the world of his past and "Europe" contained within the microworld of the box:

> More than twenty curious necks crane as the frisker lifts the lid and unfolds Jacob's five linen shirts; his woolen blanket; stockings; a drawstring bag of buttons and buckles; a tatty wig; a set of quills; yellowing undergarments; his boyhood compass; half a bar of Windsor soap; the two dozen letters from Anna tied with her hair ribbon; a razor blade; a Delft pipe; a cracked glass; a folio of sheet music; a moth-eaten bottle-green velvet waistcoat; a pewter plate, knife, and spoon; and, stacked at the bottom, some fifty assorted books. (21)

The center of Dejima itself, ruled into a series of worlds-within-worlds of sequestered zones and buildings, is Flag Square—like the *Phoebus*, a world of buzzing activity that appears to Jacob, seeing it for the first time, as paradoxically exotic and uniform: "The small square bustles with more than a hundred merchants, interpreters, inspectors, servants, spies, lackeys, palanquin bearers, porters. *So these*, thinks Jacob, *are the Japanese.* Their hair color—black to gray—and skin tones are more uniform than those of a Dutch crowd, and their modes of dress, footwear, and hairstyles appear rigidly prescribed according to rank" (22). In fact, as Jacob discovers during his tenure in "The Land of a Thousand Autumns" (366), "Japan" is not a singularity, any more than is the HMS *Phoebus* or the outpost of Dejima when more thickly surveyed. In one of the novel's most evocative passages, Nagasaki is described from a bird's-eye view: "Gulls fly through clouds of steam from laundries' vats ... over bathhouse adulterers; heartbroken slatterns; fishwives dismembering lobsters and crabs; ... imprecise soothsayers; unblinking liars; weavers of mats; cutters of rushes; ink-lipped calligraphers dipping brushes; booksellers ruined by unsold books" (452). With this invocation of the multitude, *The Thousand Autumns* establishes its realism as a pastiche of imbricated worlds, small and large, and its plot a migratory itinerary of realms that reveals their variant mutuality and separation.[6]

The novel opens in a house in the hills above the city of Nagasaki in 1799; a Japanese midwife, Aibagawa Orito, who has learned Western birthing techniques by reading passages and observing illustrations from a textbook translated by her father and written by the Scottish obstetrician, William Smellie, miraculously delivers a breeched infant to the wife of Nagasaki's chief magistrate. The scene rapidly shifts to the American freighter, the *Shenandoah*, anchored in Nagasaki harbor, where we are introduced to Jacob de Zoet, a clerk in the Dutch East India Company who has embarked on a career in the merchant marine in order to earn sufficient money and status to marry his betrothed in Holland, and who has been given the task of looking into a series of corrupt accounting practices and thefts taking place on Dejima. Thus two principals are established amidst adjacent, but quite different, cultural frameworks that shift considerably as the novel proceeds, even as these characters come into and go out of focus. Jacob cannot enter Nagasaki proper and Orito is forbidden to enter those areas of Dejima where Jacob works, so that they are sequestered in island spaces that must be traversed in order for the intimated romantic subplot to be initiated—one which falters due to a combination of bad luck, weak intention, and vocational dedication. Science meets art, and European science meets Japanese practices (the male Japanese physician is forbidden to touch the magistrate's wife, even in childbirth) in the birth scene. The origin of the "shuddering newborn boiled-pink despot [who] howls at Life" (9) takes place in the midst of scenes of commerce and "business as usual" in the daily life of empire.

As *The Thousand Autumns* unfolds, narrative contraries proliferate and collide in ways indicative of the incommensurabilities of historical experience as compared to any resolutions or synthesis that a conventional narrative plot might offer. In scenes taking place in a mercantile enclave on the edge of Japan in 1799 or in the chambers of Nagasaki government officials, Jacob's story unfolds through a series of conversations, encounters, witnessed events, and anecdotal tales exchanged across captain's tables and in magistrate's chambers. On Dejima, a naive Jacob easily falls victim to a series of deceptions and double-dealings that culminate, months later, in his realization that he has been only a pawn in a game being played by the station chief, Vorstenbosch, who has ostensibly brought him to Dejima to clean up corruption while covertly advancing his own financial interests. As he makes his way through a tangle of lies and power games, Jacob, who stands out because he is a "*kômô*," or "red-haired barbarian" (20), navigates through a series of islanded zones and spaces replete with mistranslations and fractious cross-cultural encounters. In a Dejima warehouse, he first meets Orito, who is chasing a Barbary ape owned by Dr. Marinus that has escaped from the doctor's clinic with the amputated leg of a sailor. The comic scene is one of utter confusion that undermines its framing as the initial fateful encounter of future lovers, while instantiating a number of spatial violations: an animal bearing human remains running amuck in an area devoted to commerce and accountancy; Orito crossing the boundary into territory forbidden to her by virtue of the fact that she is both Japanese and a woman, and indeed coming from another space—Dr. Marinus' operating room—where she is permitted as an observer/student only as a special exception to a general rule that forbids Japanese women, especially, from engaging with foreigners or pursuing "Western knowledge." Like many of Mitchell's transitory principals, Orito is marked, not by a birthmark or a tattoo, but by the reddened scar tissue on the left side of her face resulting from an accident involving hot cooking oil that she has suffered as a child—a physical "defect" that makes her unmarriageable to a Japanese man of her caste.

The novel's first part, entitled "The Bride for Whom We Dance," refers in part to Vorstenbosch's characterization of Japanese copper as the "world's reddest, its richest in gold, and, for a hundred years, the bride for whom we Dutch have danced in Nagasaki" (36). It traces Jacob as he moves from the house/clinic of Dr. Marinus, who assists him arranging a forbidden meeting with Orito, to the labyrinthine space of the magistracy in Nagasaki, where Jacob assists Vorstenbosch in negotiating copper delivery and is scrutinized by Enomoto, a Japanese provincial warlord and abbot, whose "lips are tight, the cheekbones high, the nose hooked, and the eyes ferocious with intelligence" (45). Often conversing with a Japanese translator whom he befriends and enlists in advancing his doomed romantic interests with Orito, Ogawa Uzaemon (who, unbeknownst to Jacob, has earlier been prevented from marrying a "defective" Orito by his parents), Jacob becomes increasingly aware of the complexity of Japanese culture and the barbarity of his own in witnessing the effects of a slave's brutal beating, suffering the insults of his fellow clerks in his role as whistleblower, discussing Western philosophy and Japanese custom with Dr. Marinus, or observing the beheading of four thieves on the public square of Dejima. Ultimately, Jacob is humiliated and demoted because he will not sign a document that falsely accounts for the amount of copper being shipped to Indonesia, and eventually, Holland, on the freighter bearing the departing Vorstenbosch. In many episodes of Part One, the valences of a cultural dialectic that divides world, knowledge, and space up into binaries of "civilized" and "barbaric," "East" and "West," and "scientific" and "superstitious" simply dissolve in the face of historical event, as when Dr. Marinus seizes upon the gory executions—which occur in a rare collusion between Japanese and Dutch law and custom—as a pedagogical opportunity: "'Seminarians,' directs Marinus, 'observe the aorta; the jugular and spinal cord; and how the venous blood is, in tone, a rich plum color, while the arterial blood is the scarlet of ripe hibiscus. They differ in taste, moreover: the arterial blood has a metallic tang, whilst venous blood is fruitier'" (164). The plot of Part One of *The Thousand Autumns* refuses to resolve such historical ironies and intransigencies by advancing a felicitous meeting between "East" and "West" in the form of advancing a romance between Jacob and the bride for whom he and Ogawa Uzaemon would have danced. Orito's father dies, and in order to pay off the family debt, she is sold to Abbot Enomoto, who indentures her to a convent on Mount Shiranui for purposes that become clear in the novel's second part. From the panopticon of the Dejima watchtower, viewing her approach the boat that will take her away from Nagasaki to the isolated mountain convent where she is intended to spend the rest of her life, Jacob belatedly runs after Orito, only to catch a glimpse of her departing figure behind a closed gate; it will be his last sight of her for twelve years.

For those readers expecting *The Thousand Autumns* to remain primarily in the mode of historical fiction redefined, Part Two, "A Mountain Fastness," offers significant narrative departures in terms of genre, setting, and circumstance. While still composed as an assemblage of minor histories that converge and divide in boundaried, hybrid spaces, the novel's second part shifts the focus from Jacob de Zoet and the mercantile world of Dejima to Aibagawa Orito, sold into sexual bondage at the Mount Shiranui Shrine, and the community of women—all of them suffering from some form of physical disability or "defect"—that the Abbot Enomoto has established from putatively beneficial motives to provide a home for outcasts where they can conduct lives of spiritual devotion. In fact, the convent into which Orito is abducted and the neighboring partitioned community of monks that occupy the Mount Shiranui Shrine are part of a systematic operation of rape, forced pregnancy, and infanticide founded upon Enomoto's belief that the sacrifice of newborns and the "bottling" of infant souls into an elixir made of their blood will ensure eternal life (at one point, Enomoto claims that he is "over six hundred years old" [316]). Orito has been brought to the convent as an experienced midwife who can assist the "engifted" women—impregnated by the all-too-willing monks who are selected for stud duty on a rotating basis—but Enomoto's plan includes her own impregnation, perhaps by the abbot himself.

With its underground passages, secret chambers, supernatural stories, dark rituals, and sacred texts, with a demonic antagonist in the form of Enomoto, a maiden apparently needing rescue in the form of Orito, and a white knight assisted by a master samurai and his followers in the form of Uzaemon, Part Two of *The Thousand Autumns* is a pastiche of genres including melodrama, romance, Manichean fantasy, the gothic, road and adventure novels, and science fiction. In this, it serves as a revealing predecessor to *The Bone Clocks*, which will extrapolate the fantasy of immorality that motivates Enomoto into the twentieth and twenty-first centuries. The narrative assemblage of "A Mountain Fastness" intersperses scenes from the sequestered space of the convent with those depicting Otane in her mountain hut; Uzaemon, who has learned of Enomoto's nefarious practices, in Nagasaki and at inns and temples on the way to Mount Shiranui Shrine as he executes a plan for Orito's rescue; and Dr. Marinus in his surgery and at the Shirandô Academy discussing Eastern and Western science and superstition. On Mount Shiranui, we are given witness to the daily life of the women amidst the exchange of stories about desperate, nomadic pasts and illusory futures. Brainwashed and made passive by a regimen of drugs taken in as part of a daily communion ritual, the women are told that their infants are adopted by well-situated and loving parents, and that after twenty years of service to the mountain convent they will be provided with comfortable retirements in the world below. In fact, much like the "ascended" fabricants of "The Orison of Sonmi~451" in *Cloud Atlas*, they are murdered and buried in numbered graves behind an inn in a remote village. Unfortunately, staying at the inn owned by Enomoto's informant and crony on his way to liberate Orito from Mount Shiranui, Uzaemon is told that the graveyard is full of dead guests who await proper burial "with priests for chantin' an' a stonecutter for a nice tomb an' a plot of earth in the temple..." (303) once they are claimed by their relatives.

Orito attempts her own rescue from Mount Shiranui when, over torturous months of painful work, she digs a passage from her convent cell to an underground tunnel that leads to the hidden chamber where Enomoto's infanticidal blood rites are performed. Nearing escape at a time when Yayoi is about to give birth and in dire need of her midwifery, Orito is faced with the question of whether the "liberty of Aibagawa Orito is more important than the life of Yayoi and her twins" (271). Her decision to return to her cell in order to care for Yayoi and the future "engifted" of the shrine represents an acceptance of vocational fate, if not perpetual imprisonment in the shrine, but her escape is not curtailed before she discovers in the monastery scriptorium the fake letters, written by narratively talented monks, that "engifted" sisters receive from fictional children living happy lives with fictional adoptive parents in the world below. Mitchell thus reveals once more the tenuous relation between narrative transmission and human survival drawn in *Cloud Atlas*, where transmigratory stories essential to the continuance of collective identity are set alongside fictions of a utopian future issuing forth from the machinery of enslavement in the utilitarian destruction of human life. At the slave camp on Mount Shiranui, Orito reflects on the necessity of stories for survival:

> *The belly craves food*, she thinks, *the tongue craves water, the heart craves love, and the mind craves stories.* It is stories, she believes, that make life in the House of Sisters tolerable, stories in all their forms: the gifts' letters, tittle-tattle, recollections, and tall tales like Hatsune's singing skull.... Orito pictures the human mind as a loom that weaves disparate threads of belief, memory, and narrative into an entity whose common name is Self, and which sometimes calls itself Perception. (244)

In discovering the fake letters of a foreclosed future recounting stories of lives unlived and memories unmade, Orito implicitly recognizes the other side of the story dialectic Mitchell constructs throughout his novels: stories can kill as well as save; they can negate as well as posit a future; in the wrong hands, they can be made into the one story that equals the "truth," or they can, in their multiplicity and alterity, reflect the plurality of existence.

While Orito attempts an escape from the self-contained world of Mount Shiranui, Uzaemon attempts to free her. He has been moved to plan her rescue when he receives a visit from Otane, who has undertaken the difficult journey from her mountain hut to Nagasaki in order to inform Uzaemon of Orito's fate. Otane, in turn, has been given a scroll inscribed by an escaped monk, Jiritsu, who has heretically written down the "Twelve Creeds" of Mount Shiranui Shrine: "'Merely to *utter* them is a profanity, except for Master Genmu and the lord abbot, but to *record* them, so a layman's eyes might read...'" (185). The contents of the forbidden scroll are never fully revealed in *The Thousand Autumns*, but it can be inferred from the conversations about it taking place between several characters that it is a codex of the blood rites at the shrine disclosing what really happens to the women and infants subjected to them. The fleeing monk, a former tanner who dies in Otane's hut from poisons covertly administered because he is suspected of treachery, tells her, "I read the Twelve Creeds and saw, for the first time...the slaughterhouses of Sakai are a pleasure garden in comparison" (185). After reading the scroll, Uzaemon enlists a number of parties, including his samurai master and Jacob De Zoet, with whom he entrusts the scroll should plans fail to assault the shrine and free the women. Several episodes in Part Two recount Uzaemon's movements in Nagasaki and in the countryside as he formulates his plan and makes his way to the shrine; these offer vivid "insider" glances of the diversity of Japanese life that contrast with Western notions of uniformity and standardization, such as when he visits the Ryûgaji Temple in Nagasaki:

> The holiday crowds throng and jostle. Boys are selling warblers in cages dangling from a pine tree. Over her smoking griddle, a palsy-handed grandmother croaks, *"Squiiiiiiiiid on a stick-oh, squiiiiiiiiid on a stick-oh, who will buy my squiiiiiiiiid on a stick-oooh!"* Inside his palanquin, Uzaemon hears Kiyoshichi shout, "Make way, make way!" less in hope of clearing a path than to insure himself against being scolded by Ogawa the Elder for laziness. "Pictures to *astound*! Drawings to amaze!" hollers a seller of engravings. The man's face appears in the grille of Uzaemon's palanquin, and he holds up a pornographic wood-block print of a naked goblin, who bears an undeniable likeness to Melchior van Cleef. (248)

In the end, Uzaemon's plan fails because he has been betrayed from the outset by Shuzai, the samurai master, and he is imprisoned and murdered by Enomoto. In Uzaemon's final moments, Enomoto launches into a defense of his insane practices in which he cites Adam Smith as an authority, shows Uzaemon stolen sketches of Orito that Jacob has drawn in his infatuation, and shoots him with a gun sold to Enomoto by Vorstenbosch proclaiming, "The day is coming—you shan't see it, but I shall—when such firearms transform even our secretive world" (317). The doubled escape and rescue plots of Part Two thus conclude with a scene depicting the spectacular collision of and collusion between "Eastern" and "Western" cultural practices and beliefs.

In a third major development of Part Two, seemingly at a far remove from the dramatic adventures of Orito and Uzaemon, Dr. Marinus and his Japanese peers engage in scholarly discussions about the intersections between science and religion made manifest when "Western" and "Eastern" belief systems come into contact. The relevance of these conversations to the novel's enplotment of failed rescues, escapes, and a vampiric conspiracy that allegorizes the objectification of women as bodies whose sole purpose is reproduction is made clear in the gadfly figure of Enomoto, whose discourse seems to move seamlessly from that of the shaman and mad scientist to that of the enlightenment philosopher. The all-too-easy marriage of science and belief in Enomoto suggests both the proliferation of discursive orders in this world perched on the edge of the modern age and the singular perspective that may undergird many or all of them, even in their seeming contradictions. Enomoto thus engages in a form of scientism that manipulates the ubiquity of scientific method to bolster pernicious values and beliefs. His blood rites and experiments anticipate Nazi "programs" in racial purification, the scientific racism of "the Bell Curve," or the advocacy of cranial size as an indicator of intelligence, but it should be noted that the novel's "good" scientist, Marinus, is a disciple of Linnaeus, whose *Systema Naturae* (1767) presented a taxonomy of the human species divided into five categories based on physiological characteristics, and thus arguably a predecessor of scientific racism. Science, like religion, is not a neutral, value-free discourse in Mitchell's fiction, but oftentimes an ideologically based form of inquiry put to bad ends, such as Mo Muntervary's experiments in quantum cognition resulting in a "modest contribution to global enlightenment... used... to kill people who aren't white enough" (319).[7] For Enomoto, science and religion are interdiscursive parts of a totalistic worldview that justifies a form of cultural elitism and the evolution of a super race that portends the survival of the few at the expense of the many.

Contrastingly, in the novel's third part, set primarily in October 1800, we return to an ostensibly historical narrative that depicts Jacob learning of Uzaemon's fate and engaging in the laborious translation of the Twelve Creeds as he finds a way to inform Magistrate Shiroyama about the activities of Enomoto's nefarious cult. Meanwhile, an English ship, the HMS *Phoebus*, navigates toward Dejima with the objective of taking the trading station from the Dutch and establishing the presence of British Empire in Japan. The narrative is based on the invasion of Nagasaki Harbor in 1808 by a single British ship, the HMS *Phaeton*, which disguised its intentions by sailing under a Dutch flag. The plot of *The Thousand Autumns* follows the historical record up to a certain point in relating how the British captured and retained the representatives of the Dutch East India company who rowed out to meet the ship, thinking it was from home; how the magistrate of Nagasaki, unprepared for the attempted takeover of Dejima and required by the Japanese code of *sakoku* (translation: "chained country") to defend the interests of the Dutch and to prevent any other foreigners from landing on Japanese soil, managed to quickly gather enough samurai to leave after a couple of days; and how the magistrate's suicide ensued from his humiliation over his unpreparedness to defend the harbor.

However, as if a camera existed with the capacity to zoom in on events that occurred a century before the available technology, the narrative in Part Three focuses on localized events taking place amidst the scenes of invasion and military maneuvers occurring on the colliding, islanded entities of ship, trading post, and Nagasaki mainland, each zoned into its own sequestered, islanded space. The camera traces the itinerary of the *Phoebus* as Captain Penhaligon goes in search of the ship's doctor to alleviate the pain from his gout; it records the intimate, veiled political conversations taking place in his private chambers between Magistrate Shiroyama and Enomoto over a game of Go; it voyeuristically shadows Jacob, bereft with loneliness after the departure of Orito, awakening in a house of prostitution next to the woman who will become his wife in the aftermath of the events of 1800. Through the lens of this shifting narrative device, we monitor Captain Penhaligon, awakening from a precognitive nightmare in which he dreams his dead son, Tristram, is alive. We are given witness to the suicide of Magistrate Shiroyama, who has just murdered Enomoto in the middle of a game of Go, having learned of the abbot's schemes after a private meeting with Jacob in which he is handed the Twelve Creeds, and whose *seppuku* occurs as much from his humiliation at Enomoto's treachery as it does from his lack of military canniness. Panning seawards, we see Dr. Marinus and Jacob on the watchtower of Dejima, the latter armed with his Psalter and the scroll of the Twelve Creeds, observing the approach of the *Phoebus* into Dejima as it prepares to fire upon the fortifications and warehouses of the island. Finally, in an improbable moment in the midst of battle, we witness Penhaligon turning the *Phoebus* about and sailing out of Nagasaki Bay when he views Jacob's face and red hair as he stands his ground in the watchtower and sees his son, Tristram, reincarnated.

The events of Part Three, related through multiple perspectives that posit "history" as an admixture of legible events, dreams, games, conversations, and phantasmatic encounters, bring to conclusion the narrative trajectories with which the novel began: Jacob's arrival on Dejima; his first, chance meeting with Orito; his friendship with Uzaemon; the delicate politics of Dutch-Japanese relations; and the office politics of the Dutch East India Company. The two brief remaining parts of the novel, set temporally adrift as aftermaths to the events of 1799–1800—almost as part of the rolling credits—depict the morning of July 3, 1811, where Dr. Marinus' funeral is taking place by special permission at the Mount Isana Temple overlooking Nagasaki Bay. Jacob de Zoet, the chief resident on Dejima for many years, has married and raised a son, Yuan; at the funeral, he encounters Aibagawa Orito, who has survived Enomoto's regime and who, unmarried, continues to serve as a professional midwife in Okinawa along with Yayoi, now her assistant. Their last brief meeting ends with Orito's declaration in Dutch, "'So, Chief de Zoet, our steps together is ended'" (471). Flash forward in Part Five, "The Last Pages," to November 3, 1817, and the quarterdeck of the *Profetes* (bearing the name of futurity echoing that of the ship upon which Adam Ewing sails in *Cloud Atlas*), where Jacob has his last glimpse of Nagasaki Bay as he sails back to Holland, his work on Dejima completed, his son left behind according to Japanese law. In an inversion of the scene where Captain Penhaligon sees his dead son's face in Jacob's visage on the watchtower, Jacob refuses a telescope that would allow him to better see his son one last time waving from the shore because he'd "not see his face properly" (477). On board the *Prophetes*, "[l]ooking backward, Jacob sees pages from the months and years ahead" (477) and envisages the hard voyage to The Hague, his return to Domburger, settling into a life of respectable domesticity, marrying again and raising a family, his gift of the Psalter to his eldest son, his decline, and the visitation of the ghost of Orito on his deathbed. Mitchell thus concludes the compendium of minor histories that comprise *The Thousand Autumns* with the imagined future of a character from the from the past caught up in the present moment of departure, looking backward to a world composed of worlds with histories told and unforetold, and prophesying a singular history ("*the* future") that may never be.

"An uncertain time"

Jacob's simultaneous glances to the past and the future on the deck of the *Profetes* suggest, once more, Mitchell's interest in the elasticity of time, and particularly in *The Thousand Autumns*, how "history" as an assemblage of minor histories is related to the divergent temporalities of multiple coexisting worlds. Jacob experiences the present moment of departure as a partially known, and still partially opaque, past that stretches behind him, and an unknown future that stretches before him extrapolated from what he knows of his more distant past in Holland, sporadically updated by news from his home country over the years of his residency in Japan. The contemporary reader of *The Thousand Autumns* equally experiences the multiple pasts of the novel as prophetic and future-oriented from the perspective of the present. When we read of the magistrates and scholars of Nagasaki forecasting a future in which Japan must imitate the empire-making strategies of the West by building a great navy in order to survive, we also register the fulfillment of their prophecies in the evolution of the Imperial Japanese Navy, the dominant military force in the Western Pacific before its collapse during World War II. In the longer view, we reflect on the transiency of empire as a historical constant, depending as empire is on illusory notions of temporal permanence and succession that affect the lives and deaths of countless subjects. Temporality—the relation between past, present, and future, and the quanta of these categories that are ultimately inseparable—shifts constantly in the novel; the passing of time is perceived differently dependent on local circumstances, the succession of events, or the impact that the legible past and the indeterminate future has upon a specific moment.

Only one chapter in *The Thousand Autumns* bears a noncalendric time signature: that of Chapter Twenty-Nine, situated anomalously in "An

Uncertain Place" at "An Uncertain Time" (343): its opening depicts Jacob dreaming and waking up next to his future wife in "The House of Wistaria." But the novel's frequent instances of recollection and flash forward, dual calendars, and temporal and spatial biolocations and dislocations interspersed with conversations and events in the present tense (at times, line by line, detail by detail) suggest that all time in the novel is contingent and uncertain—affectively an indeterminate positioning of subjects as moving targets in a rapidly passing present that is reliant upon equally indeterminate senses of anteriority and posteriority.[8] In both "East" and "West" as depicted in the novel, the uncertainty of this subject position results in compensatory, overdetermined strategies that attempt to control reproduction, heritage, empire, longevity, and future in the face of the ravages of time.

The most visible and perverse example of the plan to beat time is Enomoto, who engages in infanticide in order to ensure the immortality of the members of his fanatic cult, and thus the genealogical continuance and purity of an elitist sect of "evolved" humans. A translator of Newton and reader of Adam Smith, Enomoto, defending his practices to Uzaemon who is about to die at his hands, articulates a philosophy that appears to merge Western science and political theory with occult notions of the transmigration of souls and the efficacy of newborn blood as a source of eternal life:

> Oh, evil. Evil, evil, evil. You always wield that word as if it were a sword and not a vapid conceit. When you suck the yolk from an egg, is this "evil"? Survival is Nature's law, and my order holds—or, better, is—the secret of surviving mortality.... Your Adam Smith would understand. Without the order, moreover, the gifts wouldn't exist in the first place. They are an ingredient we manufacture. Where is your "evil"? (316)

Enomoto's justification is built upon jumbled conceptions of self-interest and the "natural" law of social survival that he derives from Adam Smith, Newtonian notions of classical mechanics that stipulate the linear movement of time through space as the stable, permanent condition of the universe, and a perversion of the belief familiar to the European scientist and moral philosopher that the source of eternal life is the partaking of the blood of Christ. That arguments derived from Newton and Smith have also been incorporated into the logic that informs the building of empires and dynasties in a quest for permanent domain is relevant to Enomoto's attempt to pursue a version of what Patricia Meyers Tobin has termed "the genealogical imperative," observable in conspiring narratives—novelistic, historical and philosophical—that depend upon a linear conception of temporality undergirding the "dynastic line that unites the diverse generations" (Tobin, 6–7). Enomoto's demented plan is somewhat different: he pursues the "dynastic line" of the genealogical imperative not in familial or generational terms—just the opposite, as his continuance depends upon the extermination of the newborn; rather, his goal is to preserve forever an elitist "generation" of immortals who will be the bulwark against the passing away of generations, empires, and identities in time.

In *The Thousand Autumns*, Enomoto's destinal logic and the concept of dynastic time upon which it is built is everywhere countered by Mitchell's framing of temporality as a narrative construct that changes according to varying cultural systems, genres, and experiences. Set in the eighteenth century, the novel puts into question assumptions about history and futurity in prefigurative representations of the fractal relation between time and space iterated in the futures of *Cloud Atlas* or the contemporary microhistories of *ghostwritten*.[9] There is the aforementioned example of the novel's two calendrical systems indicative of the differential registration of time and history in distinct cultures, but following is a highly selective shortlist of the novel's relative temporalities:

1. the stochastic, multidirectional experience of time as articulated by Magistrate Shiroyama, beleaguered by the invasion of the English and wistful for the more orderly successions of a game of Go: "If only time was a sequence of considered moves and not a chaos of slippages and blunders ... My temporary reverses ... are reversed" (357);

2. Penhaligon's sense of "national" time: "Our mission here, men, is to bring the nineteenth century to these benighted shores. By the 'nineteenth century' I mean the British nineteenth century: not the French, nor Russian nor Dutch" (393);

3. Time as a machine linked to climacteric patterns, as figured by the omniscient narrator of Chapter Five: "The cogs and levers of time swell and buckle in the heat. In the stewed gloom, Jacob hears, almost, the sugar in its crates hissing into fused lumps" (46);

4. Subjective time, relative to nominal identity: "'Would you excuse me,' Jacob asks Fischer, 'for a minute?' Fischer fills his pipe with provocative slowness. 'How long is your minute? Ouwehand's minute is fifteen or twenty. Baert's minute is longer than an hour'" (81);

5. Time as the medium of mortality, as Otane posits: "Fire consumes wood ... and time consumes us" (186);

6. Time as both a condition and sublation of locale: Orito, imprisoned on Mount Shiranui, imagines the passing of days in

Nagasaki and the passing of seasons on the mountain from which she might escape, and defiantly thinks, "*The house may own me...but it shan't own time*" (188).

In the novel, time can be compressed or extended; the narrative may move from minute to minute, or jump cut forward by days, years, and decades. Each variant sense of time conveys a different and equally variable sense of futurity. For Enomoto, there is the mad illusion of a dynastic, dystopic future in which the elite survive through the enslavement and sacrifice of marginalized women and innocents—a "future" inversely realized in the Nea So Copros of *Cloud Atlas*, where the corporate elite thrive at the expense of the fabricants whose bodies are reprocessed as food so that there might be an endless supply of cheap labor. For Jacob, a *bildungsroman* protagonist who temporarily resides in between "East" and "West" on the island of Dejima, thus inhabiting the dual temporalities indicated by the novel's two calendars, the future is a mirror of the past: his tenure on Dejima is but an interim between departure and return to Holland, where he will fulfill his Western bourgeois destiny, while haunted by the specter of an alternative future that could never come to pass. For Orito, whose temporality is a succession of passing present moments in which the only constant is an abiding sense of duty and vocation, the future, irregardless of actual location, is a time space where she will continue to enact her identity as a deliverer of new life. Oppositely Penhaligon, for whom the *Phoebus*, with its sailors of many regions, is paradoxically the embodiment of a "United Kingdom," a "sociological organism moving calendrically through homogeneous, empty time which is a precise analogue of the idea of the nation, also conceived as a solid community moving through history" (Anderson, 26), the future is prefigured as a place where national destiny will be fulfilled. These contending senses of temporality and futurity are not resolved in *The Thousand Autumns*; as in *Cloud Atlas*, there is no narrative outcome that suggests one predominates over the others, or that one is more authentic, more "human."[10] Once more, Heise's notion of "chronoschisms" comes into play: the novel projects "different temporal universes that can no longer be reconciled with each other" (Heise, 7). For Mitchell, modernity—staged in *The Thousand Autumns* as a colonial encounter between East and West—is precisely a condition in which the attempt to reconcile past to present and future amidst contending temporalities undergirds fantasies of identity, nation, and empire that only reveal, in their fulfillment, their own transiency and impermanence.

"The Babel enigma"

George Steiner, the classic theorist of translation in *After Babel*, writes in "The Broken Contract" of "the Babel enigma," which "points to a vital multiplication of mortal liberties. Each language speaks of the world in its own ways. Each edifies worlds and counter-worlds in its own mode. The polyglot is a freer man" (Steiner, 56–7). For Steiner, the enigma or paradox lies in the fact that each language contends with all of the others to establish the singular reality of its enunciations, the god, world, or social order of which it speaks. This linguistic formulation of the contestation between singularity and multiplicity is apt for *The Thousand Autumns* and Mitchell's fiction writ large where, we have seen, multiple worlds and multiple temporalities overlap and collide. In the Dutch colonial encounter with an isolationist Japan, translation is crucial as a means of negotiating between diverse worlds, at the same time that it also necessarily registers intractable cultural differences; indeed difference, per se, is what gets both lost and made visible in translation. This novel of contact zone and empire contains numerous scenes of translation and mistranslation where interlingual communication can create or destroy, for, like Appiah's notion of simple conversation between embattled parties, it can serve as a bridge across cultural differences extended "not because that will bring us to agreement, but because it will help us get used to each other" in the cooperative contingencies of pragmatic cosmopolitanism (Appiah, 78). The romantic relationship between Jacob and Orito and perhaps more crucially the friendship between Jacob and Uzaemon, an official Dutch translator for the Japanese court, come about through translated discourse that enables the overcoming of cultural differences and forges connections between contingent identities who together act against self-interest for ethical ends. At the same time in *The Thousand Autumns*, translation can be used to deceive, dominate, and subjugate others to imperial will or dark design, as numerous occasions in the novel when Dutch is deliberately mistranslated into Japanese or Japanese into Dutch in order to exert force over another. As Derrida suggests, "translation practices the difference between the signified and the signifier" (*Positions*, 19) and in that practice or work reveals the particular culturally situated power of language to connect or to divide and conquer.[11]

Translation in the novel becomes a critical plot element when we consider that Jacob is compelled to hasten his learning of Japanese in order to read the Twelve Creeds. Japanese mistranslations of letters forged in Dutch under the name of the governor-general of the Dutch East India Company (thus, in a sense, doubly translated) play a key role in frustrated negotiations over copper deliveries between Vorstenbosch and Magistrate Shiroyama in "the Hall of Sixty Mats." In the larger cultural history that *The Thousand Autumns* embraces, the Japanese translation of the Dutch translation of the German *Tafel Anatomie* has transformed Japanese medical practices, but in many ways different—due to the fact that the Japanese translators have "just a few hundred Dutch words between us" (208)—than the German original had ever imagined. Translation in the novel often offers as well comedic possibilities, opening the negotiation between languages to new puns, *portmanteaux*, and figures of speech, thus operating as a third language situated between two "originals." When Jacob, having fallen in love with Orito after a brief exchange, asks Uzaemon how a man proposes to a woman in Japan, Uzaemon's reply is humorously scandalous: "The interpreter decodes. 'Mr. de Zoet want to "butter your artichoke"'? Jacob loses half a mouthful of *sake* in spectacular fashion. Ogawa is very concerned. 'I make mistake with Dutch?'" (85). Uzaemon's "decoding," which both incorrectly and correctly interprets the word "propose" in one of its literal senses as a sexual proposition while missing the intended sense of a marriage proposition, introduces Jacob to the remarkable figure of "buttering one's artichoke" for sexual activity that offers a new way of "thinking" about sex, both literally and figuratively. It also leads to an extended discussion of Japanese and Dutch marriage practices, where stark cultural differences (the Japanese practice of not meeting one's bride for the first time until the wedding day vs. the Dutch practice of a carefully organized period of courtship overseen by chaperones) occur alongside notable resemblances (when Uzaemon distinguishes between love and marriage in Japan, the latter "a matter of head...rank...business...bloodline" and asks, "Holland families not the same?," Jacob responds, "We are exactly the same, alas" [85; ellipses in text]). Translation may thus be considered as the linguistic register of the novel's circumstantiality and its constant movement between shifting cultural frameworks, tiled spaces, and multiple temporalities consistent with Mitchell's sense of history and narrative as composed of myriad "minor" stories.

The generative and fatal aspects of translation form a dialectic in *The Thousand Autumns*. The power of the translator is such that he can determine the outcome of events through a single word or intonation that can affect laws and treaties, and the wars fought over them, or determine identity, even posthumously, as when Jacob is questioned by a Japanese chamberlain about the identity of a dead sailor discovered in the wake of the British attack on Dejima in order to determine where to bury the corpse. Jacob surmises that the sailor's "father was probably European.

His mother was probably Negro" (446), but the senses of this language of identification do translate into the Japanese system, where the anonymous sailor can only be conceived of as "English" or "not-English." The distinction is important to the inquiring Japanese official since, Jacob is given to understand through an interpreter, "'If foreigner is English...body shall throw in ditch.'... 'Otherwise he rests in the foreigners' cemetery?'... 'Chief de Zoet is correct.'... 'Chamberlain... This youth is not English. His skin is too dark. It is my wish that he is buried'—*like a Christian*—'in the cemetery of Mount Inasa. Please place the coin in his grave'" (446). Multiple versions of identity—ethnic, national, and religious—circulate in this passage around how these categories can be translated, or how the reductive logics of language can be deployed to determine the fate of identities, unmarked in a ditch or commemorated in a grave, even in death.

At the same time, the circumstantialities of translation and mistranslation in *The Thousand Autumns* can result, epistemologically, in new ways of knowing that generate innovative opportunities for cultural understanding, the diversification of language in heteroglossia and multilingualism serving as a form of intercultural, cosmopolitan materiality. As Édouard Glissant suggested in an interview about the poetics of the future, "Translation will become an important part of poetics... And I think of all the infinite variations inherent in the poetic possibilities of languages, each increasingly penetrated by that fragrance, that bursting forth of a poetics of the world. There will be a new sensibility" (cited in Hantel, 110; my translation).[12] Glissant's rhizomic notion that the adventures and misadventures of translation can open out onto a "poetics of the world" and new sensibilities is evident everywhere in a novel in which political fortunes and historical outcomes, commerce and personal relationships, and identity and belief are so dependent on acts of translation. In one comic sequence, Dr. Marinus is providing his students with instructions for the day's lesson, which will include using Jacob as a test subject for a "smoke glister," an enema that forces tobacco smoke up the colon to relieve intestinal blockages:

> "Today, seminarians," says Marinus, "we have a practical experiment. Whilst Eelattu and I prepare this, each of you shall study a different Dutch text and translate it into Japanese.... to Mr. Muramoto, our bonesetter-in-chief, I proffer Albinus's *Tabulae sceleti et musculorum corporis humani*; Mr. Kajiwaki, a passage on cancer from Jean-Louis Petit... Mr. Yano, you have Dr. Olof Acrel, my old master at Uppsala; his essay on cataracts I translated from the Swedish. For Mr. Ikematsu, a page of Lorenz Heister's *Chirurgie* on disorders of the skin... and Miss Aibagawa shall peruse the admirable Dr. Smellie. This passage, however,

is problematical. In the sickroom awaits the volunteer for today's demonstration, who may assist you on matters of Dutch vocabulary ..." Marinus's lumpish head appears around the door frame.

"Domburger! I present Miss Aibagawa, and urge you, *Orate ne intretis in tentationem*." (66)

The notable bevy of original languages and translations referenced in this passage—Japanese, Dutch, Swedish, French, German, Latin, not to mention English, the language in which the novel is written—is indicative of the discourse of *The Thousand Autumns*, where, in this instance, new medical knowledge and scientifically advanced procedures (such as the smoke glister would have been in the eighteenth century) come about through an exchange of linguistic differences. In this scene, the performance of translation serves as a means to generate new words and grammars as it migrates from Latin or German or French to Dutch and then to Japanese. Earlier, we learn there is "no Japanese word" for "forceps" (7) in the scene where Orito safely delivers the magistrate's son, the implement thus preceding its name and translation as an advanced medical tool that she uses to facilitate birth, as if language is a spacing that awaits the entry of new things in the world. In such instances, language and the translation of languages enable an exfoliation of knowledges and perspectives that is as dependent upon the specific dialogic circumstances of a given situation as it is upon any conception of a systematic or totalized ethnographic encounter between languages and cultures under the category of "East meets West."

The circumstantial "fatal" relation between translation and event comes to the fore in Dr. Marinus' clinic when translation is used as the excuse for arranging a private meeting between Orito and Jacob. In this encounter, a lifelong relationship is initiated on the basis of translation, not just of Smellie's obstetrical treatise, but of culturally circumscribed personal histories and desires into another's language. Marinus invokes this dimension in his warning in Latin to Jacob as Orito enters the clinic sickroom where Jacob is temporally installed, "*Orate ne intretis in tentationem*" ("Pray that ye enter not into temptation" [66]), the famous dictum accompanying the rear view of a skeleton kneeling at an altar in Jacques Gamelin's 1779 *Nouveau receuil d'ostéologie et de myologie* [*New Corpus of Osteology and Myology*], an illustrated anatomy book that employs various religious themes). Marinus' warning is prophetic in that the subsequent conversation between Orito and Jacob touches upon matters of life, death, sexuality, family, vocation, science, and superstition as they "enter into the temptation" of intimate relations with each other, the words of a text in a foreign language that Orioto is attempting to understand with Jacob's help serving as the springboard for sharing personal information. From a confusion of tongues—Marinus' loud voice translating Latin medical terms into Japanese overheard by Orito and Jacob as they discuss names, symptoms, organs, red hair, and butterflies in Dutch and Japanese—emerges the complex mix of cultural difference and cross-cultural intimacy that translation, in its best moments, makes visible:

> "Your sister, too, have red hair and green eyes?"
> "Her hair is redder than mine, to our uncle's embarrassment."
> This is another new word for her. "'Am-bass-a-ment'?"
> *Remember to ask Ogawa for the Japanese word later*, he thinks. "'Embarrassment,' or shame."
> "Why uncle feel shame because sister has red hair?"
> "According to common people's belief—or superstition—you understand?" "'*Meishin*' in Japanese. Doctor call it, 'enemy of reason.'"
> "According to superstition, then, Jezebels—that is, women of loose virtue—that is, prostitutes—are thought to have, and are depicted as having, red hair."
> "'Loose virtue'? 'Prostitutes'? Like 'courtesan' and 'whore's helper'?"
> "Forgive me for that." Jacob's ears roar. "Now the embarrassment is mine." (68)

Shame and embarrassment, superstition and reason, virtue and vice—these will become primary elements of the narrative relationship that evolves from this consequential meeting between the Dutch clerk and the Japanese midwife. Translation, in other words, forms the material linguistic relationship between the novel's two principals; it foreshadows and registers the trajectory of their entangled histories. In one remarkable scene, Jacob meets with a group of Japanese interpreters in order to help address questions about translating Japanese into Dutch: "The group discusses an appropriate Japanese substitute, sometimes testing it on Jacob, until everyone is satisfied. Straightforward words such as 'parched,' 'plenitude,' or 'saltpeter' do not detain them long. More abstract items such as 'simile,' 'figment,' or 'parallax' prove more exacting. Terms without a ready Japanese equivalent, such as 'privacy,' 'splenetic,' or the verb 'to deserve,' cost ten or fifteen minutes …" (114). As the conversation unfolds, more complicated matters of translation arise. "'Please may Clerk de Zoet explain this word: "repercussions."' Jacob suggests, 'A consequence; the result of an action. A repercussion of spending my money is being poor. If I eat too much, one repercussion shall be'—he mimes a swollen belly—'fat'" (115). Such words and phrases as "in broad daylight," the "impotence" of mice compared to "powerful" lions, "blithely unaware," and "lack of proof positive" are given further consideration. While the questions related to these may seem to be random, the translations can also be "heard," by the reader, as predictive metafictional cues for the novel's concerns writ large: the parallaxes that exist between the lives of characters from radically different cultures who come into temporary contact; a foreshadowing of nefarious schemes that will occur in broad daylight; Jacob's naivety; the ripple effect of small actions that will have far-reaching consequences in the historical aftermath; the "proof positive" of the Twelve Creeds; Jacob's impotence in the face of Orito's forced exile from Nagasaki; and his courage in the face of death facing the guns of a British warship. Translation, as enacted in *The Thousand Autumns*, is thus yet another connective tissue in Mitchell's oeuvre, a form of contingency—like transmigration, parallel histories, and multiscaled worlds overlapping and colliding—that scores his fiction as "planetary," an assemblage of linguistic, historical, and intercultural connectivities where past and future come to meet in the present moment of possibilities realized hereafter.

And its discontents

That an ostensibly historical fiction set at the turn of eighteenth century is at the same time markedly contemporary as a fiction of the global present may seem a contradiction, but it is precisely the slippage or passage between categorical entities such as "past" and "present," "East and West," and "civilization" and "barbarism" that Mitchell navigates in *The Thousand Autumns*. The historical setting of the novel occurs at a moment when the Dutch empire is in decline and the modern Japanese empire is in its infancy during a new century that would usher in the Meiji Restoration and the rise of Japan as an international superpower. In a novel comprised in significant part of extended conversations between principals, the history of empire thus forms the backdrop to a matrix of perspectives formulated by Janus-eyed characters discursively eliciting and translating the linkages between cultures and temporalities, recollected pasts and projected futures, local experience and global current. And the pattern of that history, at least in the mind of Timothy Cavendish, invoking Gibbon in *Cloud Atlas*, is neither cyclical nor linear, but that of a sine graph, one of continuous rise and fall. The limitations of this figure for historical process are made evident, however, if one regards the entirety of the novel in which Cavendish appears, with its uneven progressions, regressions, and overlaps, or the whole of *The Thousand Autumns*, where a Venn diagram of the novel's myriad minor histories in their relation to the global flows of capital and the fortunes of empire would result in a fractal display of some complexity. This is the contemporary world as we know it, and it is the perspective from which we look back at characters and events of the novel looking forward to and foreshadowing the future.

Nevertheless, an endless succession of civilizations in ascent or decline marking the continuous bloody battle between conquerors and victims, invaders and indigents, along with the accompanying ideologies of exception and progress used to justify the brutality of the victors, comprises the narrative of "History" writ large against which all minor histories contend in Mitchell's novels. If "civilization" is the source of great beauty and scientific advance, what Freud in his classic work on the inner contradictions of modern Western culture viewed as the embodiment of "[b]eauty, cleanliness, and order," characterized by its "esteem and encouragement of man's higher mental activities—his intellectual, scientific, and artistic achievements" (Freud, 45), it is also the engine of massive violence, chauvinistic nationalism, and imperialistic xenophobia.[13] Mitchell explores the double narrative of "civilization" in *The Thousand Autumns* in multiple intersecting stories of individuals contending against the religious, military, and governmental institutions that form the backbone of organized society and—because they serve as assimilative mechanisms for the transmission of power—are inescapably corrupt and self-perpetuating.

This familiar story that hinges upon the seemingly inevitable contradiction between the highest utopic aspirations of "civilization" for order, knowledge, aesthetic achievement, commerce, and collective well-being visible in its artifacts and institutions and the inconceivable brutality historically directed against indigents and foreigners alike in the making of civilizations is encapsulated in the ancient Chinese game of Go played by Shiroyama and Enomoto in the novel. Like chess, Go is a war game that depends upon the intelligence of the player—stereotypically, a "highly-civilized" game played in a sequestered time and space with pieces that can be expensively made works of art. The world of Go, like the world of chess, is both reductively binary, divided along Manichean lines between black and white, and extraordinarily intricate with its seemingly infinite number of moves and combinations. As is the case with many scenes of conversation in the novel, Mitchell interpolates the dialogue between the two nobles with unspoken asides that reveal deep political differences between the two parties that transform the game of Go into a gaming out of rivalries, conspiracies, and strategic repositioning, possibly leading to real-world battles to come:

Lord Abbot Enomoto of Kyôga Domain places a white stone on the board.

A way station, sees Magistrate Shiroyama, *between his northern flank*... Shadows of slender maples stripe the board of gold *kaya* wood.

> ...*and his eastern groups...or else a diversionary attack? Both.* Shiroyama believed he was gaining control, but he was losing it.
> *Where is the hidden way,* he wonders, *to reverse my reverses?*
> "Nobody refutes," says Enomoto, "we live in straitened times."
> *One* may *refute,* thinks Shiroyama, *that your times are straitened.*
> "A minor *daimyo* of the Aso Plateau who sought my assistance—"
> *Yes, yes,* thinks the magistrate, *your discretion is impeccable.*
> "—observed that what grandfathers called 'debt' is now called 'credit.'"
> "Meaning"—Shiroyama extends his north-south group with a black stone—"that debts no longer have to be repaid?" (353)

The game and the conversation continue to touch upon debt, the Japanese class system, the economic theories of Adam Smith, polity, criminal justice, family trees, training in the game of Go itself, boundary disputes, the burden of rule, trade with the Dutch, and the economic and military deterioration of Shiroyama's domain: the latter is quite pertinent as the game is interrupted by the arrival of the HMS *Phoebus*, disguised as a Dutch ship, in Nagasaki harbor. Later, Enomoto and Shiroyama again play Go as a prelude to the magistrate's murder of the abbot and his own suicide upon learning of the abbot's blood cult and its practices at Mount Shiranui Shrine.

The game of Go can be viewed as a microcosm of the novel. It is a game that simulates the rise and fall of domains, nations, and civilizations in a world divisible by two where one can only dominate or submit, yet one that is also many, replete with unforeseen outcomes, moves, and agencies that— latent or unnoticeable as they might be—have the capacity to dramatically change the outcome. If we extend the metaphor of the game of Go to the view of civilization that extends across Mitchell's fiction, historically, the advance of cultures embodied in nations and empires comes at the expense of the multitude in the singular game of "them" and "us." At the same time, as we have seen, "world" in Mitchell's fiction is composed of an unknowable number of worlds in conflict and parallel, marked by fault lines running in every direction, and replete with transmigratory identities that, themselves, overlap in time and space. Go is a binary game of black and white, victory and loss, yet also a game that can signify for its participants a manifold reality where genealogy, war, commerce, justice, and personality can come into play. Equally so "civilization" can be conceived along the diagonal, bound to a logic of advance and decline that involves brutal domination of or submission to the "other," yet composed of an infinite series of differentially related moving parts that do not operate according to that logic.

Minor Histories: The Thousand Autumns of Jacob de Zoet 153

For all that, civilizations in Mitchell's hands, whether those of the eighteenth or twentieth century, or extrapolated into a millennial future, inevitably entail enslavement, xenophobia, racism and sexism enacted both internally and externally, and the wasting of nature and humankind alike. This bleak view is everywhere on display in *The Thousand Autumns*: in the scene where an Indonesian slave suspected of theft is nearly beaten to death, in the systematic raping of women on Mount Shiranui, and in a Dutch shiphand's account of colonial adventures and the extermination of the "savages" in Surinam. Civilization, "continually bathed in blood," tending toward "Empire" in Hardt and Negri's view, "posits a regime that effectively encompasses spatial totality, or really that rules over the entire 'civilized' world.... [it] presents itself... as an order that effectively suspends history and thereby fixes the existing state of affairs for eternity" (*Empire*, 61). Yet over against civilization's seemingly fatal progress toward its own perpetuity, which is belied by the historical fate of civilizations in time, Mitchell's fiction of survival registers the counterformations of temporary communities that portend a different, if fragile, future: the community of marked and disfigured women on Mount Shiranui, the community of outcasts living off the grid in twenty-fifth-century Korea in *Cloud Atlas*, and the community living spare on an island off the coast of Ireland in *ghostwritten*. Mitchell does not idealize the tenability of these alternative communities or the efficacy of identities like Aibagawa Orito, whose choice of vocation as deliverer of new life militates against the "romantic" option of the novel resulting in the union of the novel's principals. Her fate can be compared to Jacob's premonition of a bourgeois future that plays out exactly as it is supposed to, haunted by Orito's ghost. Alternative narratives and alternative futures are the evanescent, ghostly remainders of Mitchell's fiction, but there nevertheless. This is one of the intimations of the novel's title: a thousand autumns; multiple worlds and innumerable possibilities that, with the passing of days, become the specters of pasts unrealized in real time.

6

A Secret War: *The Bone Clocks*

Nothing lasts, and yet nothing passes, either. And nothing passes just because nothing lasts.
        Crispin Hershey, citing Philip Roth's *The Human Stain* (395)

It's a curse, the present, it allows us to see and appreciate almost nothing. Whoever decided that we should live in the present played a very nasty trick on us.
        Peter Wheeler, in Javier Marías, *Your Face Tomorrow* (326)

In *The Thousand Autumns of Jacob de Zoet*, the story of Abbot Enomoto and a cult that seeks immortality by drinking the blood of newborn infants is one among many, a fantasy-nightmare linked to the novel's assemblage of historical, medical, nautical, political, and romantic narratives. In *The Bone Clocks*, the Enomoto affair becomes a symptomatic incident in the ongoing narrative of a group of humans who are fated to be reborn over eons of time, their souls moving from body to body as the generations pass through history. Mitchell has been hinting at the potential centrality of this narrative throughout his career, in the ghosts and transmigrations of *ghostwritten*, the dreamscapes of *Number9Dream*, and the intermedial rebirths of *Cloud Atlas*. In *The Bone Clocks*, the cosmological fantasy of humans reborn continuously and souls journeying from body to body over millennia is the singular, subliminal script of a novel revolving around the figure of a human living in "real time," Holly Sykes, who appears to be gifted or cursed with telepathic and precognitive abilities. The novel traces Holly's life from her fifteenth year, in 1984, to her mid-seventies, in 2043, yet it is far from centered on her sole existence. The dual narratives of *The Bone Clocks*—that of the life and times of Holly Sykes on Planet Earth as it progresses from post–Cold War global capitalism in the mid-1980s to political and environmental meltdown in the not-so-distant future of the 2040s, and that of elect groups of "Atemporals" (513) warring behind the scenes for control over the destiny of mortal souls—conjoin dozens of narratives of lives intersecting on multiple temporal and spatial planes.[1]

The Bone Clocks is a big novel that touches upon everything from politics and post–Cold War history to the future of the novel and the work of memory. Like *Cloud Atlas*, it is encyclopedic and interdiscursive, containing references to quantum physics, the sociology of power, religion, popular culture across six decades (three into the future), political geography, history, and historiography. And like *Cloud Atlas*, *The Bone Clocks* comes to us in six parts, though each part is "whole" and all of the parts are arranged in chronological order, consecutively dated with the years 1984, 1991, 2004, 2015, 2024, and 2043—ostensibly, a random number sequence with intervals of 7, 13, 11, 9, and 19 years. Sequencing in another register is crucial to an understanding of *The Bone Clocks*. With its dozens of cross-references to characters deceased and reborn in his previous novels, and to the many pasts, futures, and events those novels portray, it seems clearer than ever that Mitchell is engaged in an ongoing project of mapping out a fictional multiverse with each successive novel. Above all, as its title indicates, *The Bone Clocks* engages dramatically with the fact of mortality (the "bone clock" of the body) and the thirst for immortality that has haunted all of Mitchell's novels: the "time problem" that is connected in his work to the construction of empires, the fantasy of utopia, the impact of human agency, the presence of the past, the predominance of the present, and the possibility of a future when, over time, nothing lasts, and nothing passes.

If there is a chief protagonist in *The Bone Clocks*, she is Holly Sykes, whose life trajectory is traced in the novel from three days in the summer of 1984 to three days in October 2043. During the intervening four decades, Holly appears in the novel sporadically, sometimes as the central figure, and sometimes as an important character in someone else's drama. Each of the six parts of *The Bone Clocks* are narrated from a different perspective and premised on a different timescape. The two three-day sequences set in 1984 and 2043, "A Hot Spell" and "Sheep's Head," are narrated by Holly in the first person, the earlier recounting what occurs when, at the age of fifteen, she runs away from home following a dispute with her mother over a much older boyfriend; the latter, her life with her granddaughter and adopted grandson in a small village in Ireland at a time when the planet has been devastated by war and ecological disaster. Part Two, "Myrrh Is Mine, Its Bitter Perfume" (the phrase comes from a verse of the Christmas carol "We Three Kings"), takes place from December 13, 1991, to New Year's Day, 1992. It is narrated by a Cambridge undergraduate, Hugo Lamb, who relates his adventures during a Christmas season as he travels from King's College to London for a family visit, and then to a Swiss ski resort for a holiday with three other college friends, where he meets and has a brief affair with a server in a local pub, Holly Sykes. Part Three, "The Wedding Bash," is told from the perspective of a war correspondent and Holly's husband, Ed Brubeck; it recounts events surrounding the Brighton wedding of Holly's sister, Sharon, including the brief but startling disappearance of Holly's six-year-old daughter, Aoife.

Part Four, "Crispin Hershey's Lonely Planet," is the narrative of a forty-something novelist, once the *enfant terrible* of the British literary scene, but now declining into obscurity. As the title suggests, we are taken on an alternative tour of the planet that progresses from Hay-on-Wye to Cartagena (Colombia), Perth, Shanghai, and Reykjavik, as Crispin describes his annual trips to international book festivals from 2015 to 2020. Crispin's downward trajectory (he comes to rest as an authorial has-been and a visiting instructor at a small college in upstate New York) occurs alongside his growing friendship with a fellow author, Holly Sykes, whom he sees on these yearly occasions. In Part Five, "An Horologist's Labyrinth," we are no longer, for the most part, in three-dimensional time and space. Though the preceding chapters contain glimmers and fragments of a parallel universe with its own history and ontology, Part Five plunges us fully into another dimension where Atemporals battle for ascendency and intervene in the lives of "mortals," like Holly, who by virtue of her "psychosoteric" gifts (429), sporadically tune into this alternative reality.[2] A "Horologist" (415) records the events taking place over seven days in April 2024, when a decisive battle—one that involves Holly, who has been recruited into the fray—is fought between the Horologists and the "Anchorites" (200), a contending party of Atemporals attempting to guarantee their own immortality through perverse means. In Part Six, we return to Holly and "normal" reality gone completely awry in the future, and her final contact with the Atemporals, who continue to live out their existences in the bodies of mortals.

The Bone Clocks is thus a succession of interconnected narratives occurring across scattered latitudes, temporalities, and dimensions, in which Holly Sykes serves as an intermediary—much as the novel as a whole serves to mediate—between "fantasy" and "reality." I place these terms in scare-quotes because, in all of his novels, Mitchell crosses and re-crosses the permeable boundary between the two, reflecting their frequent mergers in his fictional landscapes. If we consider Mitchell's career-long interest in quantum physics, a scientific discipline that postulates many worlds and dimensions, black holes, and the patterning of chaos, then his paralleling of multiple recognizably "realistic" sequences with a prevailing "supernatural" subtext comes into focus as a form of narrative extrapolation. In *The Bone Clocks*, amidst detailed scenes of "ordinary" contemporary existence—episodes portraying middle-class family life or the sexist camaraderie of college "mates" pub-crawling, satirical accounts of celebrity authorship and the publishing world, and depictions of environmental catastrophe and psychogeographic tours of countryside and city—there are the intrusions of a story that has been unfolding in the background for millennia and that involves entities with superhuman abilities and all-too-human desires. One of the compelling aspects of the novel is Mitchell's deftness at interweaving the imaginary and the real in a work of fiction that is, by definition, "all" imaginary, yet given over to a portrayal of the multiple worlds and realities we inhabit. It is important to note that in this admixture of realism and fantasy, as the ensuing discussion will expound, all of the participants, including the "Atemporals," are temporary, mortal, and subject to the consequences and accidents of time passing, whether their lives extend fourscore and seven or a thousand years: all, in the novel's parlance, are "bone clocks," or timekeepers of identity's continuance and limits. In more carefully tracking the novel's narrative itineraries, each taking on its own generic shape and all centered upon or adjacent to Holly's sojourn, we can observe the significant implications of Mitchell's allegory of mortality.

The title "A Hot Spell" refers directly to the three warm summer days in which Holly lights out from her home in Gravesend, Kent, as well as to a strange two-hour event—our first introduction to the world of the Atemporals—that has been erased from her mind at the time and only "recollected" decades later, as a form of recovered memory. Part One is cast in the form of a road novel, a highly compressed picaresque account of the various unusual and ordinary characters Holly meets during the brief three days of her runaway adventure as she traverses the North Kent marshlands in search of a new life. The daughter of pub owners, fifteen-year-old Holly has left home after a fierce squabble with her mother over her continued association with the mendacious twenty-four-year-old Vincent Costello: the grandson of Veronica Costello who dwells in the Aurora House of *Cloud Atlas*, he is an early addition to the novel's matrix of characters connected to those of previous novels. But before Holly has left home, she has been given a maze inscribed on a piece of cardboard by her younger brother Jacko (eerily echoing the name of Jacob de Zoet), an odd child, prescient well beyond his years, who spends his time inhabiting the fantasy landscapes of Dungeons & Dragons. The maze is a labyrinth, made of eight circles inside each other, and comes with a strange invocation from Jacko: "It's diabolical.... The Dusk follows you as you go through it. If it touches you, you cease to exist, so one wrong turn down a dead end, that's the end of you. That's why you have to learn the labyrinth by heart" (8).

The cardboard labyrinth conferred upon her by her "freaky" brother is the first hint that there is something else going on in this narrative of teenage rebellion. Holly departs in anger and haste after confronting her mother and runs off to join Vinnie in his digs, only (of course) to discover him in bed with her best friend. Confused and betrayed, Holly begins a journey to the nearest city, Rochester, where she will gain employment and start a new life. But her journey is quickly interrupted and derailed by a sequence of events: encounters with Ed Brubeck, an older boy who pursues her out of Gravesend on his bicycle out of concern for her welfare; a meeting with a strange woman fishing off a bank, whose name is Ester Little and with whom Holly makes a strange contract, exchanging Ester's offer of tea for a promise to offer the "crazy" woman "asylum...Refuge. A bolt-hole. If the First Mission fails as I fear it must" (25); her sighting of Jacko's double beneath a highway underpass, an hallucinatory scene that Holly attributes to hunger and anxiety involving dreamlike characters, a chapel, a religious icon with a "black spot...a bit above where the eyebrows meet," and the release of some form of psychic energy; and her travel to a farm on the Isle of Sheppey, where she gains employment as a strawberry picker.[3] In her diary-like narrative, Holly observes the topography and the people inhabiting it, noting, for example, the deep history of the marshland: "To my right, the A2 roars away over the marshes. Old Mr. Sharkey says it's built over a road made by the Romans, and the A2's still how you get to Dover, to catch the boat to the Continent, just like the Roman's did" (20). When she and Ed come upon a holiday park at Allhallows-on-sea, Holly sardonically surveys "the rows of caravans, and those oblong cabins on little stilts they call trailer homes in American films.... half naked kids and totally naked toddlers... Half-sloshed moms're rolling their eyes at sun-pinked dads burning bangers on the barbecue" (29). Walking on the nearby dunes, Ed points out to her concrete machine-gun nests from World War II that have been converted into picnic tables; climbing onto one to "take in the view," Holly sees that "Southend's across the wider-than-a-mile mouth of the Thames and the other way I can see Sheerness docks on the Isle off Sheppey" (30). As she travels, she occasionally "bi-locates" to imagine what her family is doing in Gravesend when they realize she is gone. Everyday scenes, an encounter with a stranger who may be crazy, the beginnings of a romance, the *schadenfreude* that accompanies the projection of parental anxiety, an hallucination born of hunger and confusion, and landscape and history opening out onto a larger world—all seem like relatively familiar elements that one might expect in the narrative of a schoolgirl who has run away from home.

Save that the narrative concludes with the news, delivered by Ed Brubeck, who has ferreted out where Holly is working, that Jacko has disappeared, never to be seen again in this world as Jacko. Holly returns home immediately, but before this startling conclusion to "A Hot Spell," intermixed with the everyday, the familiar, or the explicably strange, there are two narrative intrusions which further confirm that the real bilocations taking place in

Holly's narrative occur between a world that is only inaccurately described as "normal" and the shadow realm of a parallel universe. The first of these is a sequence of recollections that occurs just as she is leaving Gravesend and remembers the "daymares" she had as a seven-year-old in which she hears voices: "Not mad, or drooly, or specially scary... the Radio People, I called them, 'cause at first I thought there was a radio on in the next room" (16). The voices are accompanied by visits from a mysterious "Miss Constantin," an "imaginary friend" who, apparently, has the power to punish a bully who has been harassing Holly at school, and who will disturbingly reappear years later when Holly sees her with Jacko's double under the highway. When she turns eight, Holly is "cured" of her daymares and visions by a Chinese physician, Dr. Marinus, who presses upon the middle of her forehead with his thumb to affect the remedy. Is this the same Marinus as the Dutch physician of *The Thousand Autumns of Jacob de Zoet* reborn—a possibility certainly extended in *Cloud Atlas* and *ghostwritten*—or a distant relative descended from him?

We get a glimpse of an answer in a second-narrative intervention when Holly, attempting to get to the farm on Sheppey Island, hitches a ride with Heide and Ian, a pair of yuppie revolutionaries. They take her home for breakfast, at which point we know we are no longer in Kansas, for Holly, returning from the kitchen, discovers both of them dead or unconscious as "the gears what's real slip" (60), seeing in a mirror one of the figures from the underpass hallucination who possesses "piranha eyes... curly black locks... [a] busted nose" who begins to interrogate her as to whether she is "Esther Little or Yu Leon Marinus" (60). The events that follow constitute a barrage of the improbable: Marinus appears in the body of Heide, Ester Little in the body of Ian; a psychokinetic battle ensues over the possession of Holly's body between her antagonist, an "Anchorite" (67), and the two others, identified as members of "Horology." Marinus/Heide is destroyed, but not before Marinus flees the body as Esther/Ian destroys the Anchorite Joseph Rhîmes; Esther then claims her promise of asylum from the thoroughly traumatized Holly, hiding "deep, deep, deep in" while stating that she will "redact" what Holly has seen "from your present perfect, for your own peace of mind" (67). Since this tense redaction of the "has been" into the "is" has occurred as her account is written in the first-person present, Holly is clearly authoring "A Hot Spell" from the position of the future perfect, the "was to have been" of a fragment of recovered memory, and from the perspective of a much older Holly Sykes. The effect is to convert the improbable into the historical, and the fantastic into the factual within the narrative order of *The Bone Clocks*.

As the novel unfolds, we begin to piece together this shadow narrative. What Holly has observed in her underpass hallucination is the climatic event—the disastrous end of the "First Mission"—in a war between Atemporals that spells temporary defeat for the Horologists. The conflict between these "mortal immortals" (they can die, like Rhîmes, though their lives can extend for millennia) occurs, precisely, over the issue of immortality, and how it is acquired. Much later in the novel, it is explained by an elder Horologist to Marinus—who, having occupied at least thirty-six bodies and lived for hundreds of years is, indeed, the "same" Marinus of *The Thousand Autumns,* and the Horologist/narrator of Part Five of the novel—that becoming an Atemporal can be a matter of either will or chance. Those Atemporals like Marinus, who somehow can transmigrate their souls from body to body, "ingressing" to each body in the form of a memory of the past conjoined with the soul of the new body, are subdivided into two groups: "Returnees die, go to the Dusk, are resurrected forty-nine days later. Sojourners ... just move on to a new body when the old one's worn out" (483). Marinus is a "Returnee," his first identity, born in 640 A.D., that of the son of a Sumerian falconer. As he will tell Holly forty years after the events of "A Hot Spell," "We Atemporals live in this spiral of resurrections involuntarily. We don't know how, or why us" (451), each of his "resurrections ... a lottery of longitudes, latitudes, and demography" (432). But then there are others known as "Carnivores," or "metaphorically vampiric" (452) Atemporals who attempt to force immortality, not through the transmigration of an incrementally layered consciousness into successive bodies, but by consuming the souls of those humans, like Holly, to whom they are especially attracted by virtue of their paranormal capacities. While the bodies inhabited by Returnees and Sojourners constantly change as the original soul becomes multiplied, the bodies inhabited by Carnivores are unchanging and ageless as the singular soul with which they began entirely consumes those upon which it feeds.

Such is the metaphysical subtext of the novel and the basis for the ongoing "War" that implicates Holly and many others in the novel. The Horologists, keepers of time and history, Sojourners, or Returnees, all have squared off against the Anchorites, an elect, secret order of Carnivores initiated in the thirteenth century dedicated to the rites of soul extraction (Enomoto of *The Thousand Autumns* is clearly an aspirant), periodically recruiting a human into their midst who possesses an exceptional craving for the preservation of his or her singular identity. In the allegorical register of the novel that will be considered in greater detail as we proceed, the war occurs between those narcissistically tied to the preservation of a singular identity in the steady state of the present and those compiled entities for whom identity is a form of multiplicity evolving over time and space as they graft pasts onto present and future selves. On another level, the conflict exists between those who would use other humans to extend their own lives, identities, and power—here, the depictions of slavery and imperialistic brutality across Mitchell's novels take on another dimension—and those for whom "the human" signifies continuance and collectivity in the transmission of story and memory.

Holly Sykes has errantly stumbled onto a crucial episode in this war, the denouement of the "First Mission" in which the Horologists have failed in their attack upon the Anchorite stronghold. She has observed the debacle in her vision at the underpass where several Horologists have been supposedly killed, including the Horology general, Xi Lo, who is more than twenty-five centuries old, one of his avatars being that of Magistrate Shiroyama of *The Thousand Autumns* and another, his last, that of Jacko, her brother. The Anchorites believe that Ester Little, the oldest of the Horologists "whose soul predated Rome, Troy, Egypt, Peking, Nineveh and Ur" (435), has also been killed, but she has managed to secrete herself in Holly in such a way that she will remain undetected for decades. But, memory redacted, Holly knows none of this until years later: what she remembers of her vision in her adolescent mind is a "daymare" that can be explained as a temporary revisiting of her childhood malady and an overexcited imagination. Nor does she know that the events of 1984 and the failure of the First Mission directly precede the initiation of the Second Mission, according to an ethereal "Script" (61) being enacted as the war unfolds. For the next forty years, the surviving Horologists will regather and the Anchorities will recruit new blood, drawing humans like Holly, Ed Brubeck, Hugo Lamb, Crispin Hershey, and dozens of others into the conflict. Each of their stories is their own and not their own, as each is also the story of the others and the "secret war waging around us, *inside* us even" (399) that encompasses them, a history into which they are networked knowingly or unknowingly, collectively responsible for its outcome either way.

In Part Two, Hugo Lamb, a twenty-one-year-old Kings College undergraduate, anecdotally relates his experiences in Cambridge, London, and the Swiss Alps during the 1991 Christmas holiday. Readers of *blackswangreen* will recall a younger Hugo, nine years previously, as the cousin of Jason Taylor who seduced him into smoking. He was a scoundrel then, and he has continued in his ways, his surname designating a Christ-like innocence that conceals a criminal intelligence. While pretending to be a helpful friend to his college mates and a thoughtful son whom his parents admire for his work ethic and charitable activities, at Cambridge, he sleeps with the girlfriend of a classmate with no regard as to how the betrayal will affect his friend. In one of several ongoing scams that take advantage of the weaknesses of others, he cheats at high-stakes poker with another classmate, Johnny Penhaligon (a descendent of the captain of the HMS *Phoebus* in *The*

Thousand Autumns), then offers to broker a deal for the sale of Penhaligon's vintage Aston-Martin to pay off his mounting debts from which Hugo will skim the profits, thus double-dipping into the financial agony generated by Penhaligon's gambling addiction. At home, he visits a retired Brigadier Philby in an assisted living residence, ostensibly for the purposes of reading to an old man suffering from dementia. In fact, he uses the occasion to steal rare stamps from the Brigadier's collection, which he sells under the pseudonym of Marcus Anyder ("Anyder" is the name of the largest river in St. Thomas More's *Utopia* [1516]) to a London philatelist; and—Hugo being Hugo—he has hot sex with a Brazilian nurse working at the residence, then cruelly breaks off their affair during his Christmas visit after she confesses her love for him. As a student of political economics and a reader of Machiavelli and Sun Tzu's *The Art of War*, Hugo is clearly educating himself for a future life in crime, deception, and empowerment.

If Holly's narrative bears features of the road novel and the picaresque, Hugo's is a compressed *bildungsroman*, the education of Hugo Lamb. Hugo sketches scenes at school in his accounts of pub gatherings and campus conversations. He "goes up" to London, where he provides a psychogeographic tour of the city as he navigates from philately shop to bank to car dealership pursuing his various schemes (at the auto showroom, he attempts to sell Penhaligon's Aston-Martin to a car dealer who is none other than Vinnie Costello). With subtle cynicism, he portrays family life in the Lamb's comfortably middle-class household where dinner-table conversation leads to a discussion about in-laws and the future of characters seen in *blackswangreen*: Jason Taylor is pursuing a course in psycholinguistics and speech therapy at Lancaster University; Julia, his sister, has won a scholarship to study human rights law in Montreal; and their parents have been divorced for a decade. Hugo's descriptions of the young and the privileged enjoying a ski holiday in Switzerland, where he meets and briefly falls in love with Holly, is a backhanded indictment of class snobbery, misogyny, and the excesses brought about by too much money in the hands of unelevated beings.

School life, domestic life, movement from country to city, the formation of vocational identity (Hugo as career criminal), the contest between innocence and experience, and first love—these are some of the classic elements of the *bildungsroman*, but like Holly's narrative in "A Hot Spell," Hugo's self-accounting is punctuated by intrusions from another plane that result in a decision as to what side he is on: those of the innocent and formerly guilty who have given up their mendacious ways or those who lead the lambs to slaughter. As Part Two opens, Hugo, incongruously, is in a chapel listening to the King's College Choir sing Benjamin Britten's "Hymn to the Virgin"— perhaps a sporadic episode indicative of potential redemption—when his eye is caught by an attractive young woman across the aisle. She turns out to be Holly's Miss Constantin, and though he is not yet fully aware of it, she is there to recruit him to the Anchorites. Their discussion of power clarifies the interests and ideology of the Anchorites: countering Hugo's definition of power as "the ability to make someone do what they otherwise wouldn't, or deter them from what they otherwise would," Constantin responds that power is a form of energy:

> never created or destroyed.... Power is crack cocaine for your ego, and battery acid for your soul. Power's comings and goings, from host to host, via war, marriage, ballot box, diktat, and accident, *are* the plot of history. The empowered may serve justice, remodel the Earth, transform lush nations into smoking battlefields and bring down skyscrapers, but power itself is amoral.... Power will notice you. Power is watching you now. Carry on as you are, and power will favor you. But power will also laugh at you, mercilessly, as you lie dying in a private clinic, a few fleeting decades from now.... That thought sickens me, Hugo Lamb, like nothing else. Doesn't it sicken you? (100–1)

The logical chain of the argument leads Constantin to introduce the possibility of "[a] form of power that allows one to defer death in perpetuity" (101), the first gambit in his recruitment to the Anchorites, though at the moment Hugo thinks he is having something equivalent to one of Holly's "daymares." But what is most interesting in this commentary on the nature of power is that, in its garden variety forms, it is located both nowhere and everywhere, and its presence for those who temporarily have it is purely opportune, entirely dependent on the fact of mortality and the passing of time. Describing it, Constantin sounds like she is describing the transmigration of souls as they move "from host to host," and thus gives voice to one of the Anchorite's guiding principles: that the desire for the possession and control of power—the ultimate form of egoism informing everything from megalomania to empire—relies on somehow maintaining the singularity of the individual, "outside time," embracing the temporal fantasy of the impossibly long durée. For Hugo, this is the first act in an implausible sequence of events that will take him toward and away from Holly Sykes.

Hugo has one other strange, but brief encounter before he departs Cambridge for the Christmas holiday: in the "loo" of a pub, he encounters one Elijah D'Arnoq, a New Zealander (he is a descendent of the resident preacher, Mr. D'Arnoq on Chatham Island in *Cloud Atlas*) and a Corpus Christi postgraduate who Hugo dimly remembers from their days as fellow members of the Cambridge Sharpshooters. D'Arnoq mentions that he is "an Anchorite," which, though prefigurative, means nothing to Hugo at the time ("I wonder if 'Anchorite' means 'anchorman,' or if it's a Kiwi-ism or rifle club-ism. Cambridge is full of insiders' words to keep outsiders out" [106]). Like Holly, he initially lays off these intrusions from elsewhere as random strange occurrences in the ordinary; not until he becomes an Anchorite himself will Hugh have access to the insider vocabulary of *The Bone Clock*'s secret narrative.

The encounter between Hugo and Holly at a chic ski resort where she is working and he is playing with friends (one of whom is future novelist Richard Cheeseman, who will play a significant role in Part Three) takes a predictable course. Meeting by chance while skiing as Holly retrieves a ski for Hugo, who has crashed because he has gone down a run well beyond his skill level, they initiate a cat-and-mouse affair—Holly, entirely uninterested at first, is gradually seduced by Hugo's seeming charms. Amidst a sequence of scenes that ought to inspire guilt in Hugo as he receives the news that Johnny Penhaligon has driven off a cliff in his Aston-Martin over despair at his gambling debts, or listens to his heartbroken friend on love's betrayal, Hugo pursues Holly while the Anchorites, from the shadows, pursue him in dreams and phantasmatic stalkings. Events conspire to cause Hugo to take refuge in Holly's flat during a blizzard, where they commence their affair in earnest as they make love and exchange stories of stupidity and guilt: Hugo, telling of the time he stole cigarettes and seduced Jason into smoking; Holly, the period of time she ran away from home as consequential to Jacko's disappearance. While there, he notices some of Holly effects: a postcard from Ed Brubeck, traveling in Turkey, and a pendant with a maze inscribed on it, which is a rendition of the cardboard maze Jacko gave to her as she ran away from home. Their intimacy, however, is short-lived. Wandering out into the semideserted landscape of the snowbound village, Hugo is picked up in a Land Cruiser by D'Arnoq and his fellow Anchorites. In the final "intervention" of Part Two, he is introduced to the current Anchorite leader, Mr. Pfenninger, who claims to have been born in 1758. Pfenninger explains, "[w]e are the Anchorites of the Dusk Chapel of the Blind Cathar of the Thomasite Monastery of Sidelhorn Pass" (200), transports Hugo to the ethereal realm of the Dusk Chapel where he awakes two days into the future, and inducts him through a portal opened by Miss Constantin into the order of the Anchorites.

The plot elements of Part Two underscore the ethical choice faced by several characters in the novel, but most starkly by Hugo Lamb: to engage in acts of self-preservation that inevitably come at the expense of others or to sacrifice the good of the one for the good of the indeterminate many. For

Hugo, operating on the basis of a naturalistic worldview that regards the survival of the fittest as the highest goal and the possession of absolute power as the surest means to attain it, the choice "between two metamorphoses" (197) seems clear, the "Faustian pact" (199) he is contemplating the logical outcome of his existence. True, there are moments where he has glimpses into another future that involves love and commitment, but even Hugo's version of love when he thinks he has fallen into it has the ring of domination as he compares love to lust: "This isn't lust. Lust wants, does the obvious and pads back into the forest. Love is greedier. Love wants round-the-clock care; protection; rings, vows, joint accounts, scented candles on birthdays; life insurance. Babies. Love's a dictator" (185). In embracing the Anchorite way of life, Hugo chooses another form of "life insurance" arising from a fear of the mortal future that haunts him even as he witnesses a lively scene of young people dancing at a Swiss nightclub:

> So what if Marcus Anyder builds his own empire of stocks, properties portfolios?... Look, wrinkles spread like mildew over our peachy sheen; beat-by-beat-by-beat-by-beat-by-beat-by-beat, varicose veins worm themselves through plucked calves... the dancers' hair styles frost, wither and fall in chemotherapeutic tufts... DNA frays like wool, and down we tumble; a fall on the stairs; a heart attack; a stroke; not dancing but twitching. (173–4)

As in *Cloud Atlas*, Mitchell generates a poetics of survival in *The Bone Clocks*. In staging an allegorical battle between "immortals" engaging with mortal humans in the extended fantasy environments of the novel, Mitchell underscores the two concepts of survival that form a dialectic in his fiction. There is the relatively short-term survival of the singular, powerful, and dominating individual, moiety, nation, or empire, always doomed to fail over the long haul. In contrast, there is the survival of the collective which inevitably involves the sacrifice of the self in an equally frail alternative, given that the realization of the future in Mitchell's novels is often dystopic and that the collective only continues to exist through the work of "passing on" souls or stories. Mitchell risks fantasy in *The Bone Clocks*, because it allows him to address mortality from an impossible dimension beyond its limits as, paradoxically, a condition necessary and sufficient to human survival: as Holly says at one point, "You only value something if you know it will end" (193).

To some degree, the shadow war of *The Bone Clocks* may be read allegorically as a drama of moral choice, but it is not a simple allegory as the novel advances over six decades. This is a David Mitchell novel, after all, involving dozens of characters inhabiting multiple overlapping chronotopes and working at cross-purposes. Histories, stories, and ideology-bearing agendas contaminate and cross-pollinate each other, and Planet Earth from 1984 to 2043 is in a downward spiral as environmental and political catastrophes unfold. As in the "epic" visions of *Cloud Atlas* and *The Thousand Autumns*, in *The Bone Clocks*, good and evil are not simply paired off in Manichean binaries embroiled in an eternal battle for domination of the human world. There may be "Atemporals" flitting through time and space in one or many bodies, but there are no saints and no devils, metamorphosis takes many shapes, and if there is a god that some blindly obey, it is power itself, which, as Miss Constantin suggests, is more of a form of multilocated kinetic energy than it is a force permanently possessed by the few. The third and fourth parts of the novel deepen the complexities of the novel's moral scheme in preparation for the staging of the decisive conflict between the Anchorites and the Horologists in Part Five.

In Part Three, "A Wedding Bash," the narrator is Ed Brubeck, a "hot zone" war correspondent for *Spyglass* magazine (now edited by Luisa Rey, having survived the conspiracies of *Cloud Atlas*) currently married to Holly Sykes. Ed had said at their first meeting that his dream was to travel the world "[f]rom the tip of Portugal to the tip of Norway. Eastern-bloc countries too. Yugoslavia and places. The Berlin Wall. Istanbul. In Istanbul there's this bridge, right. One side's in Europe and the other side's in Asia. I'm going to walk across it" (38). The irony inherent in the fact that because of the Cold War and Bosnian War the geopolitical landscape has changed utterly since 1984, when Ed makes these youthful pronouncements, and 2004, when his world tour now consists of visiting war zones, is painful, underscoring Mitchell's insistence on wars both earthbound and ethereal as the constant elements of human history, no matter what timescale we are considering. Ed has returned for the wedding of Holly's sister from the battle zone of the Iraq War, just over a year in progress in 2004, and his marriage is in trouble because of an ongoing disagreement with his wife about continuing as a war correspondent when they have a six-year-old daughter to consider. Holly, in effect, has taken the path of "rings, vows, joint accounts, scented candles on birthdays; life insurance. Babies" that Hugo has rejected, and her dispute with Ed involves a many-sided debate between the preservation of the nuclear family and her husband's commitment to preserving the world's memory: "if an atrocity isn't written about, it stops existing when the last witnesses die.... If a mass shooting, a bomb, a whatever, *is* written about, then at least it's made a tiny dent in the world's memory. Someone, somewhere, some time, has a chance of learning what happened. And, just maybe, acting on it. Or not. But at least it's there" (210). For Ed, as for Somni~451 and Zachry in *Cloud Atlas*, the survival of a narrative, a report, or an accounting of the past, no matter how minor, is essential to any chance for change in the future.

But the disputed choice between self-interest (in this case, the "self" as family) and world interest is not that simple, for Ed has been drawn to the battlefields of Iraq, Syria, and Bosnia out of the combination of an aversion to domesticity, an attraction to war's "excitement," and overriding guilt for the death of two colleagues during the intervention in Iraq. The conflict in Iraq has "gone horribly off script" because, in Ed's view, "the script was written referring not to Iraq as it was, but to a fantasy Iraq as Rumsfeld, Rice, and Bush et al. wanted it to be, or dreamt it to be or were promised by their pet Iraqis-in-exile it would be" (250). Ed's narrative interpolates horrific scenes from Iraq with scenes from the ongoing wedding, illuminating the jarring contrasts and disturbing connections between the disastrous outcomes of a national political fantasy and the domestic fantasy of idealized love, marriage, and family that any wedding (even the one viewed through Ed's war-wearied eyes) symbolizes. Once more, the complexities of the novel, viewed as an allegory of choice, emerge through the network of linkages between fantasy and reality and the multiple directions that the paths laid out in any "script" may take, whether that of the Atemporals or that of the invasion of Iraq. For Ed, whether pursued in the name of family, love, or war, premised on whatever ideological scripts are being followed, all human actions are interconnected, each leading to others, as he suggests to a British interlocutor who wonders how all the "wise, compassionate, and decent" Americans he knows could be behind the Iraq War:

> I suspect that the Americans you have met...aren't high-school dropouts from Nebraska whose best friend got shot by a smiley Iraqi teenager holding a bag of apples. A teenager whose dad got shredded by a gunner on a passing Humvee last week while he fixed the TV aerial. A gunner whose best friend took a dum-dum bullet through the neck from a sniper on a roof only yesterday. A sniper whose sister was in a car stalled at an intersection as a military attachés convoy drove up, prompting the bodyguards to pepper the vehicle with automatic fire, knowing they'd save the convoy from a suicide bomber if they were right, but that Iraqi law wouldn't apply to them if they were wrong. Ultimately, wars escalate by eating their own shit, shitting bigger and eating bigger. (253)

Ed's take on "Americans" and Iraq clarifies the relation between the "home" and "abroad" (a high-school dropout from Nebraska and a teenager in Baghdad; a wedding in England and a bombing in Iraq), and the knotted narratives that connect all into a chain of mutual responsibility.

"A Wedding Bash" provides a context for understanding the multiple fantasies of *The Bone Clocks*, including the novel's master fantasy of a war between Anchorites and Horologists—serving, as all other fantasies, including those of the domestic order—as a coping mechanism, a way of structuring reality, and a future over against the bare fact of mortality. As in other parts of the novel up to this point, intrusions upon the narrative present arrive from the realm of the Atemporals. On a walk with his daughter, Aoife, on the Brighton Pier, Ed encounters Imaculée Constantin, out recruiting, and Dwight Silverwind (the New Age guru of *Cloud Atlas*), manning a fortune-teller's stand. At the wedding reception, Ed converses with Eilish, Holly's Irish great-aunt, who speaks knowingly of Holly's precognitive abilities and of the disappeared Jacko, reading Beckett, Spinoza, and Kant at the age of six, a "changling" who has informed her that he is "inside" Jacko, "a well-intentioned visitor ... keeping Jacko's memories safe" (258). In Part Three's climatic episodes, Aoife disappears, just as Jacko did, but only temporarily: in a sequence involving Ed and Dwight Silverwind, who mentions that he has been "scripted" to join him, and in a display of Holly's psychosoteric gifts, Aoife is found hiding in an empty room at the hotel at which they are staying for the wedding. A wedding and its aftermath, a journalistic account of a contemporary war, and flashes of another war taking place on the esoteric plane—all are conjoined in Part Three as contingent narratives that reveal the contradictions underlying tenuousness of existence and the fantasy of continuance: "they lived happily ever after" placed against "until death do us part" in a wedding ritual; the living death of "immortality" experienced by the Anchorites and the body counts of the real war that Ed Brubeck experiences when he is most alive.

In Part Four, the author Crispin Hershey engages in a world tour quite different from Ed Brubeck's tour of the world's battlefields. "The Lonely Planet of Crispin Hershey" can be viewed as a cosmopolitan novel unto itself, the location of each international literary festival Crispin visits in the quest to bolster his sagging career both locally distinct and globally connected. Crispin's impressions of Shanghai offer a revealing example:

> The Shanghai Bund is several things: a waterfront sweep of 1930's architecture with some ornate Toytown set-pieces along the way; a symbol of Western colonial arrogance; a symbol of the ascension of the modern Chinese state; four lanes of slow-moving, or no-moving traffic; and a raised promenade along the Huangpu river where flows a Walt Whitman throng of tourists, families, couples, vendors, pickpockets, friendless novelists, muttering drug-dealers and pimps... The sun disintegrates into evening and the skyscrapers over the river begin to

flouresce: there's a titanic bottle-opener; an outsize 1920's intersteller rocket; a supra-Ozymandian obelisk, plus supporting cast of mere forty, fifty, sixty-floor buildings, clustering skyward like a doomed game of Tetris.... When I was a boy the USA was synonymous with modernity, now it's here. So I carry on walking, imagining the past.... If city's have auras...then Shanghai's aura is the colour of money and power. It's emails can shut down factories in Detroit, denude Australia of its iron ore, strip Zimbabwe of its rhino horn, pump the Dow Jones full of either steroids or financial sewage... (343-4)

Here, Crispin provides a pocket history or lonely planet entry on global capitalism and modernity that reveals both the centrality and capriciousness of power over time. Serving as *The Bone Clocks*' flâneur without portfolio, Crispin's mobility and his perceptive, if jaded, authorial eye allow him to register psychogeographically the deep history and the global connectivity of cities like Shanghai and Cartagena, or islands like Iceland when he drives through the Asbygri Forest on a break from a festival in Reykjavík, and the prison island of Rottnest, near Perth, where he goes to see the famous lighthouse located there.

Crispin's tour also charts a sequence of meetings and a growing relationship with Holly Sykes, who has become a fellow author with the publication of her bestselling book, *The Radio People*, which recounts her childhood contacts with the "other world." Crispin is initially jealous of Holly's success, as he is of the success of any competitor for literary attention. Indeed, his authorial envy leads Crispin to pull a practical joke on a bitter adversary, literary critic Richard Cheeseman, last seen at Cambridge as a member of Hugo Lamb's crowd—one with disastrous consequences. Crispin hides a packet of cocaine in Cheeseman's luggage just before the celebrity critic departs for the airport in Colombia, and then alerts the customs authorities; the "joke," intended merely to generate an international scandal and embarrass Cheeseman, results instead in a long jail term in a Colombian prison for his unfortunate rival. Crispin feels guilty enough about the prank to lead an ongoing artist's initiative to "free Cheeseman," but not guilty enough to confess the truth.

At the same time, another side of Crispin Hershey and the key role he will play in the War of the Atemporals comes gradually into view as he is drawn into friendship with Holly, now a widow after her husband died in an attack in Syria. In several key episodes, Crispin experiences interruptions in his life's tour as he comes into involuntary contact with figures from another reality that lead to his unwitting fate, in death, as an encoded marker for

Esther Little's whereabouts. At Rottnest Island in 2017, he witnesses Holly having a psychosoteric "fit" in which she channels the voices of the aboriginal people who have been departed to and imprisoned on the island. At the 2019 Reykjavik Book Festival, he has an eerie encounter while on a wander in an Icelandic forest with Hugo Lamb, now an Atemporal, who interrogates him about Holly. Throughout his narrative, he recounts unplanned and unwanted run-ins with a strange woman, Soleil Moore, who attempts to impose upon him her chapbook of poetry entitled *Soul Carnivores*, and winds up stalking him to the scene of his demise in 2020. All of these occurrences, as well as his writing which contains coded messages between Horologists that have been channeled through him, signify Crispin's "unconscious" involvement in the ethereal conflict. As in the novel writ large, fantasy and social realism butt heads in "The Lonely Planet of Crispin Hershey," which gives Mitchell the occasion to parody the cult of authorial celebrity, advance the ongoing metafictional dimension of his work that reflexively deploys fictional devices to locate the reader in many worlds and multiple temporalities, and provide a richly detailed itinerary of earthly locales.

Above all, the annual encounters of Holly and Crispin described in Part Four trace a certain history, for we learn later that Esther Little, buried deep in Holly Sykes, has left signs of her location in Holly since 1984 for her colleagues to discover. These clues, scattered about in texts, minds, and bodies across decades, all "glimpses of the Script" (411), lead to the Blythewood cemetery where Crispin is buried and a meeting between Marinus and Holly that culminates in the seven-day Second Mission of the Atemporal War in April 2024. Part Five of the novel, "An Horologist's Labyrinth," told from Marinus' perspective, combines autobiography (perhaps the genre should be renamed for entities like Marinus, composed of several lives and selves), the detective novel, and other-worldly fantasy in depicting Marinus' sojourn over the centuries, his hunt for the location of Esther Little "in" Holly, and the final conflict (for now) between the Anchorites and the Horologists. The complexities of the battle that takes place in the dimension of the Chapel of Dusk are such that no summary could do it justice. Holly (now, "just" Holly, once Ester has evacuated her asylum) is drawn into it because her brother, Jacko, has been killed in the First Mission serving as a vehicle for Xi Lo, who may still somehow be alive in the Chapel of Dusk. And while the Horologists appear to have achieved a pyrrhic victory—almost all of the combatants die, though among the survivors are Marinus, who will live other days in other bodies, and Holly, who will live to the end of her natural life in Part Six thanks to her escape from Chapel via an underground labyrinth navigated by tracing the maze on her pendant—it is not entirely clear what has been won in this allegorical battle between those who live and die as one and those who evolve as many. For here, as throughout Mitchell's fiction, the question of survival hangs in the tenuous balance of the future.

The novel's aftermath suggests both how much and how little the trajectory of the future, collective and individual, is affected by the War of the Atemporals. True, a few lives have been saved: after all, the Anchorites, itself a select body of eight, only requires each member to "decant" the soul of one "engifted" with psychosoteric powers four times annually in order to "fuel their atemporality" (456). On the other hand, the planet as a whole has taken the predictable death-spiral course charted from the beginning of the novel, reflecting Mitchell's general view of civilization as self-destructive and transient. The sole remaining superpower of China (previously, America; previously, the Soviet Union; previously, the British Empire, etc.) wields its authority carelessly and unilaterally; the Earth is dying in the wake of global warming and nuclear meltdowns; the social order has nearly broken down entirely as gangs of raiders roam the landscape terrorizing and destroying what is left of communities; the very few are enormously rich; and the vast many barely survive. Holly Sykes has retreated to Sheep's Head (also known as Muntervary), a promontory jutting into the Celtic Sea in Cork County, Ireland, where she lives with her granddaughter, Lorelei, and an adopted boy, Rafiq, in a bungalow on ancestral lands owned by Mo Muntervary, the quantum physicist of *ghostwritten*. Lorelei has come to Holly after the death of her mother, Aoife, and her father, Örvar, in an airplane crash that occurred in 2036 when global-warming-induced "Gigastorm" hit, causing the downing of "theirs and two hundred other airliners crossing the Pacific" (549). Rafiq is a child refugee who has washed up on Irish shores and whom Holly adopts as her own. The year is 2043 and the times are more treacherous than usual within the parameters of a new normal that includes a return to the bartering system, a social order based primarily on agriculture, and survival heavily dependent upon the unreliable delivery of supplies from the government/corporate entity that operates within the protection zone.

In this tenuous social order, the political, racial, and class divisions of the past are in full operation as the populace barely gets by through a combination of survivalist techniques and technological remnants: there is an internet, but it is slow, unreliable, and on the verge of breaking down altogether, as are the aging computers and tablets used to access it; the bungalow is roofed with solar panels while Holly tends small "cash" crops that help to maintain the insulin supplies that must be delivered for the diabetic Rafiq. Holly mourns the passing of Aoife along with planet Earth destroyed by human hands:

It's not just that I can't hold Aoife again, it's everything: It's grief for the regions we deadlanded, the ice caps we melted, the Gulf Stream we redirected, the rivers we drained, the coasts we flooded, the lakes we choked with crap, the seas we killed, the species we drove to extinction, the pollinators we wiped out, the oil we squandered, the drugs we rendered impotent, the comforting liars we voted into office—all so we did not have to change our cozy lifestyles. (560)

Life, in short, is far from idyllic, but tenable, until the Chinese pull out of a protection and trade agreement with parts of Europe, including Ireland. The local village is destroyed in a battle between raiders and militia, and Mo, Holly, and the children retreat to the bungalow, where they are threatened by a group of militia who attempt to strip them of all usable possessions. In a narrative movement reminiscent of *Cloud Atlas*, at the moment when Holly is considering desperate alternatives to ensure at least the survival of the children, a ship arrives with a Swedish diplomatic official aboard, offering Lorelei asylum in Sweden as the child of a Swedish-born subject. Like the "Prescient I." of *Cloud Atlas*, having preserved the positive aspects of advanced technology in its ecological practices, Sweden in 2043 appears to be an enclave of civilization's continuance (with all of the ambiguous entailments that "civilization" offers) where the possibility of survival beyond bare life remains intact. The official is Marinus reborn (until this moment, Holly is not aware that he had survived the cataclysmic battle of Part Five), who, at Holly's urgent bidding, arranges for Rafiq to accompany Lorelei, saving him from a death sentence on Sheep's Head, where anarchy reigns and the insulin deliveries have ceased altogether. Thus having assured, at least temporarily, the salvation of dependents from the coming "Endarkment" (561) that will overtake much of Europe and the rest of the world as the power systems based on destructive technologies fail, Holly signs off on her life and the novel with an acceptance of mortality—the shelf life of her own bone clock—not as a vehicle of extinction but of tenuous continuance as she watches Lorelei and Rafiq depart: "Incoming waves erase all traces of the vanishing boat, and I'm feeling erased myself, fading away into an invisible woman. For a voyage to begin, another one must end, sort of" (624).

* * *

Holly's narrative in "Sheep's Head" makes it clear that the interacting narrative dimensions of *The Bone Clocks* exist as fabrications born of the collective need for explanatory stories of how everything came to be as it is, and how it will be in the future. All of them are "entirely man-made," as she says of the reality that existed before the Earth's winding down, which, in itself, is a narrative that crosses over and simultaneously contradicts the evolutionary, naturalistic, and supernatural narratives that the novel touches upon, operating behind the scenes of everyday life:

> For most of my life, the world shrank and technology progressed; this was the natural order of things. Few of us clocked on that "the natural order of things" is entirely man-made, and that a world that kept expanding as technology regressed was not only possible but waiting in the wings. Outside, the kids're playing with a frisbee older than any of them—look closely, you'll see the phantom outline of the London 2012 Olympics logo. (595)

If we consider Louis Althusser's foundational "Thesis 1" in "Ideology and Ideological State Apparatuses," "Ideology represents the imaginary relationship of individuals to their real conditions of existence" (*Lenin*, 162)—a relationship that is narratively represented as "the natural order of things"—then Holly's insight deepens our understanding of what Mitchell is attempting in providing a fantastic or paranormal "foundation" to the labyrinthine narrative architecture of the *Bone Clocks*. Althusser writes of the "ideological state apparatuses" or "ISA," made up of institutions of all kinds, including those of state, church, and education, that our "own devotion contributes to the maintenance and nourishment of th[e] ideological representation of the School, which makes the School today as 'natural,' indispensable-useful and even beneficial for our contemporaries as the Church was 'natural,' indispensable and generous for our ancestors a few centuries ago" (*Lenin*, 157). His critique of the false naturalness of the social order echoes Holly's reflections on a "man-made" world and her thoughts during an exchange with a local politico and right-wing religious fanatic in "Sheep's Head" who is trying to convert her to the party of faith: "The conversation heats up but I may as well be listening to children arguing about the acts and motives of Santa Claus. I've seen what happens after death, the Dusk and the Dunes, and it was as real to me as the chipped mug of tea in my hand…. There Is No God but the one we dream up … but my truth sounds no crazier than their faith, no saner either …" (574).

Many of the narratives of *The Bone Clocks* occur in settings that we commonly recognize as parts of the "natural" social order: school, resort, domicile, wedding reception hall, city, village, town hall, pub, and convention site; indeed, like *The Thousand Autumns*, much of the novel might be seen as a navigation of these bordered zones by multiple characters. The "other" narratives of the novel—whether the horrific and grotesque scenes of war in the Middle East, depictions of conflicts between entities operating in another spatiotemporal dimension, hallucinatory memories of redacted experiences, or the voice and memory of an alterity hiding within—intrude upon those taking place in conventional settings, giving the lie to the "naturalness" or "truth" associated with realism. Just as Mitchell often challenges the conventions of genre within the imaginary space of the novel and, particularly in *The Bone Clocks*, challenges the reader to accommodate high fantasy to social realism, so Holly, who has traversed multiple dimensions and realities within that space, questions the naturalness of any narrative that claims to be fundamental to the construction of a monolithic reality, whether it be technological or religious, identificatory or esoteric. For Holly, as for Mitchell, they are all "true" in that they have all had a defining relationship to "the conditions of existence" represented in the intersecting narratives and worlds of *The Bone Clocks*, and they are all "false" in their relation to any inherent claims they might make to being foundational, natural, or permanent. In the many metafictional gestures of *The Bone Clocks* (some of them sardonically self-referential, as when Crispin Hershey claims that "[i]n publishing it is easier to change your body than it is to switch genre" [295]) and the (re)cycling of narratives and narrative agencies over time in patterns of dispersal paralleled to the chronological narrative of Holly's life, Mitchell provides us with a deepened sense of the transient "truth" of narrative, available only in its passing and passing on.

The primary condition of existence—indeed, the only truth underlying orders natural and unnatural in *The Bone Clocks*—is that of mortality, time's perpetual dance partner. As we have seen in the itinerary of the novel's parts, the actuality of death or the fear and futile avoidance of it in an attempt to preserve the singularity of identity or the retention of power inform the novel's allegory of continuance and the counternarrative of time passing. As throughout Mitchell's fiction, in his sixth novel, the narrative fabric is threaded with time's circumstantiality as the present vanishes into pasts remembered and repressed, and prefigures futures that might have come to be in the rear-view mirror. The forms and shapes temporality takes in *The Bone Clocks* are as variable as the dimensions its characters inhabit. For Dave Sykes, Holly's father, time past, divisible into the artificial construct of the decade, is a refuge: speaking avuncularly to Ed Brubeck in a bathroom at the wedding bash, he opines that "[l]ife's more like science fiction by the day. It's not just that you get old and your kids leave: It's that the world zooms away and leaves you hankering for whatever decade you felt most comfy in" (246). Time becomes elastic when life-changing events occur. Examples include Holly's encounter with Rhîmes ("[b]ut I'm slowing, slowing...it's like the brake and the accelerator are being pressed at the same time...it's time slowing up or gravity pulling harder" [62]), Ed's recollection of the frantic moments before Aoife's birth ("a dash to the maternity ward, where Holly got axed and shredded alive by a whole new pain called childbirth; and clocks that went at six times the speed of time, until Holly was holding a glistening mutant in her arms" [289]), or Crispin Hershey's account of being lost in the Asbyrgi Forest just before he comes across Hugo Lamb ("[t]he glass of dusk is filling by the minute, and I don't really know where I left my Mitsubishi. I feel like Wells's time traveller separated from his time machine" [369]).

Echoing the centrality of time pieces in *blackswangreen*, watches, clocks, and time mementos of various kinds are to be found throughout the novel, including Holly's pendant, which can be regarded as a "souvenir" upon which is inscribed a labyrinth that she will have to navigate in the future. Various formulations of temporality, ranging from the trite to the profound, dot the novel's landscape. Moments before he is murdered, Ian of "A Hot Spell" glibly states to Holly, agog at seeing her first microwave oven, "The Future... Coming soon to a Present near you" (58); on the phenomenon of jet lag, Aoife, in generational voice, comments that "Australia and New Zealand're, like, invasion-proof. Any foreign army'd only get halfway up the beach before the time difference'd kick in, and they'd just like *woah*, and *collapse* in the sand and that'd be the invasion over" (333). More disturbingly, Hugo Lamb addresses Holly at the climactic moment of the Battle of the Second Mission as "a desiccated embryo, a Strudlebug... a veined, scrawny, dribbling... bone clock, whose face betrays how very, very little time you have left" (526; ellipses in text). Time comes to a halt altogether when the Anchorites or the Horologists "hiatus" a mortal, fast-forwarding them instantaneously to a different time altogether, or when Holly has one of her daymares, when she skips several hours forward in chronological time. Throughout the novel, characters experience the splitting of time as they mentally bilocate—Ed Brubeck from Iraq to the wedding in Brighton; Holly from the byways of the Kentish marshes to imagined concurrent scenes of life at home in Gravesend; and Crispin Hershey, simultaneously occupying past and future as he approaches Richard Cheeseman's hotel room to "extract his due" as a "minnow of déjà vu darts by" (322).

These figures of temporality, and dozens of others that occur in the novel, suggest the degree to which time is material in *The Bone Clocks*. Both the worldly and fantasy plots and subplots of the novel can be considered, in part, as responses to the omnipresence of mortality, or identity at its limits, as the consequence of time passing and of the fact that we are all historical entities. The range of responses that Mitchell offers in *The Bone Clocks* runs from that of the Anchorites, who seek to preserve a single "soul" within an unchanging body (more precisely, the static body that they possessed upon entering the order) for as long as inhumanly possible, to the example of Holly Sykes, whose response to her own near-future death at the end of the novel is to ensure a future for her granddaughter and the stranger who has come into their midst (Rafiq) through an act of hospitality. In between, there are a host of characters caught up in this drama of temporality whose identities are shaped in relation to mortality and circumstance. Ed Brubeck is drawn to scenes of political violence and the devastation it brings to bodies and cultures for personal reasons (he seeks something other than the boredom of the everyday in a kind of death wish brought about by overwhelming guilt) as well as a self-sacrificial sense of responsibility for telling the stories of the unknown dead. Crispin Hershey, possessed of a guilty conscience born of envy and the need to preserve a singular authorial identity, is caught up by chance and his largely unacknowledged attraction to Holly Sykes in the War of the Atemporals. While it turns out that what he regards as chance has been "scripted," thus a matter of "fate," the larger terrain of *The Bone Clocks* is so replete with dreams, visions, fortunes, prefigurations, and impaired memories that the script itself is in question as determinate in any way, and the singularity of identity—for Crispin, a matter of "authorial intention" at its limits—subject to a chaotic conflict of forces, both temporal and atemporal.

The Horologists are subject to the same forces: indeed, mortality and a constant shifting between bodies, identities, and chronotopes as the registrars of historical accumulation is their métier. As the embodiments of time's measurement across the ages (in comparison to "normals," whose "bone clocks" measure only the hours of a single life), they bear some resemblance to Benjamin's "angel of history," a figure arising from his response to Klee's *Angelus Novus*:

> His eyes are staring, his mouth is open, his wings are spread. This is how one pictures the angel of history. His face is turned toward the past. Where we perceive a chain of events, he sees one single catastrophe which keeps piling wreckage upon wreckage and hurls it in front of his feet. The angel would like to stay, awaken the dead, and make whole what has been smashed. But a storm is blowing from Paradise; it has got caught in his wings with such violence that the angel can no longer close them. The storm irresistibly propels him into the future to which his back is turned, while the pile of debris before him grows skyward. This storm is what we call progress. ("Theses," 257)

Benjamin's figure, reflecting the cultural devastation wrought by a first world war and the commencement of a second, is apocalyptic as it presides over a past in ruins and a future disavowed, its back turned to what is to come.[4] Like

Benjamin's angel, the Horologists of *The Bone Clocks* have been involuntary witnesses to multiple histories over time—those of discrete individuals as well as empires, nations, and regimes. They have watched history accumulate, and they are a form of historical accumulation themselves as they move from body to body and identity to identity, amassing knowledge, experience, and memory over generations. They are, in a sense, double agents since, rather than consuming the souls of the bodies they inhabit, they conjoin with them, each new element of the identity-assemblage becoming part of the whole. They are both one and many, both singular and plural, both transhistorical and confined by the history of a single subject at any given time. Ultimately, they are doubly mortal, for death precedes their passage to each new body, many deaths thus enabling their longitudinal continuance, which has its own mortal limit should death within an identity occur before there is "time" to migrate to another.

Benjamin's angel has its back to the future; in the allegorical register of *The Bone Clocks*, the Horologists are, by contrast, like Jacob de Zoet on the prow of ship returning to Holland, looking back at Dejima, Janus-eyed. As it moves from 1984 to 2043, the novel's six parts proceeds by turns through time chronologically, presciently, and through recursive flashbacks and recovered memories as characters cross paths and experience intrusions from the Atemporal dimension. Thus, as a narrative aggregate, *The Bone Clocks* dwells both in the past and the future at the same time. So, too, do the novel's Horologists who, like Marinus, remembers his first meeting with Ester Little in the 1870s. At the time, the oldest known Atemporal with "a metalife stretching back approximately seven millenia" (432), Esther is inhabiting an aboriginal identity named "Moombaki." Flashing back to their initial encounter in Australia 150 years later from a point in the future that, according to the timescale of a single mortal life, is both distant from the time of that meeting and near to our own contemporaneity, Marinus recalls,

> Esther and I sat across the fire from each other at the mouth of her small cave and subspoke about empires, their ascents and falls; about cities, shipbuilding, industry; slavery, the dismemberment of Africa, the genocide of Van Dieman's Land; farming, husbandry, factories, telegraphs, newspapers, printing, mathematics, philosophy, law, and money and a hundred other topics. I felt like Lucas Marinus, lecturing in the houses of the Nagasaki scholars. (434)

For Horologists, age is as important as it is for normal mortals. The scale of one's perspective on mortality and the relation of past to present and future shifts over time—the younger one is, the more distant seems the future and the temporal limitations consonant with the inhabitation of an identity; the older one is, the more distant the past seems. This scalar aspect of human mortal time is dramatically emphasized in this conversation between the two Atemporals whose existences are composed of an indeterminate number of consecutive life spans, the scale of Esther's seven millennia unthinkably large in comparison to Marinus' relatively paltry number of centuries, in itself unthinkably large in comparison to the biblical "three score years and ten" of normal life expectancy.[5] As they consider the passing of the centuries and countless mortal lives, for both Marinus and Esther, the sense of the future is entirely dependent on the sense of how much time one can expect to have. Here, more than in any previous work, Mitchell makes it clear that temporality—the quanta of past and future—is limned by mortality as the impossible "outside" of time.

When we get to it, the future in *The Bone Clocks*—that of its final part— looks a lot like Benjamin's pile of debris growing skyward, an apocalyptic storm blowing through that portends, if nothing else, the end of many aspects of modern existence as portrayed in the life and recollections of Holly Sykes and those connected with her. The utopic future promised by technocratic capitalism—universal access to knowledge, information, and an infinite array of products in a global consumerist social order—has mutated during the single generation of Holly's lifetime into its dystopic counterpart: the planet is suffering the inevitable consequences of runaway global warming, technology (the solution) has become technology (the problem) with a nuclear meltdown taking place downwind of Holly's village, and Europe has become a third world to the economic superpower of China as the world repurposes the same politics and brutal, divisive strategies that got it here in the first place.

While *Cloud Atlas* depicted a primitivistic "far" future as the fate awaiting modernity, *The Bone Clocks* speeds up the humanly induced processes that may lead to Western civilization's downfall in portraying the disastrous "near" future associated with Holly Sykes's life span. The urgency of the future raises the stakes of mortality in Mitchell's sixth novel, for the survival of all of the interconnected parts of the social order is in question: person, village, nation, region, and planet. On one level, the near-future dystopia of *The Bone Clocks* is a matter of the same old same old, just with different players: the thirst for power, territorial brutality, divisive politics, religious intolerance, and the destruction of nature—all of the maladies of the present and of the deep past in Mitchell's many narratives of civilization's rise and fall remain fully in place, even as the social order has become chaotic. On the other hand, the world really is on the brink in 2043, at the end of Holly's life, which suggests that, for Mitchell, the single lifetime—"threescore years and ten"—must remain the yardstick for measuring what the future might be. Holly's life is exemplary in this sense, for it is a life that leads to the survival of a generation to follow, and the tentative possibility of a future—perhaps a better one—beyond herself. At the same time, if the allegory of the Atemporals is folded into the picture as Ester Little is folded into Holly, the single lifetime is not really single, but a collective assemblage of pasts, memories, and experiences that took place elsewhere, in other bodies, times, and worlds. Even more, the collectivity of identity that Mitchell fictionalizes works both vertically and horizontally, back to the past, into the future, and across the present in the connectivity to be seen in the concurrent parallel lives and worlds of his novels. Futures, near or far, are not fated to be the way they are in *The Bone Clocks* or *Cloud Atlas*; as the metafictional gestures of Mitchell's fiction writ large surely indicate, these are narrative trajectories that arise out of the constellations of plot, character, topography, and concept that he invents. But the invention manifests a belief: that futures *do* depend on what "we"—one and many, mortals all—have done with the past, what we do in the present, and how we relate and change the story of what will have happened in what is still to come.

Epilogue: Toward a Fiction of the Future

Ever since the reviewer of *The Thousand Autumns of Jacob de Zoet* for *Washington Post* made the comment that David Mitchell is "the novelist who has been showing us the future of fiction" (Charles, n.p.), I have been pondering both the veracity and the implications of that statement. That Mitchell's fiction takes on the future—its possibility, its inevitability or unpredictability, and its wholly provisional nature—is unquestionable; the many ways in which the future is figured as a condition of temporality in Mitchell's work has been a dominant concern of this book. But the degree to which his work actually shows *a* future for fiction (Mitchell himself would reject the "the" of reviewer's formulation) is another matter altogether, especially in a time when the future of the novel seems to be in doubt, as it always has been in one form or another since its inception as a genre.

In the wake of the novel's apparent apogee in the form of the three-deckers of the nineteenth century, its death notices have appeared with increasing regularity throughout the twentieth century and into the twenty-first. Most recently as of this writing, there is the example of Mitchell's fellow British novelist Will Self proclaiming, in a *Guardian* piece entitled "The Novel Is Dead (This Time It's for Real)," that "The literary novel as an art work and a narrative art form central to our culture is indeed dying before our eyes." Self specifies further:

> I do not mean narrative prose fiction *tout court* is dying... nor do I mean that serious novels will either cease to be written or read. But what is already no longer the case is the situation that obtained when I was a young man. In the early 1980s, and I would argue throughout the second half of the last century, the literary novel was perceived to be the prince of art forms, the cultural capstone and the apogee of creative endeavour. The capability words have when arranged sequentially to both mimic the free flow of human thought and investigate the physical expressions and interactions of thinking subjects; the way they may be shaped into a believable simulacrum of either the commonsensical world, or any number of invented ones; and the capability of the extended prose form itself, which, unlike any other art form, is able to enact self-analysis, to describe other aesthetic modes and even mimic them. (Self, n.p.)

What are the reasons for the death of the literary novel, a "type" eloquently summarized in a description that could be an apt characterization of the novels of David Mitchell? For Self, the answer lies in "the active resistance" of contemporary culture "to difficulty in all its aesthetic manifestations, accompanied by a sense of grievance that conflates it with political elitism" (n.p.). For David Shields, no enemy to the literary novel or aesthetic difficulty, the question is more about the contemporary relevance of the novel than its demise, and the answer more time-bound as he diagnoses the passing away of the "traditional novel," inferentially equivalent to Self's "literary novel": "Why is the traditional novel c. 2013 no longer germane (and the postmodern novel shroud upon shroud)? Most novels' glacial pace isn't congruous with the speed of our lives" (Shields, 196). Shields goes on to list other traditional irrelevancies—a fascination with the myth of individual "consciousness" in the age of genetic cloning and DNA mapping, the "tidy coherence of most novels" that "belies the chaos and entropy that surround and inhabit and overwhelm us" (196–97), the hardwired self-reflexivity of fiction. What is wanted instead, Shields argues, what would be more "germane," is a form that possesses "as thin a membrane as possible between life and art" (197).

For Will Self, the literary novel is dead because of the aesthetic demands it makes upon readers too impatient to engage in the difficulties of close reading; for David Shields, the traditional novel is irrelevant because it is out of sync with the hurriedness of contemporary life and is too "thick," creating too dense a layer of mediation between the reader—with his multitasking ways, her Google-searching need for immediate, interactive access to information—and "reality." Other forms of the question about the incipient, recent, or not-so-recent death of the novel along with the reasons for its passing abound: indeed, a quick googling of "death of the novel" yields several days worth of reading for which, naturally, we have no time. While Self and Shields are at intellectual loggerheads on the issue—Self mourns the loss of our tolerance for difficulty; Shields waves the traditional novel a cheerful goodbye as he embraces new forms that satisfy our apparent need for ultimate transparency—and while they have quite different ideas about what "the novel" is in the first place, both refer to the novel's mortality in terms that have clear relevance to the novels of David Mitchell. Mitchell's novels, I have suggested, are both traditional and experimental; they are "literary," in Self's sense, inherently "difficult" and complex, and yet readily engage in thinner-skinned popular genres—the thriller, the airport novel, sci-fi. A single Mitchell novel, indeed, a single *chapter* of a Mitchell novel, often combines intensive descriptive realism with high fantasy, dreamscape and hallucination, and reflexive formal experimentation. Given this, does the death-of-the-novel question apply to the fiction of David Mitchell, to the future of (his) fiction?

A partial response lies in one of the signature features of Mitchell's fiction: its navigation of genres and its peripatetic impulses in the portrayal of multiple intersecting realities and worlds. The novel has always been a hybrid entity, assimilating other genres into its own "cannibalistic" assemblage.[1] Indeed, the word "genre" itself is associated with kind, kin, and gene, and the intermixing of these in various forms, offshoots, hybrid, and amalgams. We have seen how Mitchell "mixes" genres in his fiction, not just as a metafictional exercise or a tour-de-force, but because the forms, narrative trajectories, and linguistic specificities of a given genre are the elements of an emergent fictional world that mingles with others in the traversal and hybridization of multiple genres that occurs in all of his novels. The result has formal, identificatory, aesthetic, and philosophical consequences. As the novel is made up of mixed forms that will continue to evolve into new imaginative phyla and species, so human identities, as represented in Mitchell's novels, are conceived as hybridities in their singularity and as collectivities inhabiting multiple universes that connect across time and space through gene, narrative, and memory.

How humans will "evolve" in the future is, for Mitchell, an open question: indeed, "evolve" is a wrong word, since it often indicates a progressive development in body or consciousness moving toward greater complexity or enlightenment. The future is far too tenuous and unpredictable in Mitchell's novels for it to be read as a site for "evolution" in these senses. Perhaps a better word is "adapt." In Mitchell's novels, those who survive into the future adapt to circumstances in the two dramatically opposed ways illustrated by the allegory of *The Bone Clocks*: either in the naturalistic mode of survival of the fittest and the most powerful rooted in the old singular story of the ego or by accommodating a changing sense of human identity as collective, worldly, beyond oneself and one's own mortality in a counterintuitive "giving up" of the sole self. Both paths are explored in Mitchell's futures, formally and thematically. For him, what is always at risk, in the mix of human desire fulfilling its goals, the serendipitous course of unfolding events in patterns prefigured or coincidental, and the collisions of identities and agendas that make up history, is the continuance of life—not just human life—on the planet. It is a risk that should be clearer to us as each day passes. Mitchell's confrontation of this risk in novel after novel is the clearest sign of his imaginative investment in having a future.

As I have discussed his fiction in this book, it is apparent that for Mitchell the work of the novel is twofold. First, as a hybrid "post-genre" itself, the novel formally incorporates multiple narratives taking place on different spatiotemporal planes and dimensions. The novel's commitment in Mitchell's hands is, thus, to manifest connections, syncopations, and collisions between narrative contact zones, wherever these linkages may lead us. Second, the novel offers for Mitchell an imaginative space for figuring out how multiple narratives, brought together in varying combinations, might affect and transform the future in relation to many pasts and an ongoing present where happenstance and intention conspire. The possibilities offered in regarding the novel and its shaping as a channeling of compound stories and a navigation of many worlds include that of a different story emerging in the future, often a story of difference within, like that of Sonmi~451 or Holly Sykes, that will radically change the narrative as it is being formulated.

For Mitchell, the important thing is that the stories get passed on in their mutability and capacity for alternation. We might compare this summation of Mitchell's investments in the transmission of narrative to that of Mr. Compson's evocative speech to his son, Quentin, in Faulkner's *Absalom, Absalom!*:

> We have a few old mouth-to-mouth tales; we exhume from old boxes and trunks and drawers letters without salutation or signature, in which men and women who once lived and breathed are now merely initials or nicknames out of some incomprehensible affection which sound to us like Sanskrit or Chocktaw; we see dimly people, the people in whose living blood and seed we ourselves lay dormant and waiting, in this shadowy attenuation of time possessing now heroic proportions, performing their acts of simple passion and simple violence, impervious to time and inexplicable... They are there, yet something is missing; they are like a chemical formula exhumed along with the letters from that forgotten chest, carefully, the writing old and faded and falling to pieces... you bring them together in the proportions called for, but nothing happens; you re-read, tedious and intent, poring, making sure that you have forgotten nothing, made no miscalculation; you bring them together again and again [but] nothing happens: just the words, the symbols, the shapes themselves, shadowy inscrutable and serene, against that turgid background of a horrible and bloody mischancing of human affairs. (80)

Mr. Compson's gazes to the past as a time of "heroic proportions" and the present as the site of the future "dormant." From his perspective, the future itself is under erasure because the attempt to bring the lives and stories of the past into consonance, in "the proportions called for," has failed. Mr. Compson's past-obsessed, fatalistic view of narrative possibility is far from Faulkner's own (though perhaps uncomfortably close to the "death of the novel" views of Self and Shields), but it is indicative of the extent to which Faulkner regards the novel as a form dedicated to reincarnating the past in the present, or as the "most splendid failure" to do so.[2] This clearly contrasts with Mitchell's perspective on the novel as a site for testing the relation of possible futures to what will have come before in hindsight as the circumstantiality of the past. While Faulkner and Mitchell both see the important relationship between narrative continuance and temporality—both, in quite different ways, equating the transmission of stories as integral to the survival of the species—Faulkner views the past as the repository of the future, while Mitchell, appositely, regards the future as the repository of the past, and in this, he figures a future for the novel premised on forms of engagement and identity not fully comprehended in the "death of the novel" debate.

The many rebirths, transmigrated souls, and identities of Mitchell's fiction, the dystopic portrayals of utopia gone wrong, the cross-hatched narrative collisions and collusions leading to surprising results, the hidden or untold stories revealing a past only visible in the future, the demands on the reader to make her own connections between rhizomic and reappearing narrative threads, trajectories, and characters across his novels—all speak to the notion of a body of work pointed toward a future of relating and retelling stories, changing them as new specificities and details come to the fore. As I have discussed throughout this book, Mitchell's narratology is deeply linked to his portrayals of identity as collective alterities (the "others" within and without, across time and worlds, conflated with the "one" of the I), and his view of human survival as a narrative problem, as well as a political, climatological, and economic problem. Above all, his narrative work is "about" time, and how our temporary condition in any tense—our difference from ourselves from moment to moment—is the only constant, in the present, on planet Earth in the twenty-first century. In his novels, Mitchell affords us the opportunity to achieve, as Kenneth Burke states it in *Permanence and Change*, "an altered conception as to how the world is put together" (81), and he does so by inviting us, as readers, to participate in the "putting together" of the worlds he creates as assemblages.[3] We can then consider the novels of David Mitchell as models for thinking about the future, and our transitive role in making it, without any guarantees beyond that of perennial change in our temporary inhabiting of the world.

Notes

Introduction

1 This second-oldest of British literary prizes, its first award made in 1942, unfortunately has been suspended since 2011 for lack of funding; in addition to Mitchell, it has gone to a remarkable succession of young writers who have gone on to become major figures, including Margaret Drabble, V.S. Naipaul, Angela Carter, and Jeanette Winterson.
2 Robert Alter's *Partial Magic: The Novel as a Self-Conscious Genre* remains the most compelling discussion of metafictional reflexivity in the history of the novel.
3 My use of the word "thick" here follows Clifford Geertz's notion of "thick description" in ethnographic narrative, where the anthropologist/narrator must be attentive to "a multiplicity of complex conceptual structures, many of them superimposed upon or knotted into one another, which are at once strange, irregular, and inexplicit, and which he must contrive somehow first to grasp and then to render" (Geertz, 5). In this introduction and the readings to follow, I will be suggesting the several ways in which Mitchell's fictional techniques are analogous to the ethnographic approach to "other" cultures that Geertz famously recommends.
4 My use of the term "hybridity" here and throughout this book reflects the notion of both the grafting or mixing of species and genres, and the now familiar sense of the term generated by Homi Bhabha's *The Location of Culture*, which regards hybridity in the formation of identities and communities outside or beyond the dominant culture/species as enabling "difference without an assumed or imposed hierarchy." For Bhabha, this concept is deeply historical, and offers the possibility of a different horizon for the future other than the trajectory laid out by Western imperialism: "The social articulation of difference, from the minority perspective, is a complex, on-going negotiation that seeks to authorize cultural hybridities that emerge in moments of historical transformation" (Bhabha, 2). Mitchell's fiction, as I will discuss it, is "hybrid" in terms of form, style, and the thematic throughlines observable across his novels.
5 Perhaps coincidentally, in his review of *Gods and Men* in the *New York Times Book Review*, Douglas Coupland invents the term "Translit" as "a new literary genre" that includes Kunzru's novel along with Mitchell's *Cloud Atlas* and Michael Cunningham's *The Hours* (1998) as works that "cross history without being historical; they span geography without changing psychic space. Translit collapses time and space as it seeks to generate narrative traction in the reader's mind. It inserts the contemporary reader into other locations and times, while leaving no doubt that its viewpoint is relentlessly

modern and speaks entirely of our extreme present" (Coupland, 10). There is much to disagree with in this reductive formulation as it applies to Mitchell—or Cunningham and Kunzu for that matter; not the least troubling of Coupland's errors here is that he contradicts himself in asserting that "Translit" "collapses time and space" while, at the same time, inserting the reader into "other times and locations." Still, Coupland's notion of the "new genre" of Translit along with LeClair's more illuminating conceptualization of the anthropological novel suggest that Mitchell is at the center of significant developments in the contemporary novel in the age of globalization.

6 For a (now) classic discussion of encyclopedic narrative, see Mendelson; for a revealing set of discussions of contemporary encyclopedic fiction, see LeClair 1989; for an equally revealing book-length consideration of fiction as palimpsest—a form that radiates encyclopedic tendencies—by the editor of the first collection of essays on Mitchell, see Dillon 2007.

7 For an excellent book-length discussion of this history, see Coverley.

8 In Mitchell's own comment on islands, it would appear that he sees islands quite differently than this description suggests. Asked about his "obsession" with islands by an interviewer, Mitchell responds, "Islands are controllable.... There's no vastness on an island. The perplexity of vastness isn't something that troubles you on an island. In a way, a novel is an island as well. It's got its own shores and borders and a horrible little tyrant rules over it and says what goes on" (Jewell, n.p.). In Mitchell's fiction, this view of islands may be, indeed, part of the story. But in comparing (tongue firmly in cheek) his novels to islands and himself to a "horrible little tyrant," he is indicating by contraries the story's other side: Mitchell's "islands" may indeed be ruled over by an author whose plotting is intricate and whose signature becomes more visible with each succeeding novel, but they are also multifarious entities that provide manifold opportunities for the reader to steer her own course, discovering along the way connections and signifying chains that do not necessarily proceed from authorial intention or control.

9 Many readers will recognize the phraseology that I employ here and throughout the book when speaking of plateaus and rhizomes as that of Deleuze and Guattari (no doubt among those poststructuralist philosophers the early 1990s Cambridge in-crowd would refer to along with Roland Barthes at the pub), who define "plateau" in Geoffrey Bateson's terms as "a continuous, self-vibrating region of intensities whose development avoids any orientation toward a culminating point or external end" (Deleuze and Guattari, 22). In a restrictive sense, Mitchell's islands are "self-vibrating region[s] of intensities" notable for their provisional state, though they often have an orientation or end within their own temporal and spatial parameters (a ship sails toward its destination; a community of enslaved workers observes its mandated daily rituals). Collectively, however, as the many "islands" that make up the assemblage of Mitchell's fiction circumstantially interconnect across time and space, their orientation, and the reader's orientation toward them, changes in the to and fro of reading.

10 For another take on metamodernism, see James and Seshagiri.
11 Mitchell's implicit interest in the "many worlds interpretation" of quantum mechanics is evident in Muntervary's and Sachs' reflections on temporality, though more clearly manifest in his deployment of multiple genres and stories taking place in different spatiotemporal zones. One of the founding physicists advocating the many worlds' interpretation is Paul Davies, who explains it for a lay audience in this way:

> One argument stems from the "big bang" theory: according to the standard model, shortly after the universe exploded into existence about 14 billion years ago, it suddenly jumped in size by an enormous factor. This "inflation" can best be understood by imagining that the observable universe is, relatively speaking, a tiny blob of space buried deep within a vast labyrinth of interconnected cosmic regions. Under this theory, if you took a God's-eye view of the multiverse, you would see big bangs aplenty generating a tangled melee of universes enveloped in a superstructure of frenetically inflating space. Though individual universes may live and die, the multiverse is forever. (Davies, n.p.)

In Mitchell's fiction, there are no "god's-eye" views, but there is the sense conveyed that his characters inhabit any number of possible story-worlds resulting in a "tangled melee of universes."

Chapter 1

1 Dillon suggests that Mitchell's use of numbers—particularly the number nine—reflects a structural principle, a way of organizing his "twenty-first century house of fiction," occupied by a "cast of characters who move from room to room, unencumbered by divisions in time and space" (*David Mitchell: Critical Essays*, 6); Childs and Green complicate this perception in stating that "[t]hree of David Mitchell's novels to date were conceived in nine parts, and yet none is actually so" (25). The use of nine as intimating structure and completion and, at the same time, less than the sum of the whole is further evidence of the antinomies of unity and disparity, estrangement and fellowship, and simultaneity and asynchrony that I explore in this chapter.
2 A year after the publication of *ghostwritten*, Haruki Murakami, discussed in the introduction as one of Mitchell's primary influences, published a collection of interviews with gas attack victims along with his essay on the event entitled *Underground: The Tokyo Gas Attack and the Japanese Psyche* (2000). The coincidence of the first chapter of Mitchell's novel and Murakami's book being devoted to this catastrophic event is notable; in rhetoric that resonates with "cross-hatching" of seeing and unseeing

(acknowledgment and disavowal) that typifies the narrative work of *ghostwritten*, Murakami writes in *Underground* that in order to understand the attacks, and terrorism in general, it is necessary to recognize the "them" of the terrorists as part of the larger "us" of the nation or planet: "We will get nowhere as long as the Japanese continue to disown the Aum 'phenomenon' as something completely other, an alien presence viewed through binoculars on the far shore. Unpleasant though the prospect might seem, it is important that we incorporate 'them, to some extent, within that construct called 'us'... by failing to look for the key buried under our own feet, where it might be visible to the naked eye, by holding the phenomenon at such a distance we are in danger of reducing its significance to a microscopic level" (Kindle Edition; Locations 4165–72).

3. My use of "thin" to describe the assemblage of information networks that comprise virtual reality is purely descriptive; as I have suggested in the Introduction, this is in comparison to Geertz's notion of the "thick description" that characterizes Mitchell's writing. Mitchell is at once interested in the connectivity of information and neural networks at the same time that he wishes to suggest that there are multiple dimensions or layers beyond the cognitively mapped or known, and that it is the dense and open-ended interconnectivity of these that constitutes the substance of narrative writing. For a different understanding of networks and connections in *ghostwritten* based on general systems theory, see Ballard.

4. A startling passage in the novel encapsulates the combination of natural forces and unnatural political policies that contributed to the famine when the old woman recalls a visit from a monk: "A monk called that day. His skin wrapped his hungry face tightly. 'According to Mao's latest decree, the new enemies of the proletariat are sparrows, because they devour China's seeds. All the children have to chase the birds with clanging things until the birds drop out of the sky from exhaustion. The problem is, nothing's eating the insects, so the Village is overrun by crickets and caterpillars and bluebottles. There are locust clouds in Sichuan. This is what happens when men play at gods and do away with sparrows'" (128–29).

5. For a discussion of the contradictions of hospitality as central to the examination of nationalism and identity politics in which the host or master of the house and the guest, self and other, or native and foreigner both counter and constitute each other, see Derrida's *Of Hospitality*.

6. The term "singularity" has multiple valences in a number of disciplines, from philosophy and cultural theory to astronomy and computer studies. I use it initially in a very general sense as indicative of the notion that each human identity is in some way transhistorically unique, a concept that moves very easily from individuals to nations in narratives of national exceptionalism and manifest destiny. The intensive interconnectedness of characters in Mitchell's narratives contests this notion of singularity in that they reflect Derrida's far more complex notion of singularity as a plurality of others. Insisting on the absolute alterity of each "other" (and, therefore,

each "self"), Derrida suggests that existence is a matter of living for the vast assemblage of others that constitute, in other terms, community or world, rather than engaging in the sole project of building one's own identity or viewing the purpose of life as a journey to self-fulfillment traced through an identificatory quest narrative. The difference between these concepts of singularity has dramatic consequences for cosmopolitan ethics, identity politics, and the concentric or eccentric relationship between self, nation, and world—all matters of deep interest for Mitchell in his fiction. See Derrida (1997); see also Morin for an illuminating discussion of Derrida and Nancy on singularity and community.

7   In this book, I do not delve into Mitchell's interest in Buddhism, which mentions occasionally in interviews. One recent interviewer summarizes: "He talks nostalgically about Japan, revealing that while he isn't a Buddhist—'in terms of the afterlife, I'm a reasonably content agnostic'—he does practise Zen Buddhist techniques he learned 15 years ago in Okinawa" (Eyre, n.p.). Stephenson refers to this interest in citing Mitchell's BBC interview where he remarks on the "marking" of characters in *ghostwritten* and *Cloud Atlas* with comet-shaped birthmarks as signs of "the same soul reincarnated" (238)—indicative, Stephenson suggests, of Mitchell's ongoing concern with the exposition of many worlds and multiple universes.

8   There is a famous painting entitled *Eve and the Serpent* (1907), but by Henri Rousseau, the French Post-Impressionist; the Hermitage does contain several paintings by Eugene Delacroix, including *Lion Hunt in Morocco* (1854) and *Moroccan Saddling a Horse* (1855), but again, both "Lemuel Delacroix" and his painting are entirely fictional, which provides an additional layer of complexity to the chapter's engagement with questions of originality and forgery, and the simulation of life through art.

9   This foreshadows the reverse effect seen in *Cloud Atlas*, where the contemporary adventures of Timothy Cavendish have been transformed into a film seen centuries later by Sonmi~451, a "fabricant" slave living in twenty-second-century Seoul. Here, the film is described as having been seen before the narrative upon which the film is based will have been read. Such intermedial reversals are intrinsic to Mitchell's fiction.

10 This gloss on the "twinning" of (sexual) desire and economy in "Petersburg" is informed by Jean-François Lyotard's *Libidinal Economy*, where he asserts that "the system of capital" manifests "libidinal values" or "pulsations of desire" that reveal the sexualization of an economic system that commodifies desire (Lyotard, 82); for this reason, Lyotard views the prostitute as the most visible agent of capitalism. See Lyotard, pp. 43–94; 155–200.

11 Following in a succession of thinkers about the wanderer in the city that runs from Charles Baudelaire to the French sociologist Georges Simmel, Benjamin considers the flâneur to be an embodiment of the modern metropolitan subject; see, in addition to *Baudelaire*, *The Arcades Project*, pp. 416–55.

12 For a seminal overview of the merging of mathematics, quantum physics, and philosophy that underlies "many worlds" theories such as that to which

Mo refers, see Penrose's *The Road to Reality*. This reference, like those which link capitalism and sexuality, or Buddhism and "the music of chance" in *ghostwritten*, is a clear instance of Mitchell's "interdisciplinary" perspective discussed in the Introduction.

13 The character of Bat Segundo appears to be a conflation of such figures as Howard Stern and Larry King (in the United States), or Nick Abbott and James Stannage (in the United Kingdom). In 2004, Edward Champion established the "Bat Segundo Show" podcast in the name of Mitchell's character. The show is comprised largely of interviews with contemporary writers and artists in conversation with "Mr. Segundo," who, according to the show's website, "is believed [to be] 49 years old, although he often claims to be younger. Mr. Segundo suffered some unspecified indignity sometime in the 1980s, which is vaguely alluded to within the show's introductions. He spends most of his time living in a Motel 6 room and is very fond of tequila" (http://www.edrants.com/segundo/about). Currently, the show has exceeded 450 podcasts featuring an extraordinary range of contemporary writers; the interview with David Mitchell, discussing the recently published *Cloud Atlas* by telephone, was the first Bat Segundo Show broadcast conducted on October 6, 2004.

14 Zookeeper might be then seen as a frustrated embodiment of Walter Benjamin's historical materialist whose "weak messianic power" allows him or her to discern in the debris of the past a path toward a redemptive or orderly future in the instantaneous present, but whose powers are primarily observational, and who is entirely upon the disparities and incomplete patterns of the past to, in effect, do his or her work (*Illuminations*, 254).

15 This description of a "fractionally coherent object" derives from John Law's *Aircraft Stories*, which develops a philosophy of the object in "technoscience" based on the building of a military airplane. Viewing a novel and an airplane as homologous fractionally coherent objects seems particularly appropriate given the interdisciplinary reach of *ghostwritten* and its development of embodiments of artificial or alien intelligence such as Quancog and the noncorporeal sentient intelligence.

16 For an illuminating discussion of how this Derridean notion of temporality interfaces with representations of utopia in Mitchell's novels, see Edwards.

17 For a discussion of this paradox in Nabokov's *Pale Fire*, see my *Passionate Doubts*: pp. 3–22.

Chapter 2

1 Posadas reflects upon the moment in Eiji's dream, late in the novel, of an imaginary conversation with John Lennon in the realm of the dead, when "John Lennon tells Eiji that '#9dream' is a descendant of 'Norwegian Wood'. One can of course read this literally as Lennon talking about songs he has written, but it also simultaneously points to the title of the novel itself and

2   It is interesting to compare Eiji's relation to his father with that of Jason Taylor in *blackswangreen*: in quite different ways (and at different ages—Eiji is twenty; Jason is twelve), they become disenchanted with what Robert Con Davis has termed "the romance of paternal authority" (Davis, 3) or an acculturated narrative of the father that regards his power as natural and essential, both in its withholding and its transference, to the son's identity formation. In *Number9Dream*, Eiji recognizes that the power he has conferred upon his fiction of a father is vestigial and self-ordained. Once he comes to see his father as an empty vessel, he can reject him, though not without a consequent emptying of himself, which suggests that the *narrative* efficacy of the father in the construction of the self is extant as a still-powerful remnant, even when demythologized. In *blackswangreen*, as will be more fully elaborated in Chapter 4, Jason's adolescent recognition that his father has no power in the world at large does not inspire rejection, but a form of sadness at the loss of a narrative (the paternal romance) that, like narratives of national exceptionalism or romantic genius, had formed the basis for a cohesive childhood.

3   Posadas revealingly compares Mitchell's representation of Tokyo in *Number9Dream* to those to be found in contemporary sci-fi/cyberpunk film and fiction, including *Blade Runner* (1962)—he notes that Eiji specifically references the film in his opening fantasy of infiltrating the PanOpticon building James Bond style—William Gibson's *Neuromancer* (1984), and Chris Marker's film *Sans Soleil* (1983). In his view, *Number9Dream* both partakes of and critiques stereotypical technologized Western images of Japan and Tokyo to be seen in these works through its "self-reflexive hypermediation of these motifs [which] calls attention to the pervasiveness of the circulation of cultures as image-commodities" (80). My psychogeographic reading of the novel focuses more on Tokyo as "affect," mediated by Eiji's need to both locate and, subsequently, remove himself—as nascent metropolitan identity—from the all-too-"coherent" array of interlocking systems and structures underlying the seeming chaos of the city.

Chapter 3

1   See the "Coda" to this chapter for a brief discussion of the film adaptation of *Cloud Atlas*.
2   The term "chronotope" will be familiar to readers of the Russian formalist Mikhail Bakhtin, who developed the term in *The Dialogic Imagination* to describe "the intrinsic connectedness of temporal and spatial relationships

that are artistically expressed in literature" (84). In her book on postmodern narrative, Ursula Heise significantly revises Bakhtin's notion of the time/space relation as part of a "concrete whole" in suggesting that many contemporary narratives are "chronoschisms" that manifest the "disintegration of narrator and character as recognizable and more or less stable entities, and their scattering or fragmentation across different temporal universes that can no longer be reconciled with each other" (7). In *Cloud Atlas*, the reconciliation or irreconcilability of widely varying temporal and spatial regimes becomes one of the novel's primary subjects.

3   In discussing Mitchell's narrative strategies in this section as a "poetics of relation," I am once again relying on Eduard Glissant's formulation of a poetics—an assemblage of tropes, forms, and movements—that "diversifies forms of humanity according to infinite strings of models brought into contact and relayed" (Glissant, 160).

4   Mitchell indicates in the Acknowledgements to *Cloud Atlas* that his portrayal of the Frobisher-Ayrs relationship is informed by Eric Fenby's *Delius as I Knew Him*, an autobiographical account of the author's relationship with the famous British composer for whom he served as an amanuensis (another form of ghostwriter) during Delius' declining years.

5   "Half-Lives," as well as *The China Syndrome*, are clearly based on the 1970s controversies surrounding the building of the Diablo Canyon nuclear power plant near the city of San Luis Obispo in California and in close proximity to the Hosgri fault line.

6   As noted in the Introduction, the intertextuality of Mitchell's fiction has been widely discussed, but for a meticulous, thoroughgoing discussion of intertextuality within the theoretical framework of postmodernism in *Cloud Atlas*, see Hrubes.

7   A sardonic extrapolation of Mitchell's "ahem" and his own preferred narrative strategies is evident in one of Timothy Cavendish's editorial apostrophes: "As an experienced editor, I disapprove of flashbacks, foreshadowings, and tricksy devices; they belong in the 1980s with M.A.'s in postmodernism and chaos theory" (150).

8   In his post-Soviet analysis of Russian culture, *Russia in Search of Itself*, James H. Billington provides a brief history of the Russian doll and writes that the "matryoshka ... suggest[s] ... the different layers of belief inside the Russian psyche"; he describes the first Russian doll as modeled on a figure imported from Honshu Island in Japan: "They substituted the figure of a Russian peasant mother for the bald old man on the Japanese original and created the first matryoshka. It contained eight wooden dolls. The total ensemble represented the members of a united and happy family—the basic unit of sobornost' [community]. The outermost doll was a mother; the innermost doll an infant in swaddling clothes" (148–49). Whether or not the matryoshka signifies the belief system of a virtual entity termed "the Russian psyche," it is interesting that in its materiality the Russian doll

evidences a generative relationship between encapsulating and encapsulated figures that informs the more complex and fractal set of generative relationships between the narratives of *Cloud Atlas*.

9   In his commentary on the novel's "Russian doll" structure, McMorran notes that "it may work as a temporal model, according to which the past encases the present, and the present encases the future—although it is a bleakly deterministic model" ("Fragmentation and Integrity," 163). As will be clear, I argue just the opposite here: the structure of the novel viewed as a "temporal model" suggests the degree to which multiple, local, *seemingly* disconnected "pasts" and "presents" moved always toward a future-in-process that is ad hoc in prospect and only fatal or determined in retrospect. In the novel, Sach's distinction between the actual and the virtual is key to understanding the ways in which *Cloud Atlas* navigates between an ethics of futurity and sheer determinism. Edwards' commentary on the "fleeting instances" and "moments of possibility" in *Cloud Atlas* is more aligned with the view of structure and temporality in the novel that I am advocating ("Strange Transactions," 184–5). McMorran goes on to complicate the generative relationship between encapsulated and encapsulating narratives organized on the model of the "Russian Doll" in explicating the "effect of texts within texts asserting authority over texts that embed them" (164); the interesting "reverse matryoshka effect" that he describes as emanating from the ways in which the stories of *Cloud Atlas* are embedded, however, is contested, in my view, by the actualities of their scale and asymmetry in relation to each other.

10 In their comprehensive discussion of Mitchell's narrative strategies, Childs and Green point out that "meronymy" informs the relations between characters on multiple levels: "In Mitchell's fiction everything seems to be demonstrably a part of the larger whole. Each character is a meronym of the web of relations entangling all the others.... meronymy additionally seems to operate at the level of language: the minds of narrators are unconsciously in counterpoint across temporal and spatial distances; there are also a range of subtle repeated motifs that recur and mutate provocatively in new contexts" (32).

11 See in its entirety the entry in the online *Orthodox Wiki*, "Nestorianism," for the complex schisms and heretical history that evolved in the debates over the unity or bifurcation of Christ's "nature."

12 In his *Paris Review* interview, Mitchell claims he got the title of the novel from the title of "a piece of music by the Japanese composer Toshi Ichiyanagi, who was Yoko Ono's first husband. I bought the CD because of that track's beautiful title. It pleases me that *Number9Dream* is named after a piece of music by Yoko's more famous husband, though I couldn't duplicate the pattern indefinitely" (n.p.). The *Paris Review* interviewer had noted that the phrase "The cloud atlas turns the pages over" [352] had occurred previously in Mitchell's fiction in *Number9Dream*, to which

Mitchell responded, "Wow, is that in *Number9Dream*. Then the phrase was haunting me earlier than I realized" (n.p.).

13 Mitchell's aspirations for how novels might affect future readers are revealing; in an interview, he states that "[r]eally good books work because you don't consume them like a pack of freeze-dried pasta. Books will take up residence inside you, and even afterwards they'll stay there and alter slightly how you think about things" (Martin, n.p.). The notion of "really good books" inhabiting the reader, as identities inhabit each other in Mitchell's fiction, is opposed in his view to books as commodities, consumed and easily digested like the fast food of the Papa Song restaurants in "The Orison of Sonmi~451." Thus, for Mitchell, the dialectic of inhabitation/consumption extends to the relation between narrative and reader as well as the construction of identity and the survival of the species—a set of connections elaborated most fully in *Cloud Atlas* and *The Bone Clocks*.

14 Several of the essays in the Dillon collection, including those of Childs and Green, Posadas, and Edwards, make reference to Hardt and Negri's notion of "multitude," suggesting that it is a central concept (one I touch on lightly here) for future considerations of identity and community in Mitchell's fiction.

15 See Young's discussion of hybridity, race theory, and colonialism in *Colonial Desire*. Apposite to my discussion of identity in *Cloud Atlas*, Young states that identity as a concept aligned with notions of purity, fixity, and singularity came about in Britain at the apogee of colonialism in the nineteenth century—precisely where *Cloud Atlas* begins. Young writes: "In the nineteenth century, the very notion of a fixed English identity was doubtless a product of, and a reaction to, the rapid change and transformation of both metropolitan and colonial societies which meant that ... such identities needed to be constructed to counter schisms, friction, and consent" (3) brought about by increasing contact with "others" both at home and abroad. *Cloud Atlas*, I contend, reflects this process of transformation (and countertransformation) across the centuries of its time frame in portraying a continuous dialectic of identity: "Fixity of identity is only sought in situations of instability and disruption, of conflict and change"; because, for Mitchell, all of the time of the novel is one of constant conflict and change, a "fundamental model" or dialectic of identity emerges where "fixity implies disparateness; multiplicity must be set against at least a notional singularity to have any meaning.... identity is ... articulated through setting one term against the other" (Young, 3).

16 Mitchell reveals in the *Paris Review* interview, "I was ... reading Jared Diamond's *Guns, Germs, and Steel*, and I found a bit about the Moriori, the inhabitants of the Chatham Islands east of New Zealand, and that was irresistible. I wanted to work a way of getting that story in, and I read about someone in San Francisco whose name was actually Ewing, someone lost to history—except that one of the last Moriori told his story to him" (n.p.).

17 I rely here on Bhabha, who, citing Fanon, remarks on the dialectic process evident in the formation of cultural identity that exists between the homogenizing of cultural differences into unitary categories (i.e. we are all different from each other, but we are all Americans, or all humans, etc.) and "the zone of *occult instability* where the people dwell" (155) when intransigent differences in relations of power, time, and location are sufficiently observed.

18 The phrase, perhaps more familiar to many readers as a line from T.S. Eliot's *The Waste Land* (1922), originates in Charles Dickens *Our Mutual Friend* (1865). It is used by the character Betty Higden to describe the abilities of another character, Sloppy, who "is a beautiful reader of a newspaper. He do the Police in different voices." The phrase also aptly describes Dickens' ability to ventriloquize multiple voices in his novels, a gift assuredly shared by Mitchell.

19 My use of the expression "utopic desire" as illuminated by Jameson in *Archaeologies of the Future*, who is engaged in understanding the "dialectic" of utopia which, on the one hand, is a representation of a political desire to establish a permanent state of totalized historical conditions (such as "global capitalism") that are supposed to guarantee happiness, wealth, equality, etc., and a counterdesire "to conceive of… alternative systems… a representational meditation on radical difference, radical otherness, and on the systematic nature of social totality, to the point where one cannot imagine any fundamental change in our social existence which has not first thrown off Utopian visions like so many sparks from a comet" (4).

20 Edwards cites this passage in her important essay on utopia and temporality in *Cloud Atlas*, referring to the colony as an example of a "microtopia" and an instance of the multitude in Hardt and Negri, a society "composed of multiple irreducible individuals" (185). She goes on to suggest that Mitchell's use of transmigration, or the dispersal of connected individuals across time and space forming "a trans-historical community," is the temporal engine of such microtopias: "transmigration becomes a utopianized literary strategy in which a post-individual mode of community and political agency can be posited at a symbolic level" (191). As will be seen, my reading identity, community, and temporality in *Cloud Atlas* is informed by Edwards' compelling view, but differs somewhat in that I consider the anti-utopian conditions of temporariness and contingency—even the accidental—to be fundamental to the survival of the "human" in Mitchell's fiction. In this state of affairs, the "trans" ceases to be an operative term in drawing the connection between identity, community, and time.

21 See Hicks' interesting discussion of temporality in *Cloud Atlas* in terms of cyclical and linear notions of time that Mitchell explores and delimits. My view of temporality in the novel is one that moves to a third conceptualization of "haecceic" temporality.

Chapter 4

1. The cited title of the novel varies from *blackswangreen* to *Black Swan Green*. The cover of the first U.S. edition shows the words "black" and "green" in white lower case against, respectively, green and black backgrounds, with a drawing of a white swan on a white background in between, such that the cover title is a combination of words and image: this resonates in the novel with the images of handwriting, newspaper headlines, and initials carved into a tree that appear sporadically amidst the printed words of the text. The title page of the novel has it *blackswangreen*, but the name of the village that the title echoes is "properly" cited as "Black Swan Green" throughout the novel. In many of the reviews, interviews, and criticism that mention the novel, the title is *Black Swan Green* (it is listed thus on Amazon); the Library of Congress information on the copyright page has it as "Black swan green" (typically, LC titles put all words following the first word of the title in lower case), while the British Library lists the title as "Black Swan Green." It may seem like a miniscule point, but I find the "title confusion" of the novel interesting, given its frequent depictions of adolescent name-calling and the multiple, often derogatory, names imposed upon Jason that symptomatically reflect his own confused and marginalized identity, as well as his own obsession with name, which I discuss later in this chapter. Throughout, I will refer to the novel with what I take to be its intended title, *blackswangreen*, as this echoes the enjambed or uncapitalized titles of *ghostwritten* and *Number9Dream*.
2. In a 2012 *Slate* article, Jessica Roake proposes that *blackswangreen* replace *The Catcher in the Rye* in U.S. high schools as the prototypical coming-of-age novel. Mitchell's interest in this subgenre—whatever autobiographical elements might be detected in *blackswangreen*—certainly continues in *The Reason I Jump*.
3. Mitchell writes in an article on the film *The King's Speech* and what he regards as its intelligent and compelling representation of a speech defect that "[d]espite growing up in a much saner family than the Duke of York's, my open and kind parents and I discussed my speech impediment exactly never, and this 'don't mention the stammer' policy was continued by friends and colleagues into my thirties. I'd probably still be avoiding the subject today had I not outed myself by writing a semi-autobiographical novel, *Black Swan Green*, narrated by a stammering 13 year old" ("Lost for Words," n.p.).
4. Stephenson's discussion of *Number9Dream* provides an insightful discussion of the reach of Mitchell's "anthropology," or cognitive mapping within the global environment of late capitalism: "Mitchell's fictions ... force the reader into a new and exhilarating form of cognitive cartography, a re-territorialization of the plural, decentred, estranging present and the already emerging future that is reality in the early twenty-first century" (240). I will be discussing the ways in which, in his fourth novel, Mitchell locates

and localizes this "global" impulse in the dawning world-awareness of a thirteen-year-old living in the parochial environment of a village in 1980s Worcestershire.
5   Not entirely fanciful, the faint echo of Wallace Stevens' "Thirteen Ways of Looking at a Blackbird" might be heard in the narrative structuring and even the titling of *blackswangreen*.
6   For many Falkland Conflict historians, the skirmish can be seen as an important, if somewhat sideways, chapter of the larger Cold War or imperial narrative as well. In their 1997 Introduction to *The Battle for the Falklands* (Mitchell cites the book as a reference for his research on the Conflict in the Acknowledgements to *blackswangreen*), Max Hastings and Simon Jenkins write that the conflict "retains its fascination as a freak of imperial history" (n.p.). In *Containment Culture*, Alan Nadel offers a compelling analysis of how American popular culture artifacts—including the cultural icons to which Jason is powerfully attracted such as *Star Wars*—reflect a "national narrative" of containment and its discontents:

> Containment was the name of a privileged American narrative during the Cold War. Although technically referring to U.S. foreign policy from 1948 until at least the mid-1960s, it also describes American life in numerous venues and under sundry rubrics during that period: to the extent that corporate production and biological reproduction, military deployment and industrial technology, televised hearings and filmed teleplays, the cult of domesticity and the fetishizing of domestic security, the arms race and the atoms for peace all contributed to the containment of communism, disparate acts in the name of these practices joined the legible agenda of American history as aspects of containment culture. (2–3)

In his imbibing of both U.S. and British popular culture and in the commoditization of his identity that I will discuss shortly, Jason reflects the connectivity of Nadel's "American" containment narrative unfolding in the life of a thirteen-year-old taking place on British soil in 1982, reflecting its reach as an international Cold War narrative. For Jason, *Star Wars* and The Falklands Conflict take place in the same imaginary terrain.
7   See *Cosmopolitanism*, 87–99.
8   Comparing it to the features listed in Mendelson's essay on encyclopedic narrative, *blackswangreen* bears some, though not all, of the qualities of an encyclopedic narrative as Mendelson defines it, and is less related to the epic than Mendelson suggests for the tradition of encyclopedic narratives running from Dante to Pynchon. But all of Mitchell's novels, as I mention in the introduction, are encyclopedic in their deployment of multiple genres, their discursive variety, and their mapping of multiple imaginary landscapes. The protagonist of *blackswangreen* accomplishes all of this "at home," within the constricted confines of a suburban village.

9   Mitchell reveals in the *Serendipity* interview that while *blackswangreen* was not as research intensive as other novels, he did "research the Falklands a bit, which was the case of reading a couple of books. I got a lot of stuff from Friends Reunited, where I was a lurker. The internet is quite good for nerdy kind of areas, like a pop chart from 1982" (n.p.). "Friends Reunited" is a British social networking website that collects, among other things, "memories" about popular culture from various decades.

10 I take the nickname of "maggot" for Jason to be one of a few subtle references to John Fowles in *blackswangreen*. The Cornish resort that Jason and his father visit in "souvenirs" is Lyme Regis, the setting for *The French Lieutenant's Woman* (1969) and Fowles' home in the last part of his life; *A Maggot* (1985)—a title that does not primarily refer to insect larvae but to an older sense of the word, a whim or obsession—was Fowles' last published novel; and like Charles Freeman, the protagonist of *The French Lieutenant's Woman*, Jason is, in the words of his father's repulsive boss, Craig Salt, a "bit of a fossil collector" (184), implicitly echoing as well the title of Fowles' first novel, *The Collector* (1963).

11 There is some irony in the fact that the proliferation of the "real life" David Mitchell's name is a source of confusion and (for the author) humor. In her profile/interview with Mitchell, Hermione Eyre inspires Mitchell to reflect on the doubling of his name with that of the popular British comedian David Mitchell: "There is inevitably confusion between David Mitchell (author) and David Mitchell (comedian). 'My mum found an audiobook edition of [my second novel] *Number9Dream* that had his face on the back!' Not all authors would find this as funny as he does. As we leave the restaurant, he says: 'That was the best sushi I've had in London.' They can put that on their flyer, I say. 'I don't think anyone would care,' he says. 'Except they might, because they'd think I'm the other David Mitchell'" (n.p.).

12 The theoretical work that I rely on here in order to make these connections will be familiar to many as that of Julia Kristeva in *Powers of Horror*, especially pp. 1–31; Jason uncannily "tracks" Kristeva in making scatological comparisons to the act of speaking. See also my *Echo Chambers* for discussions of the relation between voice, identity, and writing in the modern novel from a Kristevan perspective.

13 In *The Sense of an Ending*, in metronomic terms, Frank Kermode has famously reflected on the relationship between clock-time—a form of imposed sequentiality—and narrative as a means of organizing what would otherwise be the randomness of existence: "[t]he clock's 'tick-tock' I take to be a model of what we call a plot, an organisation which humanizes time by giving it a form; and the interval between 'tock' and 'tick' represents purely successive, disorganised time of the sort we need to humanize" (45). In contrast to Kermode—or at least as a complication to his notion of clock-time and narrativization—the figuration of stammering in *blackswangreen* suggests the degree to which writing and speech must necessarily

incorporate the random and the inarticulate (the halting of the stammer) as foundational to the construction of narrative.

14 The reader interested in the (now) classic theoretical elaboration of the temporalized relation between speech and writing is encouraged to consult Derrida's *Of Grammatology*, especially pp. 95–164.

Chapter 5

1 Mitchell uses two calendars in this novel where every chapter bears some kind of time signature: the novel's "double-dating" and the variations in the dating of chapters will be discussed later in this chapter. For the "Dutch" chapters (those told primarily from the perspective of the European "foreigners"), Mitchell uses the Gregorian calendar, which had been adopted by most states in current-day Holland by 1701; for the "Japanese" chapters (those related from the perspective of the Japanese characters), the adapted Chinese lunisolar calendar is used. This calendar, for which the names of months correspond to their numerical equivalents in the calendrical year ("first month," "second month," instead of "January," "February," etc.), used in Japan from the sixth century B.C. until 1873 when the Gregorian calendar was adopted under the modernization polices that came about in the Meiji Period, runs three to seven weeks "later" than the Gregorian calendar depending on the time of the year.

2 The (now) classic formulation of "orientalism" occurs in Edward Said's foundational discussion of postcolonialism, *Orientalism*, where he defines the term as follows, interestingly within a historical framework that corresponds with the temporal framework of *The Thousand Autumns*: "Taking the late eighteenth century as a very defined starting point, Orientalism can be discussed and analyzed as the corporate institution for dealing with the Orient—dealing with it by making statements about it, authorizing views of it, describing it, by teaching it, settling it, ruling over it: in short, Orientalism as a Western style for dominating, restructuring, and having authority over the Orient" (*Orientalism*, 4). Clearly, Mitchell's novel is interested in the corporate institutions of the Dutch East India Company and the competing British Navy as the agent of Orientalism in 1799–1800—institutions that the Japanese scholar Yoshida Hayoto, in a passage to be discussed momentarily, argues the Japanese should imitate in constructing their own counterorientalist empire.

3 The term "minor history" has varying connotations depending on the context. It has been conceptually developed by historians such as Carlo Ginzburg (*The Cheese and the Worms: The Cosmos of a Sixteenth Century Miller*, 1980) and Natalie Zemon Davis (*The Return of Martin Guerre*, 1983) to indicate the symptomatic significance of "minor" lives of peasants and the working class, and local events taking place alongside the "major"

events of European history in the succession of kings and international warfare. Their work was preceded by that of the French "annales" school of historiography, which views history as made up of countless everyday lives, environmental factors, and microhistories that constantly interact much in the way narratives interact fractally in Mitchell's fiction: interestingly, Fernand Braudel's magisterial *The Mediterranean and the Mediterranean World in the Age of Phillip II* (1972) begins with a precise description of the Mediterranean topography and climactic weather patterns. "Minor history" has acquired another set of associations via the work of Giles Deleuze and Félix Guattari in *Kafka: Toward a Minor Literature* (1986) and *A Thousand Plateaus* (1987), and that of Jean-François Lyotard in *The Postmodern Condition: A Report on Knowledge* (1979). All of these works resist the notion of "grand" cultural narratives (to use Lyotard's expression), including totalizing historical narratives that convey hierarchies of power and experience as determinative and causal. The "truth" of history is to be found elsewhere. For Deleuze and Guattari, it is to be found in the myriad, semirandom intersection of identities, temporalities, environments, and events at the "molecular" level: history as a "rhizomic" assemblage of "ceaselessly establishe[d] connections between semiotic chains, organizations of power, and circumstances relative to the arts, sciences, and social struggles"; history as having "no beginning or end; it is always in the middle, between things, interbeing, *intermezzo*" (*A Thousand Plateaus*, 7; 25). As I shall discuss the notion of "minor history" in relation to *The Thousand Autumns*, Mitchell creates adjacencies between the global narratives of nation, imperialism, and empire, and the "insignificant," often inconclusive stories (in that they have no proper place in the semiotics or causalities of the grand historical narrative) of minor functionaries, slaves, seamen, and secreted women. The nature of the connections to be mapped between these narrative planes is neither symptomatic nor asymptomatic, but existing between—"intermezzo," as Deleuze and Guattari put it—cause and effect, and happenstance and fate.

4   In a rich example of social form leading to artistic genre (analogous to my claim throughout that Mitchell's deployment of narrative form and genre parallels his view of historical and social formations), the development of the floating worlds of Edo led to the style of Japanese art named after them, *ukiyo*, or "pictures of the floating world." These are primarily mass-produced woodblock prints produced during the Edo period, in which the novel is set (1615–1868), that depict scenes from everyday life, landscapes, portraits, popular personalities, and legends; one might think of them as "works of art in the age of mechanical reproduction" in Japan.

5   See note 8 to the "Introduction" of this volume for Mitchell's commentary on the significance of islands in his fiction. James Woods takes a similar view to Mitchell's when he refers to two of the principal locations in *The Thousand Autumns*: "The floating island and the remote nunnery function

like Balzacian boarding houses, offering the novelist closed alternative worlds, tight with life" ("The Floating Library," n.p.). But it is precisely his own tyrannical authority and the "closure" of both stories and islands that Mitchell consistently "deconstructs" in his novels that contain multiple island-stories bumping up against each other in various patterns and combinations that demand the reader's interaction and discernment in tracing the connections between them; this is further complicated by the recursive structure of Mitchell's stories within stories, each "island" containing other islands, other narrative strands, and trajectories.

6   In the discussion of *Cloud Atlas*, I suggested the ways in which that novel's narrative organization complicates the "nesting" effect produced by a Chinese box or Russian doll narrative structure. While several sequences in *The Thousand Autumns* contain narratives within narratives as well as literal representations of boxes, cabinets, and trunks containing objects, each with their own implied narrative history, the constellation of narratives in the novel are, like *Cloud Atlas*, more suggestive of its "fractal" nature as dispersed narratives, large scale and small, coming into contact with each other in multiple patterns to effect what Hayles terms the "orderly disorder" of contemporary narrative. If we regard *The Thousand Autumns*—with its title inferring a continuous history with an open future—as a historical novel, then its fractal structure surely suggests that Mitchell views history itself as "orderly disorder."

7   Mo Muntervary's ancestor, Fiacre Muntervary, appears in *The Thousand Autumns* as a carpenter and former convict exiled to Botany Bay from Ireland, where he had been caught stealing clothes for a corrupt pawnbroker in order to feed a starving family.

8   As seen in *Cloud Atlas*, the temporality of *The Thousand Autumns* reflects Doane's sense of cinematic modernity in which the structuring of time is related to predominance of the contingent in modern times; cf. Chapter Three.

9   The prefiguration here can also be seen as a "post-figuration" looking forward to the temporalities of novels written before *The Thousand Autumns*. Thinking about the succession of Mitchell's novels as future anteriorities is perfectly consonant with the representation of temporality in those novels.

10 See Georges Poulet's *Studies in Human Time* for a phenomenological discussion of variant senses of temporality across epochs and cultural histories; for Poulet, as for Mitchell, conceptualizations of temporality are inextricably linked to projections of desired futures that collectively suggest there are no predestined futures as such, only those that come to pass as contingencies exfoliate and collide.

11 Mitchell's responses to questions posed to him on the Amazon.com book website about translating *The Reason I Jump* reveal some of the ways in which acts of translation illuminate and negotiate cultural differences. The interviewer is Dr. Andrew Solomon, whose *Far from the Tree: Parents,*

Children and the Search for Identity (2012) offers stunning narrative descriptions and analyses of life in families whose exceptional children contend with schizophrenia, autism, depression, deafness, and a host of other medical and psychological challenges:

> **AS:** As you translated this book from the Japanese, did you feel you could represent his voice much as it was in his native language? Did you find that there are Japanese ways of thinking that required as much translation from you and your wife as autistic ways required of the author?
> **DM:** Our goal was to write the book as Naoki would have done if he was a 13-year-old British kid with autism, rather than a 13-year-old Japanese kid with autism. Once we had identified that goal, many of the 1001 choices you make while translating became clear. Phrasal and lexical repetition is less of a vice in Japanese—it's almost a virtue—so varying Naoki's phrasing, while keeping the meaning, was a ball we had to keep our eyes on. Linguistic directness can come over as vulgar in Japanese, but this is more of a problem when Japanese is the Into language than when it is the Out Of language. The only other regular head-bender is the rendering of onomatopoeia, for which Japanese has a synaesthetic genius—not just animal sounds, but qualities of light, or texture, or motion. Those puzzles were fun, though.

12 "Les traductions vont devenir une part importante des poétiques.... Et je pense à toute cette variance infinie de nuances des poétiques possibles des langues, et chacun sera de plus en plus pénétré par toute cette fragrance, cet éclatement des poétiques du monde. Ce sera une nouvelle sensibilité." Hantel's consideration of "the space of translation" in Glissant is the source for my understanding of Glissant's concept of translations as rhizomic, informed by notions of "nomadic" and "rhizomic" in Deleuze and Guattari. The turning of Glissant's thought toward Deleuze and Guattari in his major work can also be seen in *The Poetics of Relation*, particularly in the chapters "Errantry, Exile" (11–22) and "A Rooted Errantry" (37–44).

13 The well-known crux of Freud's argument in *Civilization and Its Discontents* is that the "trouble" with civilization and the mechanisms of socialization that promote the cleanliness, order, and disciplinary advances it so prizes necessarily involves the repression of individual instinct and desire paralleling the human attempt to control "nature." For Freud, instinct will come out in the forms of collective aggression that finds their ultimate expression in war, colonial exploitation, and cultural genocide; implicitly, Freud's argument suggests that the more "advanced" the civilization, the more aggressive it will become in asserting its superiority over all others. Mitchell does not exactly follow the Freudian line in his portrayal of two self-regarding "advanced" cultures coming into contact in *The Thousand Autumns* that, in the historical reach, now seem anachronistic. He does,

however, suggest in his fictions of past and future civilizations that the process of formation, empire, and collapse is always ongoing, ever the backdrop for the survival of the human in another, countervailing register involving the transmission of narrative and memory—like a genetic code—across time, space, and generation.

Chapter 6

1. Mitchell's short story, *The Siphoners*, a fractured nightmare/fairy tale of climatological change and disaster, forecasts the near future of ecological devastation and its effects on "civilization" portrayed in *The Bone Clocks*. The story was published in a collection of fiction on ecological change and the survival of species entitled *I'm with the Bears*, along with stories by Margaret Atwood, Paolo Bachgalupi, T.C. Boyle, and Kim Stanley Robinson, among others.
2. As will be seen in the ongoing discussion, in *The Bone Clocks* Mitchell develops a specialized vocabulary to describe the beings, elements, and events occurring both in the Atemporal and "normal" dimensions of the novel. "Psychosoteric" is used to refer to beings who have paranormal abilities—precognition, clairvoyance, bilocation, and psychokinesis—that enable voluntary or forced contact with the Atemporals, or those who live multiple lives as their souls transmigrate from body to body over time. For Holly, who possesses some of these abilities, being "psychosoteric" allows her sporadic entry into a larger long-term narrative with "cosmic" consequences, but it also intensifies her knowledge of her own mortality, indentured to the passing present. The term connotes both the "esoteric," that is, the knowledge of the elect, and "soteria," or the principle in Greek philosophy of self-actualization along a guided path.
3. Later we learn that this is the "chakra-eye" (479) of the Atemporals, the "third eye" in Tibetan Buddhism, a central point in the nonphysical or spiritual body.
4. Benjamin wrote the "Theses on the Philosophy of History" in 1940, while in France after fleeing the Nazi regime in Germany, and shortly before he would escape to Spain from the Vichy government and commit suicide. The "angel of history" is one of the most controversial figures of Benjamin's opus. It is often read as preceding the end of history and a wholly indeterminate, posthistorical future that would commence once the pressures of the accumulated past have led to a breakthrough in the blockage represented by the angel of/witness to history.
5. The phrase comes from Psalm 90:10, which is devoted to the brevity of human life on earth: "The days of our years are threescore years and ten, and if by reason of strength they be fourscore years, yet is their strength labor and sorrow: for it is soon cut off, and we fly away." Toward the end, the Psalm contains the invocation, "So teach us to number our days, that

we may apply our hearts unto wisdom" (*Psalms*, 90:12), one of the "lessons" of mortality that gains force as the complex set of interactions between "mortals" and "Atemporals" evolves the novel.

Epilogue

1. This is the claim made by Michael Holquist, the translator of M.M. Bakhtin, whose prominent views of the novel as a "carnivalesque" entity that incorporates all other preceding and contemporary genres are foundational to our current understanding of the novel as a form. Hoquist writes in the "Introduction" to his translation of Bakhtin's *The Dialogic Imagination* that the novel "is best conceived either as a supergenre, whose power consists in its ability to engulf and ingest all other genres ... or not a genre in any strict, traditional sense at all" (xxix).
2. The phrase occurs in Faulkner's response to a question posed to him while at the University of Virginia about feelings of satisfaction and equilibrium after completing *The Sound and the Fury*: "That's the—the one that I love the best for the reason that it was the most splendid failure. I think that— that they all failed. Probably the reason the man writes another book is that he tried to—to tell some very important and very moving truth and failed. He's not satisfied, so he tries again. He writes another book, trying to tell some—the same moving truth, since there's only one truth, and they fail" (Faulkner, n.p.).
3. Mitchell's "invitational" approach as an author is dramatically evident in the conversation he has with Tom Twyker and the Wachowskis recorded in one of the bonus features of the *Cloud Atlas* digital video. Lana Wachowski recounts before a surprised Mitchell one of the many visual connections the directors made in adapting the novel to film: in this instance, the decision to use the removed slave collars of the fabricants in "Sonmi~451" as binding material for the book of revelations that will be passed into the hands of the Abbess in "Sloosha's Crossin'". Mitchell's pleasurable astonishment at this revelation and his statements scattered across several interviews about readers seeing connections between characters and events he had not in authoring his novels corresponds with Courtney's Hopf's future-oriented conception of the reader interaction in Mitchell's fiction: "Mitchell's novels train the reader to inhabit multiple positions at once, making connections across discursive worlds in what is ultimately a satisfying process in the era of mass connectivity. This process is ongoing as each new novel is bound to introduce characters readers have seen before and to expand upon or fully rewrite their histories and identities" (Hopf, 121).

Works Cited

Alter, Robert. (1975). *Partial Magic: The Novel as a Self-Conscious Genre.* Berkeley, CA: University of California Press.
Althusser, Louis. (1971). *Lenin and Philosophy and Other Essays.* New York, NY: Monthly Review Press.
Anderson, Benedict. (1991). *Imagined Communities: Reflections on the Origin and Spread of Nationalism.* London: Verso.
Annesley, James. (2006). "Market Corrections: Jonathan Franzen and the 'Novel of Globalization.'" *Journal of Modern Literature,* 29.2: 111-28.
Appiah, Anthony Kwame. (2006). *Cosmopolitanism: Ethics in a World of Strangers.* New York, NY: Norton.
Bakhtin, M. M. (1981). *The Dialogic Imagination: Four Essays.* Trans. Caryl Emerson and Michael Holquist. Austin, TX: University of Texas Press.
Ballard, Shawn C. (2010). "Complex Systems and Global Catastrophe: Networks in David Mitchell's *ghostwritten*." *New Directions in Ecocriticism,* www.ideals.illinois.edu/bitstream/handle/2142/25241/ballard_shawn_markup3.html.
Baudrillard, Jean. (1994). *Simulacra and Simulation.* Trans. Sheila Faria Glaser. Ann Arbor, MI: University of Michigan Press.
———. (1996). *The System of Objects.* Trans. James Benedict. New York, NY: Verso.
Benjamin, Walter. (1968a). "Thesis on the Philosophy of History," in *Illuminations.* Introd. Hannah Arendt. Trans. Harry Zohn. New York, NY: Schocken Books: 253-64.
———. (1968b). "The Storyteller," in *Illuminations.* Introd. Hannah Arendt. Trans. Harry Zohn. New York, NY: Schocken Books: 83-110.
———. (1983). *Charles Baudelaire: A Lyric Poet in the Era of High Capitalism.* Trans. Harry Zohn. London: Verso.
———. (1999a). *The Arcades Project.* Trans. Howard Eiland and Kevin McLaughlin. Cambridge, MA: Harvard University Press.
———. (1999b). *Selected Writings, Volume 2, Part 2: 1931-34.* Eds. Michael W. Jennings, Howard Eiland, and Gary Smith. Cambridge, MA: Harvard University Press.
Bhabha, Homi K. (1994). *The Location of Culture.* New York, NY: Routledge.
———. (2006). "Cultural Diversity and Cultural Differences," in *The Post-Colonial Studies Reader.* Eds. Bill Ashcroft, Gareth Griffiths, and Helen Tiffin. New York, NY: Routledge: 206-09.
Billington, James H. (2004). *Russia in Search of Itself.* Baltimore, MD: Woodrow Wilson Center Press.
Bordwell, David. (2008). *Poetics of Cinema.* New York, NY: Routledge.
Burke, Kenneth. (1954). *Permanence and Change: An Anatomy of Purpose.* 3rd Edition. Berkeley, CA: University of California Press.

Charles, Ron. (2010). "Review" of *The Thousand Autumns of Jacob de Zoet*. *Washington Post* online, 30 June. http://www.washingtonpost.com/wp-dyn/content/article/2010/06/29/AR2010062904512.html.

Childs, Peter and James Green. (2011). "The Novels in Nine Parts." in *David Mitchell: Critical Essays*. Ed. Dillon S. Canterbury, UK: Glyph: 25–48.

Conrad, Joseph. (1946). *The Mirror of the Sea* and *A Personal Record*. Dent Edited Collection. London: Dent.

Coupland, Douglas. (2012). "Convergences" (review of Hari Kunzru's *Gods and Men*). *New York Times Book Review*, 1: 10.

Coverley, Merlin. (2010). *Psychogeography* (Pocket Essentials). Harpenden, UK: Oldcastle Books, Kindle Edition.

Davies, Paul. (2003). "A Brief History of the Multiverse." *The New York Times* online, 12 April. http://www.nytimes.com/2003/04/12/opinion/a-brief-history-of-the-multiverse.html.

Davis, Robert Con. (1993). *The Paternal Romance: Reading God the Father in Early Western Culture*. Urbana, IL: University of Illinois Press.

Debord, Guy. (1955). "Introduction to a Critique of Urban Geography." in Knabb: 8–11.

———. (1959). "Theory of the Dérive." in Knabb: 62–65.

Deleuze, Gilles and Félix Guattari. (1987). *A Thousand Plateaus: Capitalism and Schizophrenia*. Trans. Brian Massumi. Minneapolis, MN: University of Minnesota Press.

De Man, Paul. (1979). "Autobiography as De-facement." *MLN*, 94: 919–30.

Derrida, Jacques. (1982). *Positions*. Trans Alan Bass. Chicago, IL: University of Chicago Press.

———. (1997). *Politics of Friendship*. Trans. G. Collins. London: Verso.

———. (1998). *Of Grammatology*. Ed. and Trans. Gayatri Chakravorty Spivak; orig. 1976. Baltimore: Johns Hopkins University Press.

———. (2000). *Of Hospitality*. Stanford, CA: Stanford University Press.

———. (2004). *Spectres of Marx: The State of Debt, The Work of Mourning, & The New International*. Trans. Peggy Kamuf. New York, NY: Routledge.

Dickens, Charles. (1865). *Our Mutual Friend*. London: Chapman and Hall.

Dillon, Sarah. (2007). *The Palimpsest: Literature, Criticism, Theory*. London: Continuum.

———. Ed. (2011a). *David Mitchell: Critical Essays*. Canterbury, UK: Glyph.

———. (2011b). "Introducing David Mitchell's Universe: A Twenty-First Century House of Fiction," in *David Mitchell: Critical Essays*. Ed. Dillon S. Canterbury, UK: Glyph: 3–24.

Doane, Mary Ann. (2002). *The Emergence of Cinematic Time: Modernity, Contingency, and the Archive*. Cambridge, MA: Harvard University Press.

Edwards, Caroline. (2011). "'Strange Transactions': Utopia, Transmigration and Time in *ghostwritten* and *Cloud Atlas*," in *David Mitchell: Critical Essays*. Ed. Dillon S. Canterbury, UK: Glyph: 177–200.

Eyre, Hermione. (2013). "In the Clouds: David Mitchell on Gender Bending and the Future of Civilisation." *London Evening Standard* online, 21 February.

http://www.standard.co.uk/lifestyle/esmagazine/in-the-clouds-david-mitchell-on-gender-bending-and-the-future-of-civilisation-8505001.html.
Faulkner, William. (1936; rpt. 1990). *Absalom, Absalom!* New York, NY: Vintage.
———. (1957). Transcript of conversation with Frederic Gwynn at the University of Virginia, 15 February. Audio recording at the "Faulkner at Virginia" website: http://faulkner.lib.virginia.edu/display/wfaudio01_1.
Freud, Sigmund. (1989; orig. 1930). *Civilization and Its Discontents*. Trans. James Strachey. New York, NY: W. W. Norton.
Friedman, Susan Stanford. (2010). "Planetarity: Musing Modernist Studies." *Modernism/Modernity*, 1.3: 471–99.
Geertz, Clifford. (1973). "Thick Description: Toward an Interpretive Theory of Culture," in his *The Interpretation of Cultures: Selected Essays*. New York, NY: Basic Books.
Glissant, Édouard. (1997). *Poetics of Relation*. Trans. Betsy Wing. Ann Arbor, MI: University of Michigan Press.
Gunning, Tom. (2007). "To Scan a Ghost: The Ontology of Mediated Vision." *Grey Room*, 26: 94–127.
Hantel, Max. (2013). "Rhizomes and the Space of Translation: On Edouard Glissant's Spiral Retelling." *Small Axe*, 17.3: 100–112.
Hardt, Michael and Antonio Negri. (2000). *Empire*. Orig. Cambridge, MA: Harvard University Press; Kindle electronic book edition.
———. (2004). *Multitude: War and Democracy in the Age of Empire*. New York, NY: Penguin.
Hastings, Max and Simon Jenkins. (2010). *The Battle for the Falklands*. London: Pan Macmillan E-Book.
Hayles, N. Katherine. (1990). *Chaos Bound: Orderly Disorder in Contemporary Literature and Science*. Ithaca, NY: Cornell University Press.
Heise, Ursula. (1997). *Chronoschisms: Time, Narrative, and Postmodernism*. Cambridge: Cambridge University Press.
Hicks, Heather J. (2010). "'This Time Round': David Mitchell's *Cloud Atlas* and the Apocalyptic Problem of Historicism. *Postmodern Culture*, 20.3. http://muse.jhu.edu/journals/postmodern_culture/v020/20.3.hicks.html.
Hocking, Ian. (2007). "Interview with David Mitchell." Serendipity, www.magicrealism.co.uk, n.p.
Hopf, Courtney. (2011). "The Stories We Tell: Discursive Identity Through Narrative Form in *Cloud Atlas*." in *David Mitchell: Critical Essays*. Ed. Dillon S. Canterbury, UK: Glyph: 108–26.
Hrubes, Martina. (2008). *Postmodernist Intertextuality in David Mitchell's* Cloud Atlas. M.A. Thesis, Johann Wolfgang Goethe-Universität Frankfurt am Main.
Hutcheon, Linda. (2006). *A Theory of Adaptation*. New York, NY: Routledge.
James, David and Urmila Seshagiri. (2014). "Metamodernism: Narratives of Continuity and Revolution." *PMLA*, 129.1: 87–200.
Jameson, Fredric. (2005). *Archaeologies of the Future: The Desire Called Utopia and Other Science Fictions*. London: Verso.

Jeffries, Stuart. (2013). "David Mitchell: 'I Don't Want to Project Myself as this Great Experimenter.'" *Guardian* online, 8 February. http://www.theguardian.com/books/2013/feb/08/david-mitchell-project-great-experimenter.
Jewell, Stephen. (2011). "The Fascination of Islands" [Interview with David Mitchell]. *New Zealand Herald* online, 16 April. http://www.nzherald.co.nz/entertainment/news/article.cfm?c_id=1501119&objectid=10719736.
Kermode, Frank. (1968). *The Sense of an Ending*. Oxford: Oxford University Press.
Knabb, Ken. Ed. and trans. (2006). *Situationist International Anthology*. Rev. and Expanded Edition. Berkeley, CA: Bureau of Public Secrets.
Kristeva, Julia. (1982). *Powers of Horror: An Essay on Abjection*. Trans. Leon S. Roudiez. New York, NY: Columbia University Press.
Law, John. (2002). *Aircraft Stories: Decentering the Object in Technoscience*. Durham, NC: Duke University Press.
LeClair, Tom. (1989). *The Art of Excess: Mastery in Contemporary American Fiction*. Urbana, IL: University of Illinois Press.
———. (2012). "Review" of Hari Kunzru, *Gods Without Men*. *Barnes and Noble Review* online, 6 March. http://bnreview.barnesandnoble.com/t5/Reviews-Essays/Gods-Without-Men/ba-p/7083, n.p.
Le Guin, Ursula K. (1975). "The Ones Who Walk Away from Omelas," in *The Wind's Twelve Quarters*. New York, NY: Harper & Row: 275–84.
Linklater, Alexander. (2010). "Review" of *The Thousand Autumns of Jacob de Zoet*. *The Guardian/The Observer* online, 8 May. http://www.theguardian.com/books/2010/may/09/thousand-autumns-jacob-zoet-mitchell.
Lyotard, Jean-François. (1993). *Libidinal Economy*. Trans. Iain Hamilton Grant. Bloomington, IN: Indiana University Press.
Mandelbrot, Benoit. (1983). *The Fractal Geometry of Nature*. New York, NY: W. H. Freeman and Company.
Marías, Javier. (2004). *Your Face Tomorrow: Fever and Spear, Volume 1*. New York, NY: New Directions.
Martin, Mark. (2010). "A Conversation with David Mitchell." *Barnes and Noble Review* online. http://bnreview.barnesandnoble.com/t5/Interviews/David-Mitchell/ba-p/2811.
McMorran, Will. (2011). *"Cloud Atlas* and *If on a Winter's Night a Traveler"*: Fragmentation and Integrity in the Postmodern Novel. in *David Mitchell: Critical Essays*. Ed. Dillon S. Canterbury, UK: Glyph: 155–76.
Mendelson, Edward. (1976). "Encyclopedic Narrative: From Dante to Pynchon." *MLN*, 91: 1267–75.
Mitchell, David. (1999). *ghostwritten*. New York, NY: Random House. Rpt. New York: Vintage, 2001.
———. (2001). *Number9Dream*. New York, NY: Random House. Rpt. New York: Random House Trade Paperback Edition, 2003.
———. (2004a). *Cloud Atlas*. New York, NY: Random House. Rpt. New York: Random House Trade Paperback Edition, 2004.

———. (2004b). "Enter the Maze." *The Guardian* online, 21 May. http://www.guardian.co.uk/books/2004/may/22/fiction.italocalvino, n.p.

———. (2006a). *blackswangreen*. New York, NY: Random House.

———. (2006b). "Let Me Speak." The British Stammering Association Homepage: www.stammering.org/mitchell.html.

———. (2010a). "The Art of Fiction No. 204" (interview). Interviewed by Adam Begley. *Paris Review* 193 online. www.theparisreview.org/interviews/6034/the-art-of-fiction-no-204-david-mitchell.

———. (2010b). "On Historical Fiction." *The Telegraph* online, 8 May. http://www.telegraph.co.uk/culture/books/bookreviews/7685510/David-Mitchell-on-Historical-Fiction.html.

———. (2010c). *The Thousand Autumns of Jacob de Zoet*. New York, NY: Random House.

———. (2011a). "Lost for Words." *Prospect Magazine* online, 23 February. http://www.prospectmagazine.co.uk/magazine/david-mitchell-stammering-kings-speech/#.Ubc6gpzo5tE.

———. (2011b). "The Siphoners." in *I'm with the Bears: Short Stories from a Damaged Planet*. Ed. Mark Martin. New York, NY: Verso.

———. (2014). *The Bone Clocks*. New York, NY: Random House.

Morin, Marie-Eve. (2006). "Putting the Community Under Erasure: Derrida and Nancy on the Plurality of Singularities." *Culture Machine*, 8. http://www.culturemachine.net/index.php/cm/article/viewArticle/37/45, n.p.

Murakami, Haruki. (2000). *Underground: The Tokyo Gas Attack and the Japanese Psyche*. London: Harvill.

Nadel, Alan. (1995). *Containment Culture, Postmodernism, and the Atomic Age*. Durham, NC: Duke University Press.

"Nestorianism." (n.d.). *Orthodox Wiki*. http://orthodoxwiki.org/Nestorianism.

O'Donnell, Patrick. (1986). *Passionate Doubts: Designs of Interpretation in Contemporary American Fiction*. Iowa City, IA: University of Iowa Press.

———. (1992). *Echo Chambers: Figuring Voice in Modern Narrative*. Iowa City, IA: University of Iowa Press.

———. (2005). "Metafiction," in *The Routledge Encyclopedia of Narrative Theory*, Eds. David Herman, Manfred Jahn, and Marie-Laure Ryan. London and New York: Routledge, 301–02.

Pease, Donald. (2000). "Doing Justice to C. L. R. James's *Mariners, Renegades, Castaways*." *Boundary*, 27.2: 1–19.

Penrose, Roger. (2007). *The Road to Reality: A Complete Guide to the Laws of the Universe*. New York, NY: Vintage.

Peters, Lindsey. (2008). "Private Fears in Public Places: Network Narrative and the 'Post-Smart' American Melodrama." *Synoptique*, online, 12 October. http://www.synoptique.ca/core/articles/private_fears_in_public_places/, n.p.

Posadas, Baryon Tensor. (2011). "Remediations of 'Japan' in *Numberninedream*." in *David Mitchell: Critical Essays*. Ed. Dillon S. Canterbury, UK: Glyph: 77–105.

Poulet, Georges. (1959). *Studies in Human Time*. Trans. Elliott Coleman. Orig. 1956. New York, NY: Harper & Row.
Pratt, Mary Louise. (1991). "Arts of the contact zone." *Profession* (MLA), 91: 33–40.
Roake, Jessica. (2012). "So Long, Holden." *Slate* online, 2 November. http://www.slate.com/articles/arts/books/2012/11/schools_should_replace_catcher_in_the_rye_with_black_swan_green.html.
Said, Edward W. (1978). *Orientalism*. New York: Vintage.
Schoene, Berthold. (2009). *The Cosmopolitan Novel*. Edinburgh: Edinburgh University Press.
Sebald, W. G. (2001). *Austerlitz*. Trans. Anthea Bell. New York, NY: Random House.
Self, Will. (2009). "Incidents Along the Road." *The Guardian* online, 6 February. http://www.theguardian.com/books/2009/feb/07/wg-sebald-austerlitz-will-self-fiction.
———. (2014). "The Novel Is Dead (This Time It's for Real)." *The Guardian* online, 2 May. http://www.theguardian.com/books/2014/may/02/will-self-novel-dead-literary-fiction.
Sen, Amartya. (2006). *Identity and Violence: The Illusion of Destiny*. New York, NY: W. W. Norton.
Shields, David. (2013). *How Literature Saved My Life*. New York, NY: Alfred A. Knopf.
Simmel, Georg. (1950; orig. 1903). "The Metropolis and Mental Life," in *The Sociology of Georg Simmel*. Ed. and Trans. Kurt H. Wolff. New York, NY: Free Press: 409–24.
Simpson, Kathryn. (2011). "Or Something Like That: Coming of Age in *Number9dream*," in *David Mitchell: Critical Essays*. Ed. Dillon S. Canterbury, UK: Glyph: 49–76.
Sontag, Susan. (1977). *On Photography*. New York, NY: Farrar, Straus & Giroux.
Steiner, George. (1975). *After Babel: Aspects of Language and Translation*. Oxford: Oxford University Press.
Stephenson, William. (2011). "'Moonlight Bright as a UFO Abduction': Science Fiction, Present-Future Alienation and Cognitive Mapping," in *David Mitchell: Critical Essays*. Ed. Dillon S. Canterbury, UK: Glyph: 225–45.
Tobin, Patricia D. (1978). *Time and the Novel: The Genealogical Imperative*. Princeton, NJ: Princeton University Press.
Vermeulen, Pieter. (2012). "David Mitchell's *ghostwritten* and the Novel of Globalization: Biopower and the Secret History of the Novel." *Critique*, 53.4: 381–92.
Vermeulen, Timotheus and Robin van den Akker. (2010). "Notes on Metamodernism." *Journal of Aesthetics and Culture*, 2: 1–13 (online.pdf). http://www.aestheticsandculture.net/index.php/jac/article/view/5677.
Walkowitz, Rebecca. (2006). *Cosmopolitan Style: Modernism Beyond Nation*. New York, NY: Columbia University Press.

Woods, James. (2010). "The Floating Library." *New Yorker* online, 5 July. http://www.newyorker.com/arts/critics/atlarge/2010/07/05/100705crat_atlarge_wood.

Young, Robert J. C. (1995). *Colonial Desire: Hybridity in Theory, Culture, and Race*. London: Routledge.

Ziegler, Heide. (1998). "Interview with William H. Gass," in *Into the Tunnel: Readings of Gass's Novel*. Eds. Steven G. Kellman, and Irving Malin. Cranbury, NJ: Associated Universities Presses: 12–19.

Žižek, Slavoj. (1998). "Psychoanalysis in Post-Marxism: The Case of Alan Badiou." *South Atlantic Quarterly*, 97.2: 235–61.

ns.

Index

Note: The letter 'n' following locators refers to notes.

Aa, Michael van der 3
Ackroyd, Peter 13
Akker, Robert van der 15–16
Alter, Robert 186n. 2
Althusser, Louis 174
Annesley, Michael 11
anthropological novel 9–10, 186n. 5, 197n. 4
apocalypse 20–1, 37, 41–2, 53–5, 71–3, 80, 95, 117–18, 177–9
Appiah, Anthony 112, 145, 198n. 7
assemblage, novel as 1–4, 15–16, 31, 33, 45–8, 54–5, 59, 76, 88–9, 97–9, 135–6, 183, 201n. 3
Austen, Jane 106, 107
autobiographical novel 23, 103–5, 115–16

Bacigalupi, Paolo 12
Bakhtin, Mikhail 192–3n. 2, 205n. 1
Ballard, J.G. 13
Ballard, Shawn 189n. 3
Baudrillard, Jean 54, 113–14
Benjamin, Walter 35, 45, 59, 177–9, 190n. 11, 191n. 14, 204n. 4
Bhabha, Homi 186n. 4, 196n. 17
bildungsroman 51, 55–60, 108, 126–7, 144, 163
Billington, James H. 193n. 8
birthmark 27–8, 69–70, 72, 76, 82, 85, 96, 100, 134, 190n. 7
Bordwell, David 10
Borges Jorge Luis 4, 32, 71, 76, 81
Bradbury, Ray 65
Buddhism 41, 190n. 7, 204n. 3
Burgess, Anthony 4

Burke, Kenneth 185
Byatt, A.S. 1, 74

Calvino, Italo 4, 5, 74, 76, 81
Carey, Peter 2
Cervantes, Miguel de 9
chance 12–13, 17, 19, 25–7, 35–9, 60, 80–1, 84, 96, 127–8, 130–1, 177
Childs, Peter 81, 188n. 1, 194n. 10, 195n. 14
Chinese box 74, 75, 202n. 6
Christianity 8, 78, 85, 124
city/metropolis 12, 24–8, 31–6, 51–63, 67, 163, 169–70, 174, 190n. 11, 192n. 3
civilization 89–94, 150–3, 172–3, 179, 203n. 13
cloud atlas 79, 194n. 12
Cold War 104, 109–12, 167, 198n. 6
comet 28–9, 64, 76, 84–5
community 6, 94–5, 135, 144, 153, 189n. 6, 196n. 20
Conrad, Joseph 4, 84, 103
contact zones 10–11, 23, 69, 184
contingency 1, 6, 9–10, 12, 19, 39, 44–6, 60, 84, 96–8, 150
cosmopolitan novel 5–9, 15, 24, 48–9, 52, 57, 62, 112, 131, 145–7, 169, 189n. 6
Coupland, Douglas 186n. 5

Davies, Paul 188n. 11
Davis, Natalie Zemon 200n. 3
Davis, Robert Con 192n. 2
Debord, Guy 12, 61
Defoe, Daniel 13, 90

Deleuze, Giles 97, 187n. 9, 200n. 3, 203n. 12
DeLillo, Don 6, 9, 67
De Man, Paul 115
De Quincey, Thomas 13
Derrida, Jacques 45, 47–8, 145, 189nn. 5, 6, 200n. 14
Dickens, Charles 13, 106, 196n. 18
difference 49, 84–8, 101, 145–6, 148–9, 184–5, 186n. 4, 196n. 17
Dillon, Sarah 187n. 6, 188n. 1, 195n. 14
Doane, Mary Anne 98, 202n. 8
Duophysite heresy 77–9
Durell, Lawrence 71
dystopia 91–4, 179, 185

"East"/"West" dichotomy 51–2, 62, 124–6, 133–6, 139–45, 148, 150–1, 200n. 2
Edwards, Caroline 191n. 16, 194n. 9, 195n. 14, 196n. 20
empire 19–21, 43, 54–5, 90, 119–20, 124–5, 133, 141–5, 150–3
encyclopedic narrative 9, 112–14, 129–30, 156, 187n. 6, 198n. 8

Falklands Conflict 20, 104, 108–12, 198n. 6
fantasy 51–6, 60, 63, 66–7, 107–8, 135–6, 155–8, 164, 166–9, 175–6
Faulkner, William 184–5, 205n. 2
Fitzgerald, Ella 8
flâneur 7, 15, 35, 59–60, 170, 190n. 11
Flaubert, Gustave 71
Forster, E.M. 6
Fowles, John 199n. 10
fractal narrative 14–16, 81–2, 100, 143
Freud, Sigmund 151, 203n. 13
Friedman, Susan Stanford 11

future 12–21, 26–8, 42–9, 75–85, 88–99, 118–21, 127–30, 177–85, 202n. 10, 204n. 4, 205n. 3
future anterior 46–7, 89, 202n. 9

Geertz, Clifford 186n. 3, 189n. 3
genre 4–5, 13–16, 62–4, 73–4, 88, 103–6, 126–7, 181–3, 205n. 1
ghosts 23, 28–9, 44
Gibbon, Edward 19, 71, 75, 91, 150
Ginzburg, Carlo 200n. 3
Glissant, Édouard 48, 147, 193n. 3, 203n. 12
globalization 11, 19, 49, 83
global novel 5, 9–16, 48–9, 114, 150
Golding, William 106
Green, James 81, 188n. 1, 194n. 10, 195n. 14
Guattari, Félix 97, 187n. 9, 200n. 3, 203n. 12

Hardt, Michael 83, 153, 195n. 14, 196n. 20
Hastings, Max 198n. 6
hauntology 28, 44–5, 48
Heise, Ursula 144, 192n. 2
Hicks, Heather J. 196n. 21
history 29–31, 34–5, 37–8, 40–9, 67, 79–85, 90–7, 123–30, 140–6, 155–9, 170–1, 177–8, 183, 198n. 6, 200n. 3, 204n. 4
Hoban, Russell 4
Hollinghurst, Alan 3
Hopf 69, 75, 205n. 3
hospitality 6, 29, 32, 189n. 5
Hrubes, Martina 193n. 6
Hugo, Victor 66
hybridity 7, 27, 41–2, 56, 78, 84–8, 130, 135, 183, 186n. 4, 195n. 15

identity 48–56, 79–89, 94–8, 100–7, 115–19, 143–7, 175–80
intertextuality 74, 80, 95, 99, 193n. 6
Ishiguro, Kazuo 1, 7, 12
islands 13–15, 25–7, 123, 125–33, 170–1, 187n. 8, 201n. 5
itinerary 9–15, 30–2, 37–8, 45–7

James, David 188n. 10
James, Henry 74
Jameson, Fredric 196n. 19
Jenkins, Simon 198n. 6
Joyce, James 7, 9, 35, 76, 106, 107

Kermode, Frank 199n. 13
Kristeva, Julia 199n. 12
Kunzru, Hari 9, 186n. 5

Lady Shonogan 66
language 113–17, 145–8
late capitalism 56, 109, 113
Law, John 43, 191n. 15
LeClair, Tom 9, 187n. 6
Le Guin, Ursula K. 92
Lennon, John 191n. 1
Linklater, Alexander 124
Lowry, Malcolm 65
Lyotard, Jean-François 98, 190n. 10, 200n. 3

Machen, Arthur 13
Mandelbrot, Benoit 81
many worlds interpretation vi, 17, 39, 157, 188n. 11
matryoshka (Russian doll) 74–5, 97, 193n. 8, 202n. 6
McCarthy, Tom 9
McEwan, Ian 1, 2
McMorran, Will 194n. 9
Melville, Herman 4, 9, 71
Mendelson, Edward 112, 187n. 6, 198n. 8
meronym 78, 194n. 10

metafiction 4–5, 19, 52–4, 62–7, 82, 150, 171, 175, 180, 183, 186n. 2
metamodernism 15–16
Michener, James 10
Miéville, China 12
Mitchell, David
  novels, *blackswangreen* 3, 6–7, 20, 23, 27, 58, 70, 72, 103–22, 162–3, 176; *Bone Clocks, The* 1, 3, 8, 15, 18, 20, 31, 42, 107, 136, 155–83; *Cloud Atlas* 2–4, 10, 21, 69–102, 150, 156; *ghostwritten* 2, 4, 6, 9, 11, 13–14, 23–50, 78–9; *Number9Dream* 2, 5, 16, 49–67, 81; *Thousand Autumns of Jacob de Zoet, The* 3, 4, 8, 18, 20, 123–53, 155, 160–3, 181
  other works, "Let Me Speak," 103, 116–17; "Lost for Words," 197n. 3; *Reason I Jump, The* (trans. David Mitchell and KA Yoshida) 3, 202n. 11; "Siphoners, The," 204n. 1; *Sunken Garden, The* (with Michael van der Aa) 3
Morin, Marie-Eve 189n. 6
multitude 83–9, 94–5, 131–2, 152, 195n. 14, 196n. 20
multiverse 23, 28, 156, 188n. 11
Murakami, Haruki 4–5, 12, 49, 51–2, 188n. 2, 189, 191n. 1
music 8–9, 40, 96, 112–13

Nabokov, Vladimir 47, 65, 71, 191n. 17
Nadel, Alan 198n. 6
Nancy, Jean-Luc 6, 189n. 6
Negri, Antonio 83, 153, 195n. 14, 196n. 20
Neuman, Andreas 11

Nolan, Christopher 74
numbers 23–7, 60–1, 64–9, 77, 81, 130, 151–2, 156, 188n. 1, 204

orientalism 51, 126, 200n. 2

Pamuk, Orhan 11
Pease, Donald 46
Penrose, Roger 190n. 12
Plato 71, 121
Poe, Edgar Allan 13
Posadas, Baryon Tensor 51–2, 59–60, 191n. 1, 192n. 3, 195n. 14
postmodernism 2–6, 51–2, 75–6, 82, 98, 192n. 2
Poulet, Georges 202n. 10
power 10, 42, 61, 63, 162–7, 170, 192n. 2
Pratt, Mary Louise 10
psychogeography 12–13, 60, 67, 158, 163, 192n. 3
Pynchon, Thomas 6, 9, 198n. 8

quantum narrative 16–17, 19, 36, 38–40, 65, 157, 188n. 11, 190n. 12

raciality 49, 84–6, 124–5, 138, 172
realism 3–4, 132, 158, 171, 175, 182
rebirth 32, 69, 79–80, 100–2, 155
Roake, Jessica 197n. 2

Said, Edward 200n. 2
Schoene, Berthold 5–6, 24, 48, 52
Scott, Sir Walter 71
Sebald, W.G. 1, 7, 13, 15
Self, Will 13, 15, 181–2, 185
Seshagiri 188n. 10
Shelley, Mary 74
Shields, David 182, 185
Simmel, Georges 56–8
Sinclair, Ian 13
Smith, Adam 128, 138, 142, 152
Smith, Ali 2
Smith, Zadie 11

Solomon, Andrew 202n. 11
Solzhenitsyn 71
Sontag, Susan 121
stammering 2, 103, 110, 114–18, 197n. 3, 199n. 13
Steiner, George 145
Stephenson, William 106, 190n. 7, 197n. 4
Stevenson, Robert Louis 13
strangers 9, 23–4, 30–1, 41, 44, 48–9, 80, 95

temporality 7–21, 16–19, 28–30, 35–9, 43–8, 55–62, 74–80, 95–103, 117–29, 140–7, 150–7, 175–85, 191n. 16, 192n. 2, 196nn. 20, 21, 199n. 13, 200n. 1, 202nn. 8, 9
Tobin, Patricia D. 142–3
Tolkien, J.R.R. 71, 104
Tolstoi, Lev 71
translation 11, 49, 126, 133, 145–9, 202n. 11
transmigration 30–2, 79, 142, 150, 161, 164, 196n. 20
Twyker, Tom 69, 99, 101, 205n. 3

utopia 89–94, 156, 185, 191n. 16, 196n. 19

Vermeulen, Pieter 11
Vermeulen, Timotheus 15–16
violence 11, 30–5, 70, 84, 90–2, 94, 106, 111–12, 151, 177

Wachowski, Andrew and Lana 69, 99, 101, 205n. 3
Walkowitz, Rebecca 7
Woods, James 201n. 5
Woolf, Virginia 7

Yoshida, KA 3
Young, Robert 80, 195n. 15

Žižek, Slavoj 57

www.ingramcontent.com/pod-product-compliance
Lightning Source LLC
Chambersburg PA
CBHW062223300426
44115CB00012BA/2190